Good Boatkeeping

GOOD BOATKEEPING

ZORA AND DAVID AIKEN

with drawings by
David Aiken

International Marine
Camden, Maine

Published by International Marine®, a division of McGraw-Hill, Inc.

10 9 8 7 6 5 4 3 2 1

Library of Congress Cataloging-in-Publication Data

Aiken, Zora.
   Good boatkeeping / Zora and David Aiken ; with drawings by David Aiken.
         p.   cm.
   Includes index.
   ISBN 0-07-000747-0 (alk. paper)
   1. Boats and boating—Equipment and supplies. 2. Boats and boating—Maintenance and repair. I. Aiken, David, 1940–   . II. Title.
VM321.A36   1995
797.1'29—dc20   94-44224
                                     CIP

Questions regarding the content of this book should be addressed to:

International Marine
P.O. Box 220
Camden, ME 04843
207-236-4837

Questions regarding the ordering of this book should be addressed to:

McGraw-Hill, Inc.
Customer Service Department
P.O. Box 547
Blacklick, OH 43004
Retail customers: 1-800-822-8158
Bookstores: 1-800-722-4726

Good Boatkeeping is printed on 60-pound Renew Opaque Vellum, an acid-free paper that contains 50 percent recycled waste paper (pre-consumer) and 10 percent postconsumer waste paper.

Printed by R. R. Donnelley, Crawfordsville, IN
Design and page layout by Patrice M. Rossi
Production by Janet Robbins
Edited by James R. Babb and Dorathy Chocensky

To our families,
who encourage us.

Contents

Acknowledgments *ix*

Introduction *x*

1 ■ **Galley Gear**
Organizing the food center: what to bring, how to arrange it 1

2 ■ **Locker Stocking**
Buying ship's stores for vacation or cruise: what to buy, how to stow it 14

3 ■ **Fresh Stuff**
Adding fresh food to ship's staples: fish and shellfish, herbs and sprouts, fruits and vegetables 23

4 ■ **Cooking Stuff**
Preparing meals with what's on board: shortcuts, substitutes, menu suggestions 35

5 ■ **Cold Front**
Choosing your cool: refrigerator, icebox, or cooler; what goes in and what doesn't 48

6 ■ **Inner Space**
Solving the storage puzzle: a space for everything and everything in its space 58

7 ■ **Inside Modified**
Changing the basic plan: how to add nooks and crannies for easier living 68

8 ■ **Bucket Brigade**
Swabbing more than decks: products and ways to get cleaning jobs done fast 81

9 ■ **Clothes Lines**
Doing boat laundry: hand wash and line dry, or search for shore machines 91

10 ■ **Head and Bath**
Maintaining the boat bathroom: head aches and bath bubbles 97

11 ■ **Mechanical Maintenance**
Minding the boatworks: engine, electronics, tools 105

12 ■ **Conditioned Air**
Controlling boat atmosphere: how to heat, cool, and move air around 118

13 ■ **Outer Space**
Modifying the exterior: easier access, more comfort, better efficiency 124

14 ■ **Hook, Line, and Fender**
Securing the boat: use, storage, and care of anchors and lines 135

15 ■ **Water Everywhere**
Managing the freshwater supply: how to catch, carry, and conserve water 143

16 ■ **Water Taxi**
Tending the dinghy: how to choose, use, and maintain the water taxi 151

17 ■ **Found Time**
Using cruising time: hobbies, crafts, watersports 160

18 ■ **Warning Flags**
Staying safe and secure: what to watch for, how to deal with problems 172

19 ■ **Mess-About Time**
Keeping the boat Bristol: how to paint, varnish, fiberglass, and caulk 184

20 ■ **Hard Time**
Hauling the boat: how to make yard time tolerable and productive 198

21 ■ **Good Crewkeeping**
Exercising health options: fitness workouts and health needs 210

22 ■ **My Boat/Your Boat**
Sharing boat fun with family and friends: how to ensure good times 221

23 ■ **Best Friends**
Bringing pets on board: how to help them feel secure and happy 229

24 ■ **Worst Enemies**
Fighting the constant battle: how to get rid of crawling, flying, and scampering pests 240

25 ■ **For Sailors**
Watching rigging and sails: what to look for, how to improve it 246

26 ■ **Good Kidkeeping**
Showing children the ropes: how to make time for boathandling, learning, and play 253

27 ■ **Catch All**
Handling mail, keeping watch, playing tourist, stowing trash 262

Your Ideas   272

Index   273

Acknowledgments

It's not possible to acknowledge individually all those whose ideas are included in *Good Boatkeeping*. Though some information came directly in response to requests, more was acquired over 20-odd years of learning from other boaters. Without this collective experience, the book would not exist.

We're grateful to those friends who looked into their own long-established routines and pulled out ideas to share:

The Rumsey family—Bill, Marian, and Tom: our first (and still) cruising friends and advisers.

The Walsh family—Mickey, Joyce, and Tammy: our constant cruising companions and all-around reference resource.

Captain Michelle Walsh and Captain Charles Smith: equal partners in the care and handling of big boats.

Chuck and Jan Lowe: onetime racing captain and admiral, now accomplished sportfisherpersons.

Ted and Molly Broderson: for years of wisdom on all things bright and nautical.

Bill and Diane Biggs: who taught us to run rapids in Canada and read water in the Bahamas.

Warren and Anne Lenington: former cruisers and now our communication link to the land world.

Ron and Elaine Wolter: masters of maintenance and miscellanies.

Fleming and Margaret Sandersen: gracious house-lenders and our European cruising connection.

Carl and Nancy Lorenzen: boatbuilders, boatyard owners, and boating buddies.

For long lists of suggestions, we thank Jack and Phyllis Sabine, Bill and Barbara Keller, Terry and Dolly Dowhen, Rene and Mira Meier, Jeff and Joan Taylor, Bea Quigg, Dick and Doreen Parsons; for ongoing idea exchange, Jerry and Judy MacNab, Neal and Diane Henderson, and Captain Dick and Nancy Barnes.

We want to acknowledge the attention given to text organization and clarification by editor Dorathy Chocensky.

Special thanks to International Marine's acquisitions editor James R. Babb, and managing editor Pamela Benner, for patiently leading us through their publishing world.

Introduction

The transition from living on land to living on a boat is not always smooth, whether the switch is prompted by a short-term vacation cruise or a permanent lifestyle change. The experience can be interesting, challenging, even fun—or it can be an ongoing lesson in frustration.

In the capsulated, miniaturized world of boat life, the proverbial little things can make a disproportionate difference in attitude, comfort, and efficiency. This book is filled with tips on such little things: suggestions from scores of people who are familiar with—happy with—life afloat.

New boaters will gain the most from the collective advice, but even long-time cruisers continually learn from each other; what is routine to one boater may be a revelation to the next.

Regardless of boat style or boating activity, boaters share a lot of common concerns. Mildew doesn't discriminate between runabout and motor yacht, and the same engine can power sailboat or trawler. Galleys differ in size, but not in function, and a head by any other name would still be a pain. No boat is ever big enough to accommodate the amount of gear to be stowed.

Though problems are common, solutions may be multiple, and they apply whether the boat is used for weekend getaways, holiday cruising, or full-time living aboard.

If an idea accomplishes a chore faster, neater, easier; if it makes boat life more comfortable, more secure, more fun; if it works simply and well, we've tried to include it in this something-for-everyone collection of everyday ways to improve life on a boat.

Note: The brand names mentioned in *Good Boatkeeping* are popular with many of the people who provided information for the book, but their inclusion is not meant to suggest that those brands are the best or the only products for a particular job.

Product comparison is not the focus of this book. With the array of available choices, product longevity, manufacturer's reputation, and old-fashioned word-of-mouth are still the basic sources for product recommendation. Visit your nearest boatyard.

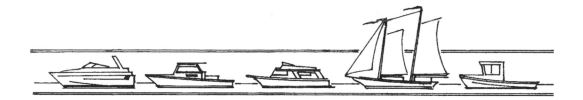

Galley Gear

A good galley is every crewmember's best friend and every cook's biggest challenge.

Size may dictate the amount of gear brought on board, but creative thinking can produce a surprising number of ways to miniaturize a food center, whether its focus is a one-pot burner on an 18-foot weekender or an apartment-size stove on a 40-foot cruiser.

Successful boat cooks adapt quickly to the tools at hand, taking the hassle out of galley duty with a minimum of equipment, effort, and fuss.

COOKING WITH ALCOHOL

Standard equipment on a lot of new boats, alcohol stoves are the most worry-free cooking option.

• You can use plain, readily available water to douse an alcohol flare-up: no foam, no powder, no mess.

• Pressurized alcohol stoves need to be pumped and preheated. Nonpressurized models are simpler to use; their absorption burners work something like lantern wick, on a larger scale. You pour alcohol into the stove's canister; the fuel soaks into a nonflammable wool material, and capillary action draws it to the surface as it burns.

• Alcohol expands when heated, so be careful not to overfill the tank. If it overflowed, it could create more fire than you want.

• Don't fill the tanks while they're in the stove, and especially don't try to fill them while they're hot, or you'll be startled by a *poof* of ignited vapor. When tanks are cool enough to touch, remove them from the stove and fill them according to the manufacturer's directions.

• If you like electric cooking at home, have it on the boat too, at least part time, with an electric/alcohol combination stove. Cook with electricity when dockside, and use the alcohol when away from shore power. (You can find a combination stove with or without pressurized alcohol.)

• While more than adequate for weekend cooking, which often consists of the quick reheating of precooked foods, alcohol is less than ideal for longer trips; cooking time is slower than with kerosene or propane, the smell bothers a lot of people, and stove alcohol is expensive.

• You can cut some of the cost of using an alcohol stove by buying ordinary denatured alcohol (sold for shellac thinner and other solvent purposes in the paint department of the local do-it-yourself home supply store) instead of "marine stove alcohol." The label will specify if it is approved for stove use.

• One average cruising couple used a gallon of alcohol every eight days for ordinary cooking, with no attempt at conserving.

• Some pressurized alcohol stoves can be converted to kerosene; kits are available to change burners on specific models.

COOKING WITH KEROSENE

Traditionalists like their trusted kerosene stoves, with their advantages of hot flame and accessible, reasonably priced fuel.

• Unless the stove has a preheat feature, you must carry alcohol for that purpose, which means more space must be devoted to stove fuel.

• Kerosene is considerably safer than propane. On the downside, it doesn't always burn clean; one good smoke puff can turn the overhead a shade darker.

• Using pure mineral spirits instead of kerosene helps some with the clean-burning problem; if the flame quits while the fuel is still flowing, there is less smoke deposit, and the odor is not as strong.

• Some kerosene burners must be cleaned often with a pricker—a well-named tool that clears the burner of deposits. Keep plenty on board, but store them carefully so they don't rust away before you've had a chance to use them. You may be able to make a substitute by taping a short length of very fine wire to the end of an ice cream stick. (Wire at a right angle to the stick.) Finding wire fine enough to do the job will be your biggest challenge.

• For a time, debates about the pros and cons of kerosene were heading toward the moot-point file, as manufacturers began phasing out kerosene stoves. But a few models stayed on the market, and parts for existing stoves continue to be available.

• Some people have successfully converted kerosene stoves to propane, but because of America's lawsuit mania, stove manufacturers and dealers won't do it; they don't want to risk being liable if there is a problem, especially if the problem stems from improper installation and not from the stove itself. This conversion must be handled by someone experienced with propane, or not done at all.

TWO-FOR STOVES

A good two-for is a combination cooking and heating stove that burns either diesel or kerosene. The heater is there when you need it, but it doesn't take up extra space when you don't. Quiet burning and dry heat are two of the more significant advantages. As might be expected, these stoves aren't cheap, but for a permanent double installation the price is reasonable. For information call Dickinson Stoves, 800-659-9768.

COOKING WITH PROPANE

Even though they require the most safety precautions, propane stoves are a popular choice.

• Gas cooking is familiar; it's clean and efficient.

• Propane is available almost everywhere, and you can cook a lot of meals for the price of a 10-pound fill-up.

• Propane gas is heavier than air. If accidentally released inside the boat, it will settle to the bilge, and too high a concentration might result in an explosion. Make prevention of propane leaks a high priority.

• When installing a propane system, don't run the line through the engine room or bilge. Cushion it when it goes through bulkheads.

Turn-on

Whenever you want to use the stove, check to see that burner knobs are in the off position before you open the gas line. (Since the usual turnoff procedure is to turn off fuel first, knob second, it is possible to forget step two after the flame is extinguished.)

Turnoff

• To be sure no gas remains in the line, always turn off the fuel supply *before* turning off the stove burner knob. The flame goes out because of lack of fuel, not because of stove knob control.

• For the safest possible propane use, one stove manufacturer recommends that you shut off the fuel at the tank when you're through cooking. Don't rely on a solenoid switch—do it yourself, manually, at the tank. Unfortunately, this is not common practice. Most propane installations have a remote-shutoff solenoid valve operated by 12-volt power. A control panel with a lighted switch mounts in the galley; turning off the switch closes the valve at the tank.

Leak Detection

There are different ways to check for leaks in a propane system. Be familiar with and use at least one method, preferably more.

• A gauge allows you to check for steady pressure by comparing two readings. The first is taken with the gas valve open, all appliances off. Close the valve, wait 10 minutes, and check the gauge again. No difference, no leak.

• A push-button version shows a leak as captive bubbles in a fluid-filled capsule.

• The simplest leak detector—a soapy-water solution that bubbles if applied over a leaky hose or fitting—is as reliable as ever. Check each time you reconnect the tank after it's gone to shore for a refill.

• A fume-sensor leak detector that sounds an alarm is extra safety insurance, but don't discount your own nose.

Buying Hints

If you're looking for a new stove:

• Be sure it is equipped with an automatic shutoff feature; if the flame goes out at the burners (because of a spaghetti overflow or a misdirected breeze), a safety valve automatically shuts off the gas flow to the burners.

• Push-button oven lighting is a nice

feature; otherwise, keep a supply of long fireplace matches for lighting the oven pilot light after the butane lighter gets tired.

Tank Talk

• Two tanks of a manageable size are better than a single large one. When the first tank runs out of propane, an immediate replacement is waiting. Then you have ample time to find a convenient place to refill the empty long before you actually need to switch again, thereby avoiding the lengthy and often costly taxi ride to the out-of-town gas company.

• A smaller tank is a lot easier to handle, whether hoisting it off and on the boat, in and out of the dinghy twice, or to—and especially from—the propane store.

• Most propane tanks are steel, mostly because they're cheaper than aluminum ones.

• Keep a can of spray enamel for the steel tanks; stop rust spots early with a good sanding and a coat of paint. Propane fillers are disinclined to refill rusty tanks, as well they should be.

• Aluminum tanks weigh less, and they're nonsparking and naturally corrosion resistant. They'll last much longer than ordinary steel tanks, justifying their added expense. Horizontal aluminum tanks are available in two sizes; vertical ones come in several sizes.

• From a safety standpoint, the way you store propane tanks is arguably the most important factor. Outside storage is safest, but tanks and fittings may suffer from the exposure. In a locker, tanks must be kept in their own storage compartment—not just a space-dividing locker, but one with a sealing gasket on its top-opening lid. The compartment must be

vented overboard, to ensure gas cannot get to the bilge.

• For cooking purposes, propane and butane are interchangeable.

CNG

Compressed natural gas (CNG) is the odd gas.

CNG does not have the heavier-than-air property of LPG; it would not go straight to the bilge, so it is much safer to use. But it is not as convenient to buy. If you choose to cook with CNG, buy the biggest tank—and spares—you can carry.

FLAME PREVENTERS

• If an opening port is situated in such a place that a breeze could blow out the stove fire, keep the port closed while you're cooking. Same if the hatch is at a bad angle to wind; close or cover it.

• Don't hang paper towels or curtains too close to the rising heat from the stove.

FLAME DROPPERS

Matchboxes with slide-off cardboard covers were designed by someone with a warped sense of humor. Many of them have almost the same printing top and bottom. To avoid unplanned games of pick-up-sticks, paint out the bottom so you'll know which way is up, even in the dim light of an oil lamp.

BACKUP BURNERS

A good choice of new one-pot portable stoves can be found, with adequate cooking surfaces and fuel options that include alcohol, kerosene, propane, butane, and CNG.

• Small stoves for small boats serve as spare stoves for big boats. No cruising boat should travel without a backup, but it will be no help at all unless it burns readily available fuel.

• The classic Sea Swing has cooked for decades. Its one-pot platform is fueled by alcohol-based solid fuel, or with kerosene or propane attachments. Available now only in closeout or secondary sales, it is still a practical one-burner choice. If you find one, make sure you own a saucepan or frying pan that will fit the stove's diameter.

• The Seacook stove, now sold by Force 10, looks to be the next classic for a gimbaled one-burner. It uses propane and accepts pots up to 8 inches in diameter.

• A fondue pot (nonelectric) can function as an emergency alternate stove; it can be an extra burner for the added cooking of holiday meals; and it allows you to vary the fare with an elegant dinner (beef and veggies), a casual lunch (cheese), or a fancy dessert (chocolate mint).

• Instead of storing multiple cans of Sterno for the fondue pot, use alcohol and cat litter. Fill an empty can (or the fondue pot's fuel container) with the litter—the plain white unscented clay variety. Pour in stove alcohol to cover and saturate the litter. Then burn it as usual. When the flame gets low, snuff it, and after the can has cooled a bit, add more alcohol and start over. (After many uses, you'll want to replace at least the top layer of litter; it gets charred.)

• The same fuel substitute (alcohol-soaked litter) is the heat source for the old standby folding campstove: a simple, collapsible metal stand that folds flat for storage on any size boat.

• For dual purpose, Origo makes a small alcohol-fueled cabin heater that could also be used as a cooking stove.

BACK-DECK BARBECUE

• A covered barbecue fits conveniently on the stern rail of many cruising boats. Great for the usual grilling, it can be used as a smoker as well. (But check to see who's downwind before starting a lengthy smoking session.)

• Buy a standard charcoal-burning model, or take along the familiar, convenient propane gas grill. Connect the grill to your onboard propane system; you'll need a pressure-adjusting adapter.

• To keep charcoal usable, take it out of its paper bag and put it in a container (preferably plastic) with a tight-sealing lid. This not only keeps the briquettes dry, it also keeps the charcoal dust confined.

• No charcoal starter? Remove the ends from a big coffee can and scallop one end with tin snips. Place scalloped end down in the barbecue tray. Put some crumpled paper and/or leaves and twigs in the bottom, and cover with charcoal. Light the kindling, and hopefully the confined heat and flame will start the charcoal. When

the coals are ready, remove the can with tongs or pliers.

• Even the smallest boats can usually find room for the smallest outdoor grill—about 12 inches in diameter—for shoreside picnics. If wood is available you can cook over a real camper's fire, but keep an emergency stash of charcoal on board so you can grill anytime.

TO PLUG

Big boats with big power supplies can use electric stoves or any ordinary household electrical appliance.

• Some kitchen helpers—toaster, microwave oven, food processor—are sold in 12-volt versions, but the standard 110-volt models can be powered by a separate generator (a very expensive add-on) or through an inverter that changes the boat's DC power to AC.

• With the right boat (and power) you can have an electric stove with a flush glass-topped surface, or with flat, round Euro-styled burners, just like a home range.

• Neighboring boats will appreciate the choice of an inverter to power appliances, since it allows the anchorage to remain undisturbed by engine noise at mealtime.

• Weekenders, vacationers, or dockside liveaboards with access to shore electric power can take advantage of rechargeable appliances like a battery-operated blender.

OR NOT TO PLUG

No external power source is needed to make your own seltzer water. With a Soda Syphon bottle, CO_2 chargers, and fruit juice or flavoring extracts, you'll always have a supply of soft drinks. You will use more of the boat's supply of drinking water, but you'll cut down on your sugar intake and on the number of cans and bottles in the trash or recycling bin, box, or bag.

PANPOURRI

• An oven is nice in a galley, but it's not necessary. You can do your baking using a pressure cooker, a Dutch oven, even a covered heavy-aluminum frying pan. A flame tamer helps to spread and control the heat. Bread may not brown on top, but if that's important, you can flip it over after it's baked and brown the top in a frying pan.

• Though sea air is a natural enemy of cast-iron cookware, many cooks will not part with their favorite frying pans; that decided, they find a way to keep and care for the pans. If and when they do get rusty, the rust can be scoured away and the pans reseasoned (though purists cringe at the word "scour"). You can season by the standard repeated oil-and-heat method; a deep-frying session will hasten the process.

• Heavy-aluminum pans work well with boat stoves, but since naked aluminum is now considered a health hazard, use those with coated, nonstick interiors. Coated frying pans are appreciated for their calorie-conserving cooking and water-conserving cleanup.

• Many cooks still favor cookware made of stainless steel with heat-conducting copper or aluminum bottoms. Those made with aluminum are generally heavier, and therefore less likely to burn their contents. Be careful not to let them boil dry; one manufacturer cautions that melting or separation of the disc might occur.

• If there's room on the boat for a big pot, it should be a pressure cooker. The smallest—4-quart capacity—would hardly be considered large by house standards, but in a galley it serves many purposes. Used with the pressure on, it shortens cooking time, thereby conserving fuel and cutting down on heat in the boat. Without the pressure cap, it's a pasta pot or a crab steamer. It's the onboard choice for canning as well.

• Some boats carry a small wok for stir-frying. While the traditional shape is no doubt best, similar results can be accomplished in an ordinary frying pan.

• The larger pots will also be used for mixing purposes, and possibly serving as well, eliminating the need for excess large bowls.

TEA OR COFFEE?

• Though whistling or basic spout-design teakettles are more readily available, those with removable lids are much easier to clean. Soaking with vinegar a few times will eventually remove a buildup of hardwater deposits from either style, but it's impossible to know when a closed pot is clean, and chunks of scale are not an appetizing addition to afternoon tea.

• With the convenience of individual-cup filters and bags, coffeepots move farther down the necessary list. If tradition dies hard on your boat, take a small percolator or tempered-glass drip pot. (Use the coffee grounds occasionally to perk up your onboard plants.)

PUT A LID ON IT

Stack frying pans with cloth pot holders (or paper plates or napkins or towels) between them so they don't rattle around, making annoying sounds and scratching the nonstick coating of the next pan down. Saucepans should also nest, and while a rack for lids could keep them quiet, they will more likely end up wedged between pan stacks.

POT HOLDER

At least one quilted mitt pot holder—the long style that extends to midarm—should hang as close to the stove as possible. A three-slot stick-on organizer can fasten to a bulkhead or locker door to hold a hand towel, a dish towel, and the mitt.

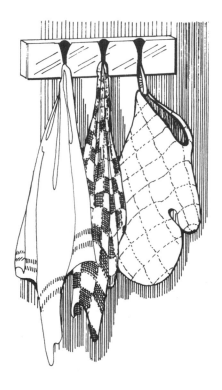

GOURMET GADGETS

Cooking gadgets that get pushed to the back of the house kitchen cabinet may be better suited to the galley.

• If you have space, take along a hot sandwich/meat pie press or a stovetop waffle maker/griddle combo.

• A small food grinder, preferably non-rusting, saves time and fingertips. It's not nearly as fast as a food processor, but it's far better than nothing. Use it to grind nuts for baking, or conch for fritters; to mince clams for chowder, or vegetables for whatever.

• A collapsible steamer will replace a colander for some uses; it doesn't take much storage space, and it's useful for steaming crabs, shrimp, and lobster, as well as vegetables.

• Even if TexMex is not a favored cuisine, tortillas are good on a boat. Use them as a basis for dinner, as an alternative to bread, or for crunchy snacks. You can make your own on board with a tortilla press—a round, handled gadget that guarantees uniform size and thickness. Be sure to buy the right kind of corn flour—"masa" or "masa harina"—or you may end up with a stack of leather tacos whose only function at a dining table is as a trivet. (You can avoid the whole corn problem by using a white-flour tortilla mix or recipe.)

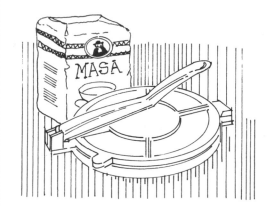

HOT OR NOT

• Large, insulated jugs with pour spouts are ideal for a weekend supply of lemonade or iced tea, especially when a house water supply is available to clean them on Sunday night.

• Thermal-lined tote bags—six-pack size or larger—keep shore lunches fresh and cool.

• Thermal cups retain the heat, just as thermal glasses keep their cool, so the last sip is as good as the first. And they don't drip.

• Standard vacuum bottles will keep liquids refreshingly cool for as long as they might stay in the bottle on a hot day. For night watches, available hot water can provide the instant pickup of coffee, cocoa, or soup, without any noisy preparation.

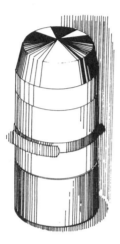

GLASS ACT

• Many new boaters assume all boat dishes should be plastic, perhaps because dinnerware aimed at the marine market is manufactured only in plastic. But Corning's Corelle plates survive amazingly well on a boat, as do some of the heavier ovenware dish sets and coffee mugs.

• Some people don't like to drink from plastic. Look for heavy, shatter-resistant glassware (probably tempered glass)—the kind that requires no special storage method and usually bounces when dropped.

• Real wine glasses can be safely stored upside down in the soft foam-rubber holders made to insulate soft drink cans. If the

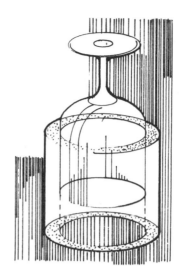

glasses are too wide for the holders, cut the foam and tape (inside and out, so tape sticks to itself) to a proper diameter. Disposable soft-plastic glasses can serve the same purpose.

• Plastic glasses with lids are handy sometimes when you're in the cockpit or on deck (provided you can keep the lids handy; such things tend to disappear just when you want them).

• Despite an antiplastic mindset, disposable plastic dishes, glasses, and utensils are convenient to take to shoreside potlucks, and help to ensure that you'll keep a matched set of everything on board. Reuse the throwaways till they crack or get lost.

CUP TAKES

• Matching mugs and glasses look nice in the locker, but they may not be practical, especially with a gang on board. Better if each person uses a particular color or pattern all day. Then nobody has to wash glasses all day.

• Thick ceramic mugs are easy enough to replace if they chip or break, particularly when you're not trying to match colors.

• Captain's mugs—the wide-bottom, narrow-top hourglass shape—may be attractive and nautically correct and keep coffee hot, but they're not easy to wash.

• The handled bowls that are so convenient for soups, stews, and other one-course meals are easy to wash, but not so easy to store—only larger galleys can afford the space luxury. The next best thing is to carry a few extra-large mugs. You can always serve half cups of coffee.

SHELF HELPS

• Sometimes—especially when underway—the less steps, the better. Arrange lockers so things are as close as possible to where they'll be used. Those items used most often will eventually end up in the front of the locker whether you plan it or not.

• If the galley has a suitable place, cups might hang on hooks, clearing locker space for other things. An overhead wood rack for stemmed glassware also works on some boats.

• Small shelves on the bulkhead take spice bottles out of the locker and make them easier to find and use. But the shelves can't be too close to the stove (excess heat will weaken the spices) or in a place sunlight enters, even for part of the day (condensation will destroy them).

• Nesting bowls conserve space and serve multiple functions as mixing bowls, serving dishes, and, if lidded, storage containers for leftovers. (Keep lids together and nearby in a plastic bag.) Stainless bowls are a good choice; they're practically indestructible and don't absorb odors.

• Nested measuring cups are neither necessary nor desirable. Why wash three cups when one does the same job?

• Don't bother with a big serving ladle either. Soups and stews can be scooped out with a handled mug or a pitcher/measuring cup.

• Line dish-locker shelves with nonskid rubber fabric. It will keep stacked dishes from sliding around. There will be times, underway or at anchor, when you may want to cushion the stacks with rolled-up towels to prevent them from tilting into locker sides or each other. The cushioning is more for noise prevention than breakage protection.

MEALS ON KEEL

Small boats without a lot of enclosed locker space often utilize a transportable, covered "dry box" to pack essentials in a three-dimensional puzzle. The box holds dishes, glasses, utensils, paper plates and towels, bread, crackers—whatever would suffer from spray. Dinghies en route to beach picnics can use canvas bags encased in large plastic bags, though such waterproofing methods do not fit a Bristol image.

CUTTING EDGES

• Serious cooks insist on seriously sharp knives, but spending time on a seriously moving platform convinces clumsy cooks to switch to serrated blades for their molded-in safety factor. Watch the knife salesman who cuts tree branches just before slicing tomatoes with his never-needs-sharpening serrated knife, and then decide.

• Loose knives are dangerous any-where. Designer woodblock holders are nice, but too bulky for a lot of boats. A separate tray inside a locker is too hard to see, but a simple in-counter knife rack leaves handles accessible while blades are safely hidden. See Chapter 7, pages 72 and 73, for more details.

• Wooden cutting boards need to be scrubbed and sanitized to prevent the growth of bacteria, which multiply eagerly in the warm, damp environment of a boat. Once the board is deeply scratched, sand it down to a smooth surface and seal it with mineral oil (*not* vegetable oil—it will turn rancid).

• Keep a separate cutting board for fish. If you have a good place to store it, use a heavy board made by Corning. Its *real* no-scratch surface guarantees no lingering smell or germs. (It is a glass product, but it's the type of glass that won't splinter; if it breaks, it will crack into chunks or squares.)

SILVER WHERE?

Even if the boat is large enough to have drawers, keeping silverware in a counter-top box may be more sensible. When you're cooking, things are accessible to one hand (not one hand for the drawer, one for the silver). You tend to keep only those items you actually use regularly, instead of a drawerful of things that only *look* useful.

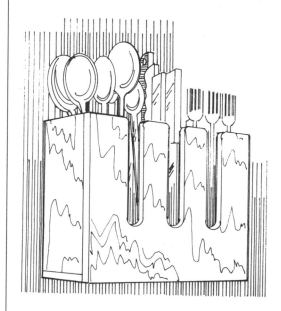

Countertop boxes are usually divided into four vertical sections, allowing room for cooking and serving pieces as well as eating utensils. Marine stores sell teak boxes, but if you're handy with wood, build your own. You can use wood that matches the boat interior, and you can customize each box to fit a specific space. (See Chapter 7, page 74.)

GALLEY GADGETS

• The old-fashioned hand-powered rotary eggbeater is likely a thing of the past in most homes, but on a boat it's much preferred to beating eggs or cake batter with a fork. Buy the best quality you can find, or rust will quickly freeze it up.

• For miscellaneous utensils, buy stain-less steel or hard plastic: potato peeler, wire whisk, small grater; a 1- or 2-cup sifter; a sieve (some have nylon screening); a handled can opener (a *good* one, like Swing-A-Way) and the old standby double-ended can-and-bottle opener that also works on oysters.

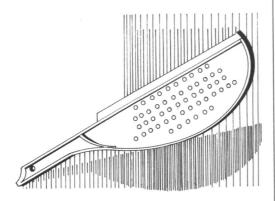

• A colander wastes too much space in a galley locker; you can try juggling pot and lid at just the right angle to pour off cooking liquid without steaming your hand, or you can use a pot-top strainer, a handled half-circle of plastic with enough holes to allow easy draining. It's not foolproof, but it does lessen the chances of the pasta or potatoes ending up in the sink along with the water.

• For use with coated cookware, take wooden spoons and plastic forks and spatulas. (When the edges get rough, sand them smooth.)

• Electric juicers are wonderful inventions, but you'll probably take a basic manual model instead. (A practical one fits over a 2-cup pitcher that is also a measuring cup and could be a drinking cup.) Your hand may not thank you if you're serving a big crew, but the fresh juice almost makes you forget the pain.

• Take a wind-up timer. It's especially useful for baking; it's too easy to get sidetracked.

• Even if you don't normally carry nuts in their shells, take a nutcracker (or two or three) for help in eating lobsters and crabs. The picks in a nutcracker kit are helpful for shellfish too.

• Take a mallet/meat tenderizer for conch. Or use a hammer.

• Don't forget an ice pick.

• An egg slicer is small enough to justify locker space. It makes quick work of slicing mushrooms or cooked potatoes.

• Besides controlling hot pasta, spaghetti-grabbers are safer than tongs for other uses, notably removing conch fritters from the deep-fry pot.

• Skewers can change ordinary cookout food into gourmet kabobs. Long-handled forks save the branches that would otherwise be cut for hot dogs and bonfire marshmallows.

OUT, DAMN DAMP
Soggy Shakers

• Salt and pepper shakers that will not clog are hard to find. Flip-top models work well for quite a while, and camper stores now sell lids only to fit over 35-mm film canisters (Kodak but not Fuji), so you can recycle the containers for shaker use.

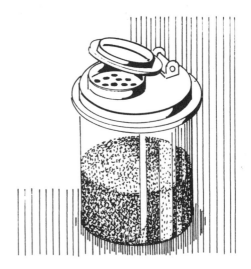

- Keeping a few grains of rice inside (to absorb the moisture) works for a while.

- Buy peppercorns and sea salt crystals and use a pepper-grinding mill for each.

- Keep a stock of small disposable shakers.

Moist Matches

- Cardboard matchboxes absorb dampness quickly, and damp matches will not light. Transfer the wooden matches to a jar, and tape sandpaper on the outside for striking the match. Replace the paper as necessary.

- Store "emergency" matches in a tight-sealing plastic container or a zip-top bag.

- Buy "waterproof" matches or make your own by dipping tips in wax.

- Use a butane lighter and keep refills or spares.

Stubborn Screw Tops

- Dampness and metal jartops don't go together; eventually, the top seals too well. A small circle of thin, textured rubber is sold to help get a grip on such lids, or you can use a piece of nonskid rubber fabric, a rubber glove, or a rubber band wrapped around the lid.

- Running hot water on the metal may allow easier removal.

SERVE YOURSELF

- When you are eating outside (in the cockpit or at a shore picnic), paper napkins

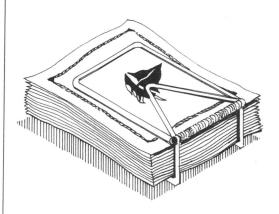

defy the breeze if placed in a simple wire frame holder with a hinged spring top.

- For everyday use, most boat people use paper towels instead of napkins. To be extra conservative about their use, slice the whole roll in half, so half a towel can be torn off.

- Straw holders for paper plates are a big help for the outdoor-dining balancing act. Some people go a giant step further and carry large, sectioned tray/plates.

- If your boat has space to store them, TV-type trays are useful for serving or for lap-dining, inside or out. They should have enough of an edge, or lip, to help prevent or at least confine spills.

- The nonskid fabric that lines lockers is also sold in place-mat form, but in a pinch, a damp towel placed on table or countertop will prevent dishes from sliding around, whether the boat is underway or anchored.

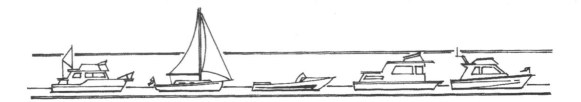

Locker Stocking

To provision for a trip of any length, ask yourself two questions: "What should I buy?" and "Where will I put it?"

"What" requires some planning and probably some list-making; the longer the time factor, the longer the list. "Where" means stowing, though stuffing, cramming, and occasional cursing are not uncommon.

The reward comes after all the stacks have disappeared behind and beneath closed doors and hatches. You're ready. Equipped. Unfettered. Independent. Free.

Fill in your favorite word, and cast off.

BACK AND FORTHING

• For weekend boating, the less stuff carried between home and boat the better. Early in the season, fill lockers (or a plas-

tic milk crate) with basics: paper plates and towels; plastic bags for food storage and trash; water or soda. Add a small stash of food: cans of tuna, fruit, soup; peanut butter, crackers, bottled cheese spreads. These can be used to welcome unexpected company; or you'll appreciate them some unplanned afternoon on the water. (Don't forget a can opener.) Restock all as needed.

• When you're boating for only a few days, nobody wants to waste any of that precious time fixing food. Cooking ahead is not only easier, the results make great boat meals. A beef roast or turkey breast can be sliced for sandwiches or cubed for a dinner casserole. Stews, meatballs, or spaghetti sauce can be frozen (and used as an ice block for a day) and, if pouch-sealed, boiled in the bag to save dishwashing.

• Make-ahead sandwiches are okay, but take the lettuce, tomato, and pickle slices separately to add just before serving. Nobody likes wet bread.

• For weekend trips, keep a few large Thermos jugs on board filled with hot coffee (or iced tea) so no one has to prepare these "anytime" drinks.

• Take fruit for snacks. Besides being good for you, it's a thirst quencher.

• Collect a set of same-size jam jars for mustard, ketchup, mayonnaise, pickle relish, barbecue sauce, jam; fill them from the big containers at home. All can fit into a plastic drawer-separator tray, which will probably pack into the same place in the food cooler. Once you've established the number of jars you'll use regularly, you'll know before you leave home if anything's missing from the tray.

• A cooler is easy to carry from house to car to boat and makes a good dry box for bread, crackers, snacks. It should have a hinged lid, not a separate top that can (and will) blow away.

• A master list of all items taken to the boat each week, posted in an obvious place, lets anyone do the packing.

LONGER HAULING

Whether you're provisioning for a three-week vacation or a six-month cruise, you need a lot of the same items; only quantities differ.

• Planning your first long cruise may seem intimidating, but it should not be; all you need is a grocery list and simple arithmetic. One simple way to start a provision list is to make up seven possible dinner menus and itemize what you will need to prepare each meal for the usual number of people on board. Your list should include meat, vegetables, pasta, rice, fruit, dessert, cooking oil, salad dressing, and spices. Multiply the items on this list by the number of weeks you plan to cruise. Do the same for lunches and breakfasts. Include a bit extra for added time or unexpected guests, and adjust for fresh foods you intend to buy or restaurant meals you plan to enjoy.

• Depending on the length of the cruise, you might want to plan 10 or 14 different menus; compile the main list the same way, and use a different multiplier.

• For ongoing cruising, you'll probably want to take as much as the boat will carry. Provision by time segments; for example, buy for two or three months, stow it, then see how much room you have left.

• If you can't fit everything you want to take, pack as many heavy items as you can. When cruising, you'll be walking to stores and won't want to carry a 25-pound sack of kitty litter or a case of corned beef hash for miles.

• If you won't be shopping regularly for basics like eggs and bread, your provisioning list should include ingredients for baking. Besides the obvious flours and leavening agents, you may need molasses, corn syrup, brown sugar, or confectioner's sugar.

• If you have a friend in the restaurant business or you can convince a local supplier to sell them to you, buy a bunch of individual serving packets of mayonnaise, ketchup, and mustard. (Buy powdered horseradish to mix with the mayo.)

CAN YOU CAN?

Before you start loading the boat with canned meat, decide if you want to do any canning yourself.

• Use a boat-size pressure-cooker (4- or 6-quart), then take it along to preserve fish or foods purchased in quantity as you travel.

• Home-canned possibilities include beef chunks, turkey, chicken, and fish. A half-pint container holds servings for two or three people. Jars can be stored in their original boxes (with separators) so they'll keep safely.

• Some people can homemade soup, spaghetti sauce, and other cooked meals. Others prefer to fix them as needed, using the individual canned foods as bases.

• It's possible to can fruit and vegetables too, but they will not taste much different than the commercially canned items, so it's probably not worth the trouble; even low-salt or no-salt veggies are available in grocery stores.

PLAN FAR AHEAD

Long before your first extended cruise, start dating things like toothpaste, shampoo, and

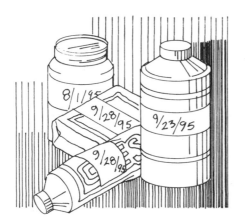

bath soap, so you'll know how much of these items you use in a given time. (You can do the same for staple foods, such as oatmeal, pasta, and rice.)

TRY BEFORE YOU BUY

Long before you're ready to buy, spend some time wandering around your local supermarkets, studying all the shelves you usually bypass, so you'll know what's available.

• Try different brands of canned goods to see which you prefer.

• Never load up on an unfamiliar item, no matter how good a sale may seem. (There are only so many ways to disguise canned sausages, and none really succeed.)

COMPARISON SHOP

• Look for *real* discount grocery stores—the no-ticketing, no-bagging, sometimes no-shelving stores. They are considerably cheaper.

• So-called wholesale or club stores have some good buys too (rice, cereal, candy, soda), but they seldom stock small cans of anything.

• Look in specialty food stores for things like vegetable bouillon, celery juice, or beef tea. Large chain stores such as Kmart and Wal-Mart stock some canned foods not usually found in familiar grocery stores: canned bacon and nonrefrigerated canned hams come to mind.

• Check health food stores, not only for sprouting seeds, but for nuts, grains, and dried fruit. Bought in bulk from the barrels, they are fresher than most packaged goods, and much less expensive. Buy a lot and make up your own trail mix (marine mix?).

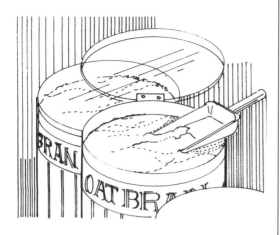

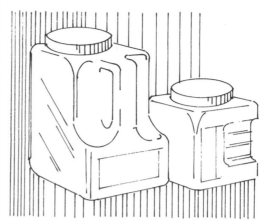

• Send for catalogs from camping and canoe outfitters or backpack suppliers to get ideas for easily packed, easily stored foods. Dehydrated or freeze-dried foods are available in an amazing assortment: One company specializes in strictly vegetarian food. Some are sold in individual or two-serving packets, some in bulk. While not inexpensive, they do answer a specific need.

For information, write or call:

Adventure Foods
Route 2, Box 276
Whittier, NC 28789
704-497-4113

Campmor
P.O. Box 700
Saddle River, NJ 07458-0700
800-525-4784

Uncle John's Foods (vegetarian)
P.O. Box 489
Fairplay, CO 80440
800-530-8733

THINK REUSE

• Buy enough same-size jars (instant coffee, peanut butter, nondairy creamer) to collect a small canister set.

• Look for widemouthed plastic containers with plastic screwtop lids. Some have molded handles, others narrower grip tops. They are sold with rice, cookies, cat food, birdseed. They're usually clear plastic, so you can see what's inside.

WHAT'S NEW?

• Some things you don't need at home are very useful on board: dehydrated onions or mushrooms, green pepper or celery flakes, real or imitation bacon bits, assorted sauce mixes, instant pudding, plain gelatin.

• You might need cream of tartar, a versatile item that you can use to make frosting, bake cakes, sour milk, or clean metal.

• If you bring freeze-dried foods, whole meals are available as emergency stores.

• Ordinary supermarkets stock complete heat-and-eat dinner packages that don't need refrigeration. Heating is accomplished by tossing a covered tray into hot water. These may look like airline meals, but you can't beat them for convenience. (If you buy Hormel's Top Shelf meals, the labeling may give only microwave directions, but it's okay to heat them in water. Don't try to immerse the tray; place it in water up to the rim, and heat in an uncovered pot about 10 minutes.)

TREATS

• Set aside locker space and a given amount of money for each person to buy his or her own personal favorite treats. These will be off-limits to other crew, except for emergency Snickers attacks.

• Take as many snacks as will fit. People on boats are always hungry.

• Even the simplest dessert can be made special. A ready-made graham cracker piecrust filled with instant pudding and topped with canned fruit and Cool Whip needs only a fancy name to border on decadent. (Use tart shells for children's portions; they like personal-size servings.)

• A basic fruit-in-flavored-gelatin mold becomes a real treat at a group potluck.

• Pack some boat gifts: chocolate mint patties, flavored teas, smoked nuts. They're a welcome way to say hello to new friends.

• Don't forget a box of birthday candles.

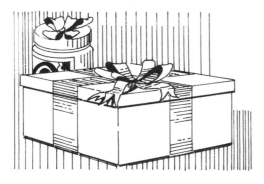

DIFFERENT WRAPPERS

Some familiar foods will be purchased in different packages for boat use.

• Buy powdered milk and sugared drink mixes in quart-size packets. (The separate envelopes may be more expensive, but if the milk goes bad and the drink mix

becomes a blob, the larger-quantity package offers no savings.)

• Danish salami, Wisconsin summer sausage, and pepperoni found on the non-refrigerated shelf in the store will last for months. So will a country ham.

• Buy margarine (vegetable oil spreads) in tubs instead of sticks; in or out of the refrigerator, it will keep neater. Better still, buy it in squeeze bottles.

• Cheese can be bought in cans, though they are expensive. Those encased in wax will keep a long time, if the coating remains intact. Once opened, the cheese will likely be eaten before it has a chance to spoil. (See Chapter 5 for cheese-keeping suggestions.)

DON'T BUY

• If they will be available where you plan to cruise, don't overbuy flour (especially wheat), cornmeal, or even pasta. These sometimes bring weevils on board. You won't necessarily see them, because they may still be invisible eggs in the package when you buy it.

• Don't overbuy baking powder, baking soda, or yeast. With time (or moisture), they may lose their reason for being. (The soda, at least, can always be used for cleaning projects.)

• Don't buy two-ply paper towels or toilet tissue. You'll get longer usage from one-ply.

• Don't buy small garbage bags. The handled bags grocery stores use for packing are just the right size for small wastebaskets. You can reuse them instead of relying on the store to recycle the plastic, even if they are a pain to fold and store. (A plastic box—one brand is appropriately named "Hold-A-Bag"—will confine at least 20.)

• Paper plates come from trees, but on board they aid in water conservation by eliminating dishwashing. Argue with your conscience about this.

• Once you've done your first long-term locker stocking, keep the master list forever.

CARRYALLS

For carrying purchases back to the boat, keep two (or four) big canvas tote bags (good), one or two backpacks (better), or a folding, wheeled shopping cart (best). The cart will also transport laundry, propane tanks, gasoline cans for the outboard, and whatever else is more easily pulled than carried.

THE STOWING GAME

• As you pack lockers, think balance. Try to distribute items so that neither side (nor bow or stern) is overweight.

• To keep dry foods dry (pasta, rice, flour, sugar, oatmeal), take as many tight-sealing plastic containers as your boat's lockers can hold. Square containers, whether tall or squatty, are better than round; there is no wasted space between them.

• If the containers aren't see-through, use plain white mailing labels or strips of masking tape to mark contents on the sides and the top of each container. Use ballpoint pen or indelible marker. If you need to change contents, sticky labels may release easier if you put hot water on the inner surface; this softens some glues.

• Keep smaller containers of foods that are used daily or weekly (oatmeal, rice, coffee creamer), and find a place for them near the front of the locker. Refill from the less accessible bulk packages as needed.

• If the boat has a big hanging locker but you don't have a lot of hanging clothes, make a pantry. Shelves can be installed, but drawers allow easier access. Each drawer holds a number of uniform-size containers, all filled with dry staples and clearly labeled on top. To keep the drawers in place even in a rolling sea, wedge a length of wood diagonally across the drawer fronts.

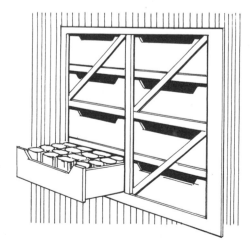

REPACKAGING

• Cardboard boxes of food are never filled by their contents. Save space by removing the inner bags from packages of snack crackers, cake mix, pudding, etc., and repack in covered plastic containers or doubled zip-top bags. Don't forget to label them.

• Store baking powder, baking soda, and yeast in double packaging. Put the baking powder can inside a jar; baking soda boxes and yeast packets will fit in square plastic containers.

• Some bouillon cubes come individually wrapped in foil, but not very well. They quickly absorb moisture and become unusable squares of goo. Instant bouillon will do the same. Double-jar both kinds.

• Jars that hold instant coffee, powdered creamer, sugar, and other dry foods will stay more airtight if a small piece of plastic wrap or a sandwich bag is used as a gasket to help seal the lid.

• After instant coffee is half gone, put the remaining half in a smaller jar. The less air space, the less opportunity for condensation.

• Keep small squeeze bottles for serving mustard and ketchup. Refill them from the big bottles stored elsewhere.

GLASS CASES

• Certain foods, like pickles and many sauces, are sold only in glass bottles. Store them in a dishpan under a seat locker, surrounded by cans or bubble wrap or boxed juices—anything to keep the glass bottles from touching each other. Breakage is a rare occurrence, but should it happen, the dishpan will confine the mess.

• Babyfood or small jam jars can be stored in a covered plastic bin. Styrofoam popcorn will prevent them from bumping.

• Small glass bottles of club soda (12-ounce size) are the exception to storing glass in dishpans. DON'T STORE THESE AT ALL. When the soda expands, whether from heat or motion, it does not just push off the bottle cap; in rare instances, the entire glass bottom can blow off the bottle. Though defective bottles were the probable cause, plastic 1-liter bottles are definitely safer; at least the bottles can expand.

DENTABLES

• Cans are usually stored in seat lockers. Organize them by type of food (soup,

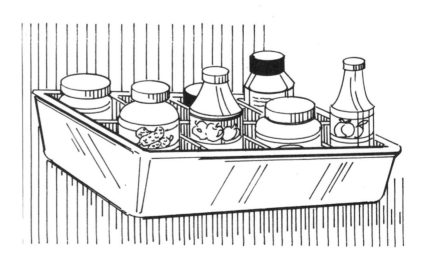

meat, fruit, vegetable) and by usual use (lunch, dinner, snack). If they are not in separate lockers, at least keep like items together in the same general area of the locker.

• It's possible that cans may lose their labels, so mark them with a quick code of initials and month and year. Make up your own code: you'll know by the shape of the can if "T" is for tuna or tomato. More important is the dating: you want to be sure to use food in the order it was purchased.

HIDDEN SPACES

• The space under some drawers is often big enough for some short cans: pet food, sardines, possibly beer or soda cans on their sides.

• There may be enough room for a roll of paper towels or a box of facial tissues *behind* the drawers.

• Some lockers have usable space hidden underneath shelves. Cut the shelf, and hinge it for access. If the space is too deep to reach easily, put storables in strong plastic or mesh bags, label them, and lower them in place with a line attached to the drawstring top of each bag. Loop the lines over a row of cup hooks inside the locker. When you need the contents of a bag, hoist it out.

• You may find other small closed spaces on the boat. Open them up and use them.

BRISTOL LAPSE

When you're stocking up for a trip to a place where food is expensive, you may not pass the Bristol fashion test in the stowing category. No matter how big the boat, for the first two or three weeks food packages may be stuffed in and spilling out of every available cranny. But as packages are emptied, the boat tidies up and you will have an extra few weeks of stores.

INVENTORY

• Very organized people keep a written record of every item on board, alphabetically filed and cross-referenced when necessary. For example, "oil" will subdivide and refer to salad, engine, or lock. Every can of food, every pound of pasta is included in the all-boat inventory, and each time an item is removed from storage, it is so noted on its file card. When it's time to restock, information for the list is immediately available.

• If you know you wouldn't keep an accurate record in the file box, try making separate lists of what's in each section. Tack up the list inside its compartment and check off each item you remove. The check marks will tell you what needs to be replaced.

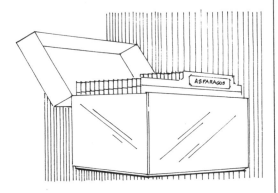

• It's almost impossible to keep a running inventory when more than one person is regularly handling ship's stores.

• When a particular locker starts looking too empty, make a rough count of what's left and restock accordingly.

• When the new cans come on board, repack lockers so older cans are on the top. Throw out any questionable cans (such as those with excessive rust spots, especially near the seams). There's no question about bulging cans: get rid of them fast, or you may suffer the consequences of a sauerkraut explosion.

• If you're going foreign for the first time, expect to pay more for many things. Familiar American products will not have familiar American prices; if the food is imported from the states, the grocer must pay duty and shipping charges on it before it ever gets on the shelf, and that cost will be reflected in the price.

• Part-time cruisers who store the boat for half the year usually leave canned goods in the lockers, but some choose to remove them and buy new each season.

• One woman keeps all provisioning receipts. At the end of her cruising time, she sells excess canned food to boaters who are just starting their trips.

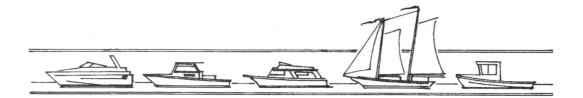

3 Fresh Stuff

A boatload of premeasured, precooked, and prepackaged food doesn't have to limit you to a revolving menu of preplanned meals. With such rich resources under your keel, fish will be caught and shellfish captured. On board, sprout jars can add greens and herb gardens refine flavors. Pots of tomato or pepper plants already decorate some decks; can hydroponics be far behind?

Properly stored, fruits and vegetables will last till it's time to resupply. Properly prepared, you can catch, grow, gather, keep, and enjoy fresh food wherever you cruise.

SEAFOOD BOUNTY

FISH FINDERS

Whether your home port is a freshwater lake or a river, or you're planning to cruise offshore, think fish.

• If you've never held a fishing rod, boating will get you started. Without investing in tournament-quality gear, you can carry a way to catch a lot of dinners. A truly fresh catch will spoil you for supermarket (and most restaurant) fish forever; there is just no comparison.

• Local knowledge is a valuable commodity, provided you can convince the locals to share it. A resident liveaboard community is usually a willing source of information about fish-finding. Failing that, eavesdropping often brings enlightenment. Finally, try following a fishing leader, as in charter boat.

• Sailboats, trawlers, and other boats traveling at a 5- to 6-knot trolling speed often drag lines as they cross between Florida and the Bahamas. They're frequently rewarded with tuna, wahoo, or dolphin (the food fish, not the friendly bottlenose).

• When trolling, you can actively seek out weed lines or look for birds as clues that suggest fish are lurking beneath the surface. But you can also hook dinner without altering course at all. (See Chapter 17 for more fish stories.)

• Check regulations in each state or country regarding licenses, seasons, species, and sizes. Watch for areas closed because of pollution. Be aware of the possible danger of seafood-related illnesses. (See Chapter 21, pages 218 and 219.)

FISH CATCHERS

• If you buy fishing gear in the general area where you'll be fishing, you might pick up some local advice along with the equipment. If you have a friend who's a fisherman, ask for recommendations. Otherwise, buy a fiberglass or graphite (or combination) spinning rod from a discount store. They're sold in lengths of about 5 to 7 feet; choose one that feels comfortable. Add a saltwater-resistant, open-face spinning reel (like a #5500 Penn) filled with 25-pound-test monofilament. Use high-quality ball-bearing snap swivels to prevent line twist. For trolling, use trolling spoons or spinners, or cut bait or worms.

• A favorite lure, used in deep water on a boat at sailing speed: Put a plastic squid body over a wire leader with a ½-ounce egg sinker inside the body, and a ⅝ hook and a swivel. The lure trolls very shallow; one trip landed Spanish mackerel, tuna, and jack.

• Recycle your old yellow foul-weather gear. Cut a bunch of strips of fabric and tie them together at one end. (Make it whatever size seems appropriate for use as

a fishing lure.) The hook hides in the tied end; the yellow strips "swim" in the water. It works, even without added bait. (Unless you go into the lure business, one old jacket will go a long way.)

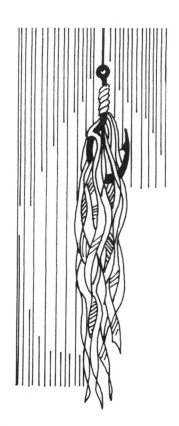

FISH BOATING

• If you manage to get a good-size fish out of the water, it won't be happy, and it can make quite a mess thrashing around the cockpit. Keep an old towel or a small tarp handy, and cover the fish to calm it down.

• A better idea is to kill the fish before it ever gets into the cockpit. Hit the fish solidly between the eyes with a winch handle, a boat hook, or the sawed-off-baseball-bat-like tool made for the purpose (called, curiously, a *priest*).

• Although we don't recommend this method, some people tie a large fish upside down alongside the boat; with its gills out of the water, it will suffocate. Be aware that doing this could attract sharks.

ALTERNATIVE FISHING

• If the alternate thrashing and calming (or whacking) of big fish doesn't appeal to you, you can use the dinghy to go after the small ones.

• When fishing for dinner, use a lighter line with mackerel spoons and hairjigs or dollhead jigs with soft-plastic grubtails.

• Leadhead jigs will catch anything, anywhere.

• In the Bahamas, you can buy a "fish pot," a wire trap sometimes disguised with palm fronds woven through the metal mesh. Bait it with conch, put it in the water near the anchor, and have fresh fish for dinner. And breakfast. And lunch. And to give to your friends.

FISH WARNING

Ciguatera—a type of fish poisoning—is not so rare that you can dismiss it. Produced by microorganisms in warm tropical and subtropical water, ciguatoxin travels up the food chain without bothering its fish carriers, but it sometimes seriously affects people who eat reef fish. (Be wary of larger barracuda, grouper, and snapper.)

Seek local knowledge regarding the known occurrence of ciguatera or the presence of a red tide (algae bloom). See Chapter 21, page 219, for more details.

FISH KEEPERS

• If you're lucky enough to catch too many fish to eat quickly, and your boat has a real freezer (separate from the refrigeration unit), keeping the fish is easy. Cut it into eating-size fillets or steaks; freeze them in water. (Use milk cartons, standard freezer boxes, or doubled zip-top bags, all labeled and dated.) If the fish are going to a home freezer, you can catch even more.

• You can also preserve your catch with your trusty pressure cooker–canning outfit. Can it plain (for fish chowders and stew) or fancy (pickled or smoked first). Chapter 4 explains basic canning procedures.

To Pickle Fish

If you're using small fish, such as herring, clean them and cut off their heads; for larger fish (tuna, bonito, dolphin), cut into ½-inch or ¾-inch chunks.

Precook the fish: Sprinkle with lime or lemon juice and salt. Bake until brown (about 20 minutes) in a medium-hot oven, or brown it lightly in a nonstick frying pan, turning once during cooking.

For 16 herrings or 2 to 3 pounds of larger fish, make a marinade with:

4 onions, sliced in rings
1 cup water
2 cups vinegar
1 bay leaf
1 teaspoon mustard seed
1 teaspoon pepper
2 cloves
a bit of sugar

Put water, vinegar, and spices into a saucepan; bring to a boil, then turn off and let stand 20 minutes.

Put a layer of cooled fish in the jar and pour some warm marinade over it. Continue to alternate fish and marinade, leaving some room at the top of the jar. Close the jar.

After two days the fish will be ready to eat as is, cold. Without being vacuum sealed, it will keep for a month. You can reuse the marinade twice.

The boaters who provided this recipe did not refrigerate their pickled fish. However, food experts do not recommend keeping it out of the cold—as they say, so much depends on the acidity of the vinegar.

To Smoke Fish

Use your stern-rail barbecue grill as a smoker. (If you planned ahead, you'll have some kind of nonresinous aromatic wood on hand.) Fillet the fish and soak it in a brine solution overnight, then smoke it for four or five hours at low heat (about 100°F), keeping a supply of damp wood chips atop the low-burning coals.

After smoking, fish will keep for three to five weeks refrigerated, or you can pressure can it (½-pint jars, 10 pounds, 60 minutes).

DIGGING CLAMS

• You'll know you're in clamming country when you see people wading in the shallows carrying buckets and rakes. If you want to join the diggers, grab your bucket and a small garden rake—the claw kind used for weeding. At low tide, look for clams in the muddy areas along the edge of the grass line, places that would be submerged at high tide. Feel with your toes, or use the rake to find and scoop out the clams.

• Back on board, scrub the mud off the shells and put the clams in a pot or bucket with clean seawater. Sprinkle in some cornmeal. Let the clams soak for a few hours so they'll clean themselves of grit.

• You can keep them for a few days in a bucket hung overboard, or in a refrigerator. When it's time to cook them, discard any that are floating, as well as those that are open and don't close when touched. (They should open only after cooking.)

Cooking Clams

Steam clams over an inch of water for about 5 to 10 minutes, just until they open. Eat them as they are or mince them for chowder, spaghetti sauce, or dip. Save the broth for chowder.

Cooking Mussels

Prepare mussels the same ways you would clams. Wash and scrub the shells; use scissors to cut off the "beards." Then steam until the shells open. Serve them as is, dipped in sauce or butter, or save them for seafood chowder or stew.

SHELLFISH CAUTION

Unfortunately, shellfish can sometimes be a health hazard. The same kinds of algae blooms that produce ciguatoxin also carry paralytic shellfish toxin and other bacteria or viruses. Areas closed to harvesting are usually posted, but always check locally before eating seafood. (NOAA weather radio may carry red tide bulletins in some states.)

NETTING SHRIMP

It's easy to find where the shrimp are: commercial shrimpboats line the East Coast and Gulf Coast waterways.

• Shrimp like light, whether it's a full moon or a lantern glow. You catch them with a casting net when the tide is running, or at slack low water in the shallows near the weed line.

• Round casting nets are available in diameters of 3 to 8 feet. A midsize (5-foot) net is fairly easy to throw and will still haul in enough shrimp to make it worthwhile. Plastic spines feed out like spokes from the center of the net, and the rim has lead weights to carry it down. A line connects your hand to the net.

Put the handline loop around your right wrist; coil and hold the line in your right hand. Be sure the drawstrings are not tangled. With the net bunched up and draped over your right arm, grasp the circular lead line in both hands and swing the net from right to left, letting go with a flourish at the end of the swing. With luck (and practice) the net will open and hit the water as a perfect circle. The weights will carry it down; when you feel it touch bottom, pull in. The line closes the circle, trapping the shrimp inside.

• A good cast will trap 10 to 30 shrimp. The same net works for minnows too.

• Some people tape a line of duct tape, inside and out, just above the weights around the full rim of the net. This makes it sink faster.

• Shrimp nets can be found at tackle shops or in the sporting goods section of family department stores.

• If you catch enough shrimp to freeze a bunch, head them and freeze in water. Use cardboard or plastic milk containers; fill about two-thirds with shrimp and add water to cover.

Cooking Shrimp

If you're not going to eat the shrimp right away, keep them in the water in a bait bucket overnight.

To cook, head the shrimp and steam them over water or beer for a few minutes, just until they turn a uniform pink. (Leave them too long and they'll get rubbery.) Peel and eat as is, or use them in shrimp cocktail or any other favorite recipe.

TRAPPING CRABS

• You can catch crabs one by one. Get a crab net and keep it close by. Dangle a baited line in the water where crabs live. (No hook required; just tie a chicken neck to a piece of string.) Soon, a crab will grab the bait. Start lifting slowly; the crab will hang onto its treasure as you pull toward the surface. Once the crab is visible, slide the net underneath and lift it out. (If you're fast enough, you can use the same bait many times.)

• Anyone who cruises the Chesapeake knows about crab pots; the bay is dotted

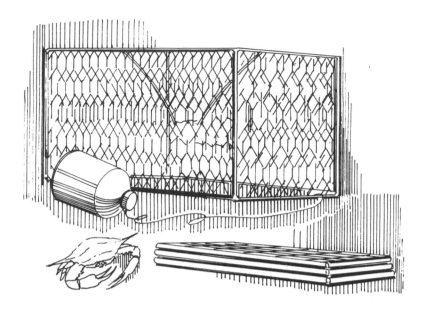

with floats marking traps belonging to the watermen who harvest blue crab commercially. Pleasure boaters can use a standard-size trap or a smaller version that folds for easy storage. (Kmart sells a 12- and an 18-inch folding trap.)

Bait the trap with chicken scraps, old salami, or whatever else might be spoiling; crabs aren't fussy. Toss the trap over whenever you're in crab country, which fortunately reaches far beyond the bay.

Cooking Crabs

Keep crabs in the trap (or a bait bucket in the water) until you're ready to cook them, preferably that evening. Scrub them with a brush before cooking. Or not— your choice. If you choose to scrub, you may have to put them into hot water for a few minutes so you can handle them safely.

Some cooks boil the crabs; most steam them. Put crabs in a colander or on a rack over boiling water and steam them for 20 to 30 minutes. You can add crab boil (a spice mixture) to the water, or not. You can add some beer or vinegar to the water, or not. You can sprinkle some of the spice mixture on top of the crabs, or not. Some like them spicy hot, some not.

Crab cooking is a very individual thing. The only constant is that blue crabs turn very red when they are cooked. Remove them from the steamer and take them to the feasting table.

PICKING CRABS

Pry off the apron flap on the underside and throw it away. Remove the upper shell with your thumb or a knifepoint. Break off the claws, but save them. Scrape off the spongelike material until you feel a hard, semitransparent membrane; this covers the good crabmeat.

Break the crab body in half and pick out the white meat with fingers, picks,

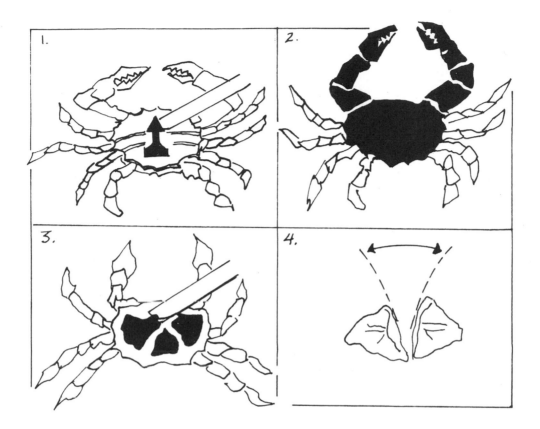

knife, or small fork. Use a hammer or a tiny mallet to break the claws and expose the meat.

It has been suggested that three or four crabs are a normal serving, but the suggesters must not be crab lovers.

• Favorite eating fest: Cover a table with newspaper or brown paper and put a stack of blue crabs in the center. Everybody grabs and picks to their tummy's content. A side dish of green salad or rice and some crusty bread makes the nutrition folks happy, though the diners could probably do without.

• If you satisfy your appetites before the crab stack is gone, pick the rest for tomorrow's crab salad or pasta sauce.

SPEARING LOBSTERS

• Some lucky cruisers catch spiny lobsters. In the Bahamas, they use a Hawaiian sling, a grownup slingshot that shoots spears instead of stones. You can look for lobster with snorkel gear, but using scuba gear is illegal.

• Lobsters hide around coral reefs and isolated heads, or under ledges. At first, you may see only the antennas. Don't shoot a female carrying eggs, which appear as a cluster of orange under the belly.

• Most of the meat is in the tail of the spiny lobster, so some people cook only that, either by broiling or steaming. There is edible meat in the legs and antenna too; steam and pick the meat for lobster salad.

TONGING OYSTERS

It is possible to gather your own oysters, but it's not easy.

• Oyster tongs are long, scissorlike rakes that scoop oyster mounds from the bottom. The tonging itself is hard work; the clumps of shells are heavy and much of what you work so hard to haul on board goes right back into the water—empty shells, small shells, other-than-oyster shells.

• Tonging is also very messy. If you want to try it anyway, and you and your clothes don't mind mud baths, find a friendly local with an oyster boat and tongs, and be an apprentice for a day.

SHUCKING OYSTERS

Keep oysters alive until you're ready to cook or eat them. (The two choices do not necessarily go together.) Throw out any that open before cooking, or before serving them raw.

To remove the oysters from their shells, insert a knife edge into the hinge; turn it to lift the upper shell enough to allow the knife blade to cut the hinge muscle. That should open them so you can serve oysters on the half shell. (They're also good grilled or sautéed.)

COLLECTING CONCH

• You can expend a lot of energy swimming around looking for conch with your snorkel and mask, or you can take the dinghy and a "look bucket" (a glass-bottomed bucket that lets you see bottom clearly).

• Conch are usually found on grassy bottoms; you'll see the conch shape, but it will probably be sandy in color. You may see a claw sticking out, but usually not. As soon as you touch the shell, the conch will disappear inside.

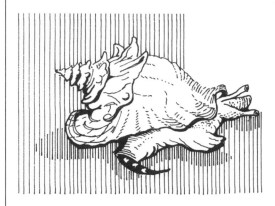

• Conch can be kept alive for a few days in the bait bucket in the water.

• When it's time to remove the conch from its shell, watch someone demonstrate the procedure. Better still, pay someone to do it for you. If you must try it yourself, good luck.

Using a screwdriver, an awl, or whatever else looks like it might work, make a hole near the top of the shell, between the third and the fourth spiral. Insert a knife tip and try to cut the muscle inside. If you succeed, the conch will fall out in a mess of slippery stuff. Until you know what's edible, use only the white meat.

• If you want to keep a perfect shell, the best way to remove the animal is to find a boat with a freezer, and put the conch inside. When it thaws, you'll be able to pull out the dead animal. Leave the shell on shore where ants can clean out what's left inside.

Versatile Conch

If after removing a conch from its shell you haven't lost your appetite, you can dice and marinate it for conch salad, beat it with a tenderizer for cracked or baked conch, or grind/chop it for conch fritters. Bahamians and brave yachties sometimes eat the meat raw.

GARDEN HARVEST

GROWING SPROUTS

When fresh produce is accessible, sprouts are a fun addition to salad or stir fry. When vegetables are not available, sprouts *are* the salad.

• Mung bean sprouts are perhaps most versatile of the sproutables. They're big enough to be the major ingredient of a sprout salad, they're good on sandwiches, and they add the finishing crunch to stir fry.

• Buy mung beans at a health food store. You can grow a lot of them in a quart-size jar, or start smaller amounts on consecutive days so you always have a supply of fresh greens.

• To sprout, put enough beans in the jar to cover the bottom. Soak them in water overnight. In the morning, drain the water and cover the top of the jar with cheesecloth or fine-mesh nylon screen secured with a rubber band. Once or twice a day, rinse the beans with a bit of water, always pouring off the excess. Keep the jars inside a locker, where it's dark, so sprouts will stay white. In a few days, you'll have bean sprouts that look just like those in the Chinese restaurant, and with much more taste and crunch than the canned variety.

• Another way to grow sprouts is to use aluminum ice cube trays. Remove the cube-dividing insert—use only the outer tray. Poke a series of small holes in the bottom so excess water can drain. (Leave trays in an appropriate place to allow for drainage.) This prevents the rotting that sometimes occurs if too much moisture stays in the bottom of a sprout jar.

• Rinse the green hulls away if you wish, but they are edible.

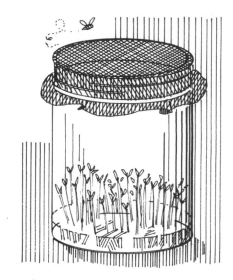

• Alfalfa sprouts are popular and easy to grow. Start them in the dark like mung beans. Once the seeds start to sprout, put them in sunlight so they'll turn green.

• Other types of seeds can be sprouted too. Personal favorites are hot radish and fenugreek (a fun word that translates as Greek hay), which add a good zing to salads.

• Even felines enjoy fresh greenery occasionally. Sprout rye grass just for your cat.

GROWING HERBS

Herb gardens are pleasing to eye, nose, and taste buds, and cruising cooks take them along for all those reasons.

• Grow a whole assortment in one large pot (a simple, squatty round shape works well) or put each in a separate small pot and keep them all together in one plastic tray. They grow well in sandy soil.

• Herbs don't like too much sea air; they do better inside the boat in filtered light. Water them often (use the water from cooked vegetables, or toss on a few coffee grounds). Set them on the back deck for an occasional bath of rainwater.

• Constant trimming of the plants will keep them confined. Cut the leaves, don't pull them. Parsley, chive, basil, and thyme are most popular; also try rosemary, sage, or mint.

HERB KEEPING

• Keep freshly cut herbs in a plastic bag in the refrigerator.

• If you have a freezer, put cut herb leaves in an ice cube tray; add about a tablespoon of water in each compartment and freeze. When you need that herb, just grab a cube.

• Keep herbs in oil. Chop leaves into a jar, add a bit of salt, and cover with salad oil. Use the oil many times for fresh herbs; eventually, use it for cooking, possibly a meat fondue.

• For long storage, dry herbs. Tie stems in small bunches and hang them upside down in an airy spot, out of direct sun. When they're dry, crush them and store in jars. (Be sure they're completely dry, or they'll mildew in the jars.)

• For short-term use, keep herbs in jars. Don't wash the leaves; place them in preserve jars and close tightly. They'll keep for two or three weeks.

VEGGIE GARDEN

If the boat has the space, and one of the crew has the ambition, you can grow cherry tomatoes and any color sweet pepper plants. Confined to whatever pot size you choose, they will produce welcome additions to salad bowl or soup pot.

COOL STORAGE

With some exceptions (as in very large yachts), boat refrigeration units do not include vegetable bins, but certain vegetables will keep even without the benefit of cold storage.

• Mesh bags help store many fruits and vegetables safely. They need good air circulation, and they must be hung in such a way that they won't swing into a bulkhead. Bruising not only hurts the produce, it makes a mushy mess.

• Wash vegetables like potatoes and carrots in a mild chlorine solution (five or six drops of household bleach in a quart of water), let dry, and store in cotton net bags hanging in the galley.

POTATO PAMPERING

• Store potatoes and onions separately, or the potatoes will suffer. Nothing smells quite so bad as a suffering potato. Check them often for soft spots.

• Check for sprouts on the potatoes and remove them before you start a potato farm.

CAULIFLOWER POWER

• Cauliflower keeps well wrapped in paper towels too. Watch for mold spots, and remove them as soon as they appear.

• Or, remove the core from the cauliflower and sprinkle a bit of water into the bottom every day.

CARROT CARE

• Don't store carrots and apples together. Apples may cause bitterness in carrots.

• Kept in plastic bags, carrots rot quickly. (Condensation seems to cook them.) Take them out of the bag, remove any green tops, and dry them. Line up three or four carrots in the bottom of a basket or tray, leaving space between them. Put a paper towel on top, then add another row of carrots. Try three or four layers, with another towel or cotton cloth over the top. (The less the carrots touch each other, the less chance of spoil spots starting or spreading.)

LETTUCE LUCK

It may surprise you to know that iceberg lettuce will keep unrefrigerated for a week to 10 days. (Longer than a single head would usually stay in the home refrigerator.) Take the lettuce out of its plastic or cellophane wrapper, and wrap it in paper towels instead. That's it. When you want to make a salad, you'll peel off an outer layer or two of dry lettuce. Inside, the rest is still good and crisp.

No such luck with romaine or other leafy varieties.

CABBAGE CONTROL

Cabbage—green or red—keeps for weeks. Treat it the same as cauliflower: out of the plastic, into the paper towels. Try the core-removing, daily-watering method too.

DEHYDRATE

Celery gets mushy in days. If you don't use a stalk quickly, dry it before it spoils. Do the same with green pepper or carrots, if you should overbuy.

Cut into thin strips or small slices; put pieces in a single layer on a paper plate, and leave them in the sun to dry. Use later for soups, gravies, rice flavorings, and other cooked dishes.

SELF SEALERS

If you've used half a green pepper (or tomato or cucumber or grapefruit or lemon), don't wrap the remaining half in plastic. Just leave it. Air will seal the cut edge; the next day, trim off the dried edge and use the rest. (This works with onions too, but you may want to cover them with paper towels, and/or set them outside, to stop your crying.)

BANANA APPEAL

Bananas—green ones included—will ripen at very nearly the same rate whether you hang them in the sun or hide them in a locker. If you buy lots, find lots of ways to use overripe bananas.

SUPER CITRUS

Oranges, grapefruit, lemons, and limes will usually keep for as long as it takes to finish them. If you have great quantities on board, look through them every few days and remove any with soft spots before the white mold spreads to a neighbor.

EXPERIMENT

If you're spending time in a place where the produce is new to you, get a local cookbook and learn how to prepare the food.

• Green papaya can be used as a cooked vegetable. Peeled, sliced, and boiled with onions, it tastes much like squash.

• Green plantains can be boiled and used as a replacement for hot potatoes at dinner.

• A mashed avocado is an unlikely ingredient in soup.

• Caribbean kallaloo replaces spinach or turnip greens.

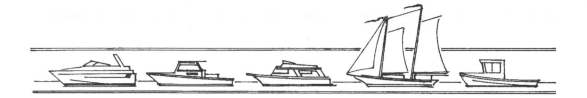

4 Cooking Stuff

Letters from boat travelers often are filled with food stories. Not about restaurants visited, but about meals prepared and enjoyed on board. New boat cooks surprise themselves by what they do with ship's stores on a small stove, and they're eager to share their revelations.

Instead of falling into a repetitious eating pattern, boat cooks develop a real enthusiasm for experimenting. Recipe invention becomes second nature as they improvise with what's available and disguise what nobody likes. The person who never baked in a house oven will turn out cakes and pies and muffins and bread on a boat stove, often prepared from scratch.

Not every boat meal will be entirely successful. But who on board would dare criticize?

CAN IF YOU MUST

First rule for using a main-dish dinner-in-a-can: Add a personal touch. Or two. Or three. Or more.

• Prepared meals such as soups, stews, and chili do serve their primary purpose of convenience. All can be improved with quick additions of onions, diced fresh vegetables, or favorite spices.

• Extend them (coincidentally diluting them, if that is your aim) with rice or pasta or biscuits or cornbread.

• A little effort put into presentation, plus a certain amount of attitude adjustment, will turn a can of beef stew into home-style beef and dumplings, Hungarian goulash, or, for the truly imaginative, burgundy beef.

FLAVOR BOUQUETS

• People who enjoy cooking are united in their enthusiasm for, and generous use of, herbs and spices. "Anybody can cook edible food; spices make food exciting." "With fresh herbs, you can do so much more with basic food." "Spices dress up an otherwise simple dish."

• People who cook because survival demands it might learn to enjoy it if they'd follow a flavoring lead.

• Buy smaller jars of spices that are seldom used, to save both space and flavor. (Spices lose strength after lengthy storage.)

• For vacation packing, buy a divided jar that holds six different spices in one container. Look for them in boat or camper stores and catalogs.

PASTA DATA

• Macaroni, shells, and other small pasta shapes can be cup-measured easily, but spaghetti and linguini recipes usually call for portions of a pound. Since you are not likely to keep spaghetti in its original box, you'll want a way to judge the amount to cook.

A half pound is a convenient measure. Before you store spaghetti in its bulk container, open a 1-pound box and divide the contents in half. Hold a half pound in a tight circle in your fist, then draw a circle that size on a piece of cardboard and store the cardboard with the spaghetti. Or look in kitchen-gadget shops for a plastic spaghetti-measurer—a long, flat rectangle with four circular cutouts indicating the amount needed to serve one, two, three, or four people.

• Cooked pasta will be approximately double the volume of uncooked.

BEANS AND RICE

• Dried beans and peas will more than double in volume when cooked (2 cups dried split peas will yield about 5 cups cooked).

• Rice (*not* the quick-cooking 5-minute variety) will triple (1 cup uncooked makes 3 cups cooked).

FLAME SAVERS

• If your stove has one burner too few for the number of items you've planned for dinner, cook the pasta off the stove. Boil the water, add the noodles, and bring the water back to boiling. Cover the pot and remove it from the stove; the pasta will continue to cook in the hot water. Watch it carefully; oversoaking will mean mushy macaroni.

• Rice will cook the same way, but without the same concern about over-absorption. When the water's gone, it's done.

WATER SAVER

• When preparing potato or macaroni salad, you can boil the eggs at the same time, in the same pot of water, as the spuds or pasta. (Save water, save stove fuel, save washing two pots.)

If the eggs are coated with vegetable shortening for keeping purposes, wipe off the excess before boiling—although a bit of vegetable oil in the water won't hurt the food anyway.

• If you choose to boil the items separately, do the macaroni/potatoes first, then use the same water to boil the eggs. (Pour the hot water into a pan with some cold water already in it, then put the eggs in, so they don't crack from a too-abrupt temperature change.)

• If you have room to store them, pasta-and-sauce dinner mixes have the advantage of absorbing all their cooking water. Canned chicken, beef chunks, or a vegetable assortment can replace the ground beef the mix recipe may specify.

• The same one-pot cooking method can be adapted to from-scratch cooking, using the provisions already on board.

EGG SAVER

When hard-boiling eggs, put a bit of vinegar in the water to keep the eggs from cracking; also, the shells should be easier to peel.

VITAMIN SAVER

When fixing mashed potatoes, use only enough water to cover; cooked over a low flame in a covered pan, the potatoes will steam as much as boil. When they're done, use some of the cooking water to mix the powdered milk you'll mash into the potatoes, thereby returning some of the good things that boiled out in the cooking process.

TIME SAVERS

• Look for potato nails, or rods, in the housewares section of hardware or kitchen-gadget stores. Potatoes bake faster with these heat-conducting aluminum nails stuck through their middles. Bake in an oven, or on the stovetop in a heavy pot on a trivet.

• Invert the lid of the potato-baking pot (or the pasta or stew pot) and put some French bread or dinner rolls on the lid to heat while dinner cooks.

• If you're using a low frying pan, inverting the lid is impractical—as in messy. Instead, lay aluminum foil over the pan top to provide a flat surface to heat the bread while dinner still steams inside.

• To heat bread on its own burner, wrap it in foil and set it on a flame tamer over low heat.

SOUP STARTERS AND FINISHERS

• Use canned tomato or vegetable juice as a soup starter. Add whatever fresh or canned vegetables or meats you choose. This is a good time to experiment with spices.

• The same juices, or canned tomato sauce, can be part of the liquid used to fix rice, providing another opportunity for recipe invention.

• Vary the color and flavor of basic potato soup (boiled potatoes in a milk-based stock) with the addition of sliced fresh carrots or diced green pepper. It easily evolves into seafood chowder with some minced clams or fish chunks and a bit of crumbled bacon. Pretend you're French and serve it cold, as vichyssoise.

• To thicken soup or sauces, use flour or cornstarch or tapioca or eggs. Easiest is to add some instant potato flakes. Do it gradually by spoonfuls until you get the right texture. The flakes take only a minute or two to absorb and expand.

BACON HANDLING

If you've never used canned bacon, don't be discouraged by your first encounter. It is packaged between layers of paper, and when first removed from the can, it is a gooey mess. Soak the bacon in hot water for a few minutes; it will be much easier to handle and separate.

DESALTERS

• Remove some of the excess saltiness from country ham or chipped beef slices by soaking them in hot water for a few minutes. Any amount of salt removal will help.

• Freshen the taste of canned shrimp and remove some of its salt by rinsing with cold water.

• A lot of canned food is too salty for many tastes. Sometimes, adding a bit of sugar may cut the excess saltiness.

TWO-FOR DESSERTS

• If your usual crew is only two people and the boat has no refrigerator for leftovers, make pudding, fruit-flavored gelatin, even cake mix by the half box. Just split the box contents and halve the added ingredients. If it's a cake, don't worry about using an extra half an egg; adjust the liquid a bit to compensate. Stow the rest of the original mix for another day.

• Instant pudding (made with instant powdered or canned evaporated milk) is a quick treat. If you miss the texture of real pudding, make it by the half package if necessary. It will set even without refrigerated chilling.

• Gelatin desserts will also set without refrigeration if you add some extra gel power. To prepare, use the usual proportion of flavor mix and water, and add one envelope (1 ounce) of unflavored gelatin for each cup of water. (If making a whole (3-ounce) box of Jello, add two envelopes of gelatin; if making only a half box, add one envelope.) The texture is slightly different than cold-set, but it's still a refreshing dessert. Setting time varies depending on temperature (overnight for a solid gel in typical Florida weather).

• Add fruit to a gelatin dessert. Use the liquid in the can as part of the water measure, and add unflavored gelatin as above.

STOVETOP BAKING

• Place a trivet into a heavy, noncoated pot (most boat bakers use aluminum pressure cookers) and it becomes a small oven. Use a flame tamer, if necessary, to control heat. Bake bread, pies, or cakes; an 8-inch cake pan fits into a 4-quart pressure cooker. Disposable foil cake or pie plates will also work.

• Don't use aluminum-bottomed stainless steel cookware for this dry cooking, or the aluminum disc may separate. There's also a possibility that a copper-bottomed stainless pot may warp if used as a stovetop oven.

• Use a frying pan (without a trivet) to bake quick bread, muffins, coffee cake, biscuits. Use a heavy pan with a lid, and keep the heat low with the flame tamer. Nonstick coatings are good for this direct baking.

• For cornbread, coffee cake, date-nut cake, and the like, pour batter into the pan, cover, and bake. Flip over briefly when done if you like a browned look.

• For muffins, mix the dough thick (use less liquid, or add extra flour). Drop by tablespoon into the pan. The muffin plops will melt together as they bake, but when done, they will break apart for easy grabbing and eating. Nobody will care that they're not round. These can be flipped too, to brown the tops, but don't turn them until they're completely baked (top pops back when pushed.)

• Sprinkle cornmeal into the frying pan when using it for baking; it helps prevent bottom burning.

• Baking times will vary depending on the thickness of the pan and the heat of the stove. Check progress frequently, and don't be discouraged if your first experiments with yeast dough are less than perfect.

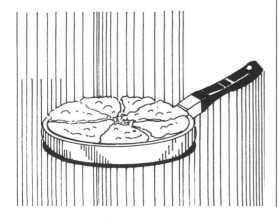

STOVETOP PIZZA

• Bake pizza without an oven. You'll find recipes for yeast-based dough, but it's a lot easier to use a basic biscuit dough, the kind that can be rolled fairly thin. Place the dough into a frying pan, letting it turn up at the sides. Pour a thin coating of tomato sauce over the dough and sprinkle on some Italian spices. Add some cheese; if you have no fresh mozzarella, use Velveeta, or whatever else you have in the individually wrapped cheese-slice department. Depending on ship's stores, add pepperoni (or salami or summer sausage), mushrooms (canned), green pepper (fresh or rehydrated flakes), onion slices, black olives, bacon (real or "bits"), ham chunks; top with a bit of grated Romano or Parmesan cheese and bake over low heat till bubbly. You will sacrifice a browned top, but you probably won't care.

• If you're close to grocery stores, buy a frozen pizza (super supreme with everything, or cheese only and add your own toppings.) Cut the pizza to whatever sizes fit your frying pans and bake on the stove.

STOVETOP TOAST

Unless your boat has sufficient power for home electrical appliances, you won't be toasting muffins or bagels in the usual way.

• The commercial stovetop pyramid-shaped toasters work, but not without some problems, storage being one and excessive drying and occasional burning the more significant others.

• Put aluminum foil over a flame tamer and lay the bread on top of it.

• Put pot holders (the metal bars that hold pots on the stove) close together and lay the bread on top to toast over very low flame.

• Sprinkle salt in a hot frying pan; put the bread in and turn when it gets brown. (The salt keeps the bread from sticking to the pan.) If you use a nonstick coated pan, you don't need the salt.

You can weigh down the bread with a coffee cup to make it brown faster. However, if you toast white cotton-textured bread this way, it will flatten out in the shape of the cup.

• Use the same toasting method (in a nonstick pan) for cheese or any kind of grilled sandwiches; no need to use butter, margarine, oil, or cooking spray. (A lid on the pan helps food heat through as the sandwich browns.)

PRE-PREPARE

Cook ahead whenever possible.

• While cleaning up supper dishes, bake muffins or stew fruit for morning.

• When fixing breakfast, cook eggs or potatoes for a lunch or supper salad.

• For weekends or daytrips, make lunch sandwiches before you get underway; it's easier while you're stationary, and food is ready for whoever gets hungry first.

• To save the ice in the main cooler, keep a separate small cooler in the cockpit for lunch and snacks.

THIRST QUENCHERS

• For weekend or vacation boating, make a big batch of cold lemonade to put into a serve-yourself pump bottle. Leave the bottle-washing to the house water resources.

• Solar tea supposedly has a smoother, less bitter taste than ordinary steeped tea. Fill a 2-liter bottle with water, dangle four teabags into the top, and let the bottle sit in sunlight till the tea is the right color. (It will "solar steep," even if you forget to put it outside, in a few hours.)

• To vary the flavor of sun tea, add some lemonade mix, or use whatever other flavors you like (raspberry is popular).

• Mix boxed fruit juices with plain seltzer for a tasty, healthy soda substitute. Or just flavor the seltzer lightly with a small amount of fresh citrus or any flavoring extract you have on board: strawberry, peppermint, coconut, vanilla. Any one will quench thirst better than sugared drinks.

MILK MIXERS

• Milk will be stored on board in liquid form in boxes (1-quart or 8-ounce size) or in cans (evaporated or condensed), and in powdered form (most are nonfat, but at least one brand has some fat). Packaged in any of these ways, it does not require refrigeration until opened or mixed. Save the boxed milk for drinking, and use the powdered and canned for cooking and baking.

• Nobody likes to drink reconstituted powdered milk, but sometimes that's likely to be all you have left. Try different brands to see which is least objectionable to your taste buds. Then add flavoring. Chocolate syrup or cocoa powder is a first choice for many, but vanilla is more versatile; even chocaholics may balk at the prospect of chocolate corn flakes. A little vanilla goes far; start with ¼ teaspoon per pint of milk. Molasses has also been suggested, but strawberry, banana, and almond seem better suited to a meal-accompanying drink.

• Another powdered milk theory suggests that the lack of flavor is due to the lack of fat; to try to fool your taster, add a rounded tablespoon of nondairy creamer to each quart of milk. Like any reconstituted milk, this tastes best if it's very cold.

• Cans of evaporated and condensed milk should be turned over every couple of weeks, or solids will settle into a thick clump at the bottom. This doesn't seem to hurt their usefulness in baking, but it doesn't look very appetizing.

COFFEEHOLICS

• If only one crewperson loves caffeinated coffee, make individual cups of real (not instant) coffee. Use a 1-cup filter/funnel, or steep the grounds as you would tea leaves and strain through a cloth or paper towel or fine mesh strainer. Either way, use about 2 rounded teaspoons per cup. Better yet, keep a supply of coffee "bags" on board.

• Mix your own gourmet coffees. Combine coffee and cocoa (or almond or vanilla) and add a cinnamon stick. Toss in some minimarshmallows if they seem appropriate. Choices are much broader now that flavored liquid or dry nondairy creamers are on the market with Amaretto or Irish cream or cappuccino options.

• For "coffee creamer," a spoonful of powdered milk is a more logical and healthful choice than the nondairy concoctions formulated for the job. It does require more vigorous stirring.

SALAD SAVERS

• When salad greens are wilting, add flavor and texture with chickpeas, green or wax beans, kidney beans, artichokes, water chestnuts, or tiny pasta shapes.

• For a quick salad dressing, mix ketchup and mayonnaise (experiment with proportions, starting with more mayo). Add a bit of pickle relish for a pseudo–Thousand Island taste. Or mix your own oil-and-vinegar with any combination of herbs.

• Mix sliced water chestnuts with canned vegetables, or add a few walnuts or almonds: the crunchy texture helps you ignore the overcooked string beans.

SANDWICH TOPPINGS

• Shredded cabbage (a much longer keeper than lettuce) is good on many sandwiches—basic sliced meat/cheese combinations, or tuna and chicken salad.

• Boat-grown alfalfa sprouts do a lot for a peanut butter sandwich.

BOAT SNACKS

• Vary the flavor of everyone's favorite snack—popcorn—with garlic or onion salt, chili powder, Parmesan cheese, or a bit of Worcestershire sauce mixed with the melted butter you drizzled on top. Fruit gelatin crystals have also been suggested, but without a lot of enthusiasm (and no hearty endorsements).

• If the raisins, prunes, or apricots get *too* dry, close the fruit in a jar with a few pieces of fresh lemon or orange peel.

BREAD SAVERS

• When you overbuy bread, dry slices in the sun. Then put them in a sealed zip-top bag and crush them with a rolling pin to save as bread crumbs.

• Cube the bread before drying, and save it for stuffing.

• Make croutons to serve with soups or salads: Spread margarine on bread slices. Cube the bread and sauté until brown. While still hot, toss in your choice of flavorings: salt (garlic or onion), paprika, parsley, Parmesan cheese, finely minced fresh herbs.

PARTY TIME

Cooking ahead lets the cook enjoy a party too. "Company" boat meals can be made from ordinary ship's stores.

• Fix any shape pasta with vegetable/tomato sauce, white or red clam sauce, ham and parmesan cheese topping.

• Make crab, salmon, or tuna croquettes, patties, or cakes.

• Tacos are fun: instead of a ground beef mixture, use chunk chicken or assorted beans in a tangy sauce.

• Ham slices served on scalloped potatoes and/or corn make hearty fare.

• Or serve a picnic of ham with potato salad and beans.

• With fresh foods, including fresh-caught seafood, possibilities grow. Kabobs on the grill are a nice surprise; a fondue is always well received.

• Do a boat version of a fish boil. Toss a bunch of fresh seafood into a big pot of water seasoned with a crab boil mix. Add potato chunks, carrots, onions, corn-on-the-cob—whatever is available. Make it a shared meal by asking everyone to bring something for the pot.

• As an easy frosting for the pressure cooker–baked cake, mix some honey or maple syrup into confectioners' sugar. When it's the right consistency, spread it over the cake and shake on some chocolate swirls or coconut flakes.

• A tablecloth might be considered an unnecessary excess, but there's no reason why you can't find room for a set of place mats and cloth napkins. (Store them under a bunk cushion.) Any meal becomes more special with an attractive presentation.

BREAKFAST ENTERTAINING

The lowly pancake can be elevated to guest status by topping it with any of a number of ordinary ship's stores. Offer an assortment in a do-it-yourself menu.

• Pour on pancake syrup, honey, maple syrup, fruit syrup.

• Spread on apple butter, pie filling, jam, canned fruit (or fresh, when available).

• Sprinkle on nuts, cinnamon sugar, wheat germ, bacon bits, coconut flakes.

• Cook in raisins, diced dried apricots, dates or prunes, sliced fresh banana or apple.

• Serve leftovers at dinner, topped with creamed or gravied meat and vegetable combinations. (If you thinned the batter earlier, you could serve real crepes.)

BOAT COMMUNE

When two or more cooks share the preparation chores, everyone enjoys the shared meal.

• If a few families are involved, an interesting experiment is to serve adults on one boat, children on another. There's usually one budding chef in the group who will be delighted with the captive guests.

• A progressive dinner on several boats is a great way to extend the enjoyment of a meal. One course per boat divides cooking chores and allows time to savor each item. Plus, one boat is not left with dishes from dinner for 12. This may be the ideal way to prepare a meal according to the local cookbook, testing new foods on an item-by-item basis.

• See Chapter 5, pages 56 and 57, for suggestions for a snack party prepared from nonrefrigerated stores.

HOLIDAY FEASTING

On a two-burner stove, you can fix a holiday meal with all the traditional trimmings. Cornish hen marinated in soy sauce and browned in a large frying pan. Stovetop stuffing baked in a small frying pan. Candied sweet potatoes, precooked, sliced, reheated with brown sugar, cinnamon, and miniature marshmallows. Green beans or peas. Simply alternate the pots on the stove; after heating one, remove it and heat another. The first will retain heat and continue to cook slowly until you're ready to switch pans again.

Bake the pies the day before. And don't forget the cranberries and possibly a fresh fruit salad.

YOU CAN CAN

Preserve the fish you catch, or prepare your own stock of canned meats.

• Canning is not a difficult process. The pressure cooker manual will detail all the steps.

A 4-quart aluminum pressure cooker will hold five ½-pint Mason jars, the size most boat cooks choose.

Wash jars and lids according to manufacturer's instructions. Prepare food and fill jars to recommended level. (This may differ according to what you are canning.) Put on caps. Place jars into pressure cooker with water. Lock on cover; follow instructions for exhausting air and bring to pressure. At the end of the specified time, turn off heat and allow pressure to drop. (Don't try to hurry the cooling process.)

• Can fish and seafood as soon as possible after they're caught. Clean your catch, and cut to size to fit jars. Soak in brine solution one hour. Fill jars and submerge, uncovered, in hot brine; boil 20 minutes. Drain jars, then put lids on. Process fish for 90 minutes at 15 pounds pressure. Shrimp, clams, and crabmeat will take about 35 minutes, lobster 45 minutes, also at 15 pounds pressure.

• If you decide to can meat and poultry, precook meat till it's light brown, poultry till it's medium done. At 15 pounds pressure, chicken takes about 40 minutes, meats about an hour.

• Always use new center lids; it's okay to reuse the screw-on rings, but always test seals according to manufacturer's directions.

SAFETY CHECK

Always check home-canned foods before using. Either bring the jars back to 15 pounds pressure, or boil the food in an uncovered saucepan for 10 minutes. Spoilage that may not be obvious in cold food will be noticeable when heated. If it doesn't look or smell right, don't even taste it.

SAFETY CAUTIONS

• Some boat cooks suggest that if you've cooked a one-pot dinner and have leftovers, you can keep the food in the pressure cooker for a day or two, after bringing it up to 15 pounds pressure and letting it sit with the lid on. However, neither the pressure cooker manufacturers nor the Food and Drug Administration's food safety consultants agree. Since this doesn't create a permanent vacuum, bacteria could still flourish. And nobody wants bacteria in their galley, particularly not flourishing types.

• The food experts also disagree with the common onboard practice of not refrigerating food items that are ordinarily kept in the home fridge. (See Chapter 5, pages 56 and 57.)

• The good news is that in 20-plus years of the authors' boating time, no illnesses relating to food-keeping practices have been experienced or observed.

• For information about keeping food safely, call:

U.S. Department of Agriculture Meat and Poultry Hotline
800-535-4555

Food and Drug Administration Seafood Hotline
800-332-4010

• While Ziploc-brand bags find multiple uses on board, they are not meant for heating foods by the boil-in-bag method. Buy the bags specifically made for meal-sealing gadgets.

COOKING LIBRARY

Everyone adopts favorite cookbooks, but the first boat cookbook should be chosen more for reference than for recipes. *Joy of Cooking* is one such food book (even if you don't agree with the title's premise). The recipes are not especially quick or boat-oriented, but the information on buying, cleaning, preparing, and preserving all kinds of food is invaluable. Once you have the basics, add specific easy-cook books.

FLOURS AND POWDERS

• Rather than buy packaged biscuit/-pancake baking mixes, many boat cooks mix and carry their own. Combine 6 cups white flour, 1 tablespoon salt, 3 tablespoons baking powder, and 1 cup instant nonfat dry milk powder (optional). Cut in 1 cup solid vegetable shortening and store in an airtight container. Use it for pancakes, biscuits, coffee cake, dumplings. Vary the mix by replacing a third of the white flour with whole wheat flour.

• If a recipe specifies 1 cup cake flour, you can substitute about ⅞ cup all-purpose flour.

• For self-rising flour, add ½ teaspoon salt and 1½ teaspoons baking powder to each cup of all-purpose flour.

• If the recipe requires 1 cup ordinary all-purpose flour and you have only cake flour, just add an extra ⅛ cup.

• Don't try to substitute all whole wheat for all white flour in a recipe, or you may play hardball with the resulting baked good.

• If you're out of baking powder, you have a few alternatives. To each cup of flour, add ½ teaspoon salt, 1 teaspoon baking soda, and 2 teaspoons cream of tartar. Or, instead of 1 teaspoon baking powder, use ¼ teaspoon baking soda and ½ teaspoon cream of tartar. Or, for 1 teaspoon baking powder, use ¼ teaspoon baking soda and ½ cup buttermilk or sour milk substituted for the same amount of whatever liquid the recipe requires.

• Check to see if the baking powder is still active by mixing 1 teaspoon powder with about ¼ cup hot water. If it fizzes, it's fine.

SUBSTITUTE SWEETS

• Granulated white sugar can be interchanged cup for cup with brown sugar.

• If you forgot to stock brown sugar, make your own (if you remembered to buy molasses). To each cup white sugar, add a couple of tablespoons molasses, less or more depending on whether you're mixing light- or dark-brown sugar.

• For 1 cup granulated sugar, substitute ¾ cup corn syrup, honey, molasses, or maple syrup; also reduce the liquid in the recipe by ¼ cup, and add ¼ teaspoon soda.

• If a recipe calls for a cup of honey, use 1¼ cups granulated sugar and add an additional ¼ cup liquid to the mix.

• If you're low on confectioner's sugar, you can use flour for part of the sugar in the icing; experiment to taste. Or make less frosting; boat cakes don't need it.

• Instead of a square of unsweetened baking chocolate, use 3 tablespoons cocoa plus 1 tablespoon margarine or shortening.

DAIRY DIFFERENCES

• Butter and margarine are interchangeable in recipes, even if the end product may look or taste a bit different. Solid vegetable shortening can also be substituted in equivalent amounts when baking.

• To measure solid vegetable shortening, you can mash it into a cup till it levels out at the required amount, then scrape it back out, leaving a well-oiled cup to wash. Or you can do it the messless way: If you need ⅔ cup shortening, put 1⅓ cups water into a 2-cup measurer. Add shortening (holding it under water with the spoon) till the water line moves up to the 2-cup level. Pour off the water; slightly damp shortening won't bother the recipe.

• Keep powdered eggs on board for cooking and baking. Order from:

Adventure Foods
Route 2, Box 276
Whittier, NC 28789
704-497-4113

• If a recipe calls for buttermilk or sour milk, add 1 tablespoon vinegar or lemon juice to each cup whole milk. Use boxed milk or reconstituted evaporated milk, and heat it slightly before adding the vinegar. Cream of tartar will also sour milk: use 1¾ tablespoons to each cup milk. (Instant dry milk is usually nonfat, so it's not suitable for souring.)

FLAVORING EQUIVALENTS

• One tablespoon instant minced onion replaces a small, fresh onion.

• Unless you are a gourmet, ⅛ teaspoon garlic powder approximates the flavor from one small clove.

• The flavor of dried herbs is much more concentrated than that of fresh ones. To replace 1 tablespoon fresh, use ½ to 1 teaspoon dry.

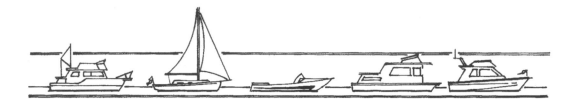

Cold Front

Boaters don't need refrigeration machinery. Even ordinary ice isn't essential to the enjoyment of boating. But on a windless, sweltering summer day, who would not welcome even the temporary soothing respite of an icy cold anything? Who would not prefer deli-sliced smoked turkey with a choice of crisp shredded vegetable toppings to a peanut butter or canned-ham sandwich?

Despite those preferences, it is helpful to know how to manage without a cold-keeper. Then the ice days may take on special status, but the do-without days won't be diminished in their pleasure quotient.

COLD BASICS

Ice is dependable and usually available, at least along U.S. waterways.

• An excellent way to ensure a constant ice supply is to travel in the company of a large boat—one equipped with a large-capacity icemaker and captained by a generous and understanding friend.

• Block ice is better than cube, cube is better than crushed, crushed is better than flaked, and that's all there is.

• With a built-in boat cooler, two or three blocks will usually fit; they'll last up to a week, depending on the cooler's insulation, how often it's opened, and the outside temperature. With a portable cooler, only one block is practical, to leave room for the food.

• Though impractical for long-term cruising, dry ice can keep vacation food so cold the only problem might be remembering to thaw each day's dinner in time. A separate cooler becomes the portable freezer; *only* frozen items are kept there. It's not a money-saving choice—to keep a week's frozen provisions would require about 25 pounds of dry ice, which costs approximately $25 to $30—but if you're not a do-without boater, it's the best solution. (One thoughtful racing skipper surprised his crew with hot fudge sundaes on their third day out. Even real refrigerators sometimes have trouble keeping ice cream solid enough to justify its name.)

COLD CARRIERS

• A canvas log carrier (a rectangle of fabric with dowels sewn into each end for handles) makes a sturdy tote for bagged or block ice. So does a handled canvas bag, provided you don't have too far to travel, in which case an insulated bag is almost a necessity.

• Wrapping ice in newspaper (sections, rather than single pages) and/or paper grocery bags will delay a premature meltdown.

• If you're transporting food between a home refrigerator/freezer and the boat's icebox, keep a Styrofoam cooler in the car so the food will stay as cold as possible en route, especially if the marina is a three-hour drive from home.

• If the cooler has been left on the boat—again—use newspaper wrap and a corrugated cardboard box.

COLD HELPERS

• Reusable blue plastic coolant containers are space-savers, but it's just as practical to make your own blocks of ice in your home freezer. Half-gallon cardboard milk cartons are fine for the ice itself, but if you use plastic containers instead, you'll have drinking water as the ice melts.

• When washing the bottles, use baking soda or a bit of chlorine bleach in the final rinse to ensure good taste.

• Don't fill the bottles completely; leave room for the expansion that freezing will cause.

• The bottle-blocks fit well either upright or horizontally in typical small coolers.

• Start each trip with as much pre-frozen food as is practical, whether it's containers of cooked stews or sauces or meat packaged for individual meals.

COLD CONSIDERATIONS

To refrigerate or not to refrigerate? The question prompts lengthy discussions.

• Criticism of early machinery, which tended to malfunction, may not be valid today, but the memory lingers, giving skeptics food for worry. On the other hand, one long-time sailor turned trawler captain observes, "Refrigeration makes cruising a civilized endeavor. A freezer, however, remains an unnecessary luxury."

• If you are converting an icebox to mechanical refrigeration, you may want to add insulation. (Even if you're not converting, the extra insulation is a good thing.) If you conserve the cold, you're also conserving the ice or the power required to produce the cold.

COOLER HELPERS

• For weekend or vacation boating, use separate coolers for food and drink. Ice in the food cooler will last longer because the cold will not escape every time someone gets thirsty.

• A cooler adjunct for any boat, though usually used with small boats on

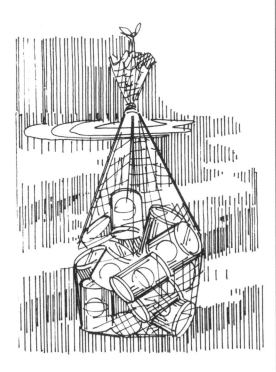

(The box can also be divided into two compartments to maintain separate refrigerator and freezer sections.)

• With the engine-driven system, it's important to read the manual and follow the instructions carefully. To maintain proper cooling, the engine should be run at the recommended rpm. If once-a-day running is supposed to cool the box for a 24-hour period and it does not, it's advisable to find and fix the problem rather than run the engine more often.

• Use an aluminum hook to attach a vertical ice cube tray to the side of a cold plate. (Use a rivet or duct tape to attach the hanger to the tray.)

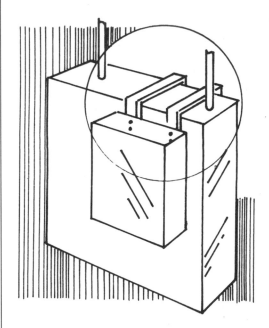

beach-party picnics: fill a strong mesh bag with drink cans and submerge the bag in the water for as long as it takes to chill them to a refreshing temperature. Those picnicking along the Gulf of Mexico will need to find other cooling plans on those days when the water is warmer than the air.

• Try not to open the food cooler any more than necessary (twice per meal: food out, leftovers in).

COLD CHOICES

Holding Plates

• Efficient but expensive, a holding-plate system powered by the boat engine can turn the boat's original icebox into a refrigerator with ice-making capability.

DC Power

The boat icebox can take on refrigerator status with a 12-volt unit powered by the boat's batteries. (The units can also operate dockside; a battery charger connected between shore power and boat battery replaces the DC power the unit is using.)

While the cooling aspect of this type of system is good, many boats have trouble compensating for the battery drain when the boat is away from the dock.

DC/AC Power

• Small, self-contained, top-opening chest-type refrigerators or freezers (or stand-up combinations) operate on either 12- or 110-volt power. For daily travel under power, the 12-volt operation is fine. Continuous running all day keeps things at maximum coldness, and the units retain enough cold overnight to keep the contents safe when the boat is at anchor. Dockside, the unit runs on 110-volt shore power.

• The chest-type unit is used as a refrigerator *or* freezer; there is no separate compartment, even for a small ice tray.

• Thermoelectric units can be used to keep food cool or warm on 12- or 110-volt power. By far the most reasonably priced alternative, they are also the least efficient. They'll keep contents cool, but not truly cold, especially in hot climates.

AC Power

Standard home appliances are an option only for those boats with an adequate power supply—usually a separate, large generator or a high-power-capacity inverter—to operate them when the boat is away from shore power.

Three-way Power

• Refrigerators made for recreational vehicles are sold with three-way operating capability, adding propane to the 12-volt/110-volt choices. The propane option is appealing to those who appreciate quiet anchorages, but these units are neither designed nor built for marine use. In a houseboat or other powerboat where the unit is mounted above the waterline (so it can be properly vented overboard), and

where heeling motion is not a problem (so the pilot light stays centered), it is acceptable. But a manufacturer specifically cautioned against using them in a monohulled sailboat.

• RV units are more likely to rust than marine products, but they can be repainted (or replaced at a fairly reasonable price) when necessary.

COLD COSTS

• The power source—both one-time and ongoing—is a big part of the actual cost of mechanical refrigeration. For a 12-volt system the boat needs a good supply of batteries plus the means to keep them charged. For engine-driven or generator-powered systems, fuel costs continue. Capturing solar power or using a wind generator may be free, but only after a considerable initial outlay.

• If the boat is equipped with a belt-driven system, and you're planning to live dockside for a time, buy a small electric motor and hook it up to do the belt-turning job usually done by the boat engine. Dockside power then oper-

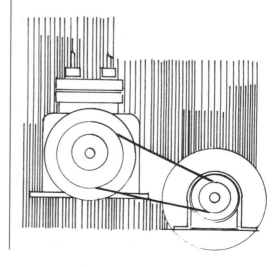

ates the refrigerator, eliminating the need to run the boat engine every day. Be sure the dockside motor matches the power provided by the boat engine's recommended rpm.

COLD PACKING

Whatever the cold-creating mechanism, the dimensions of boat boxes are considerably smaller than those of home refrigerators. You have to pay more attention to what goes in (and how) and what doesn't (and why).

• Use common sense when loading. In all cases, lowest is coldest. If the box has a holding plate, the space around the plate will also be super cold; don't put anything near it that cannot tolerate freezing. Meat and cheese can be close to the plate; keep vegetables and eggs farthest away.

• Stacking boxes (similar in design to milk crates, but smaller) make it easy to get things in and out of the box, especially

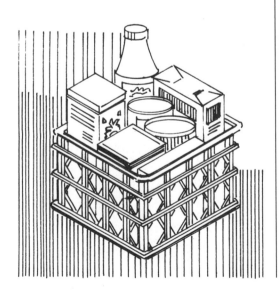

with a top-loading type. Instead of freezing your hands as you shift items around, you can remove the boxes quickly, showing the entire next layer. The faster you find your objective, the less cold escapes.

• Buy square refrigerator bottles in pint, quart, and half-gallon sizes. Clear or translucent is best, so you don't waste time opening bottles to see what's inside.

• Smaller, square, covered containers will stack easily to make use of all available space.

• You can save refrigerator or cooler space in many ways. Buy frozen concentrated fruit juice in the size that makes a half gallon. Mix it in a smaller container—the quart size, so you'll use less than half the required amount of water. When serving, pour a half glass of juice and fill with water (or whatever proportion tastes right). The juice will still be cold enough to be refreshing; you will have saved a quart of cooler space, plus the price difference between two small and one large juice can.

• Leftovers store well in zip-top plastic bags; you can usually scrunch them into whatever shape space is available in the cooler. (The bags can be washed and reused, for those so inclined.)

• Wedge egg cartons into a secure spot so you don't have icebox scramble. Transfer eggs from Styrofoam or cardboard cartons to hard-plastic egg holders, as added protection.

CRISP KEEPERS

• Boat boxes don't have vegetable crispers, but a covered plastic box will keep produce fresh and prevent it from getting lost inside the big box.

• Zip-top bags can be used with care; be sure they stay on top of things, to prevent mashed tomatoes or crushed cucumbers.

• Though not an efficient space user, a burp-top lettuce keeper is still prized for its crisp-keeping capability.

FREEZER PACKING

• When buying meat to pack the boat freezer for a long cruise, think small. Just because you have a barbecue grill and the family likes ribs, you can't justify taking too much space in the freezer for a single meal.

• Buy a lot of individual-serving cuts (steaks and chops), plus small roasts and ground meats packaged in amounts suitable for one meal for your usual crew. One possible advantage to the small-boat freezer is a forced reduction in the consumption of red meat.

• If an item is available in a can, buy the canned version and save the freezer space for those things that are not available in another form.

PREFREEZE

• Some supermarkets will cut, package, and prefreeze as much meat as your freezer will hold. Ask if the service is available, and weigh the cost against the time you'd rather spend doing something else.

• Meat packaged for the freezer should be double wrapped and clearly marked for quick identification. You can write directly on the freezer bags with a permanent marking pen, or put a piece of colored paper between the bags. Different colors indicate different types of meat.

• Date each package for timely use.

• Just as the vacationing boater cooks ahead to bring frozen meals, the cruising cook can prepare and freeze a few one-meal portions of soup or stew. Easy to prepare when you're stationary, these instant dinners will be most welcome on an overnight crossing, in a bouncy anchorage, or after a late arrival.

• Package these emergency dinners in heavy, boilable plastic bags so they can be heated in the bag. They can even be eaten from the bag when conditions are such that you choose not to handle dishes. Simple meats like sliced beef or turkey with a mild gravy provide a satisfying meal, especially with cotton bread to absorb the gravy. It's possible to package individual servings of chili in these bags, but spicy foods are not the kind you'll likely choose if you're in a situation where cooking is a problem.

ARRANGE AND REARRANGE

• Take a number of small mesh bags, and pack a selection of different meats in each (one bag might hold varied meals for one week). Otherwise, all the ground beef may end up at the bottom of the box,

requiring excessive open time and needless rummaging to retrieve it.

• If you're using your frozen food regularly and not resupplying, don't leave empty space or the unit will work overtime trying to keep the box cold. Freezer containers filled with water will soon be a solid space-filler; even rolled-up newspapers will help retain the desired coolness.

• A good boat freezer can be as efficient as a good home freezer, but be sure to keep packages revolving according to dates. Follow standard recommendations for length of time to keep each type of meat.

FREEZE OR NOT?

• Authorities don't recommend freezing lunch meat, or any cured meat, but many people do so—at home and on a boat—with no apparent problems. If nothing else, hot dogs fit a lot of meals into minimal space.

• Butter freezes well. Cheese may crumble when thawed, but the change in texture doesn't affect the taste.

• Eggs can be frozen (out of the shell, separated or whole), but most cruising boaters use other methods to keep eggs for an extended time.

FROST AND DEFROST

If the freezer compartment is the former icebox, it will have a hole in the bottom where water drains to the bilge. Keep the hole plugged (a piece of sponge will do the job) to keep warm bilge air away from the bottom of the freezer. When you want to defrost, remove the plug. If you're dockside at the time, you can use a small hair dryer to hurry the process.

COOL OR NOT?

With so many cubic feet of space in a home refrigerator, most people store food items that don't really need the cold.

• Margarine (vegetable oil spread) labels recommend keeping it in the refrigerator, but many boat cooks don't, and it lasts for weeks. Even if it melts, it just takes on its vegetable oil form.

• If you buy margarine in ¼-pound sticks, take it out of the paper wrapping and repack in sterile jars. Place the jars in the coolest part of the boat (in cool waters, probably the lowest accessible locker).

• Buying margarine in decorative tubs allows you to avoid the repack process and assures a neater serving dish.

• If you like real butter, buy it in cans for long-term storage. Once open, a pound will probably be used up before it spoils.

CHEESE, PLEASE

• Individually wrapped cheese slices are available in a wide assortment of fat and cholesterol levels, as well as theoretical flavors. While not a cheese gourmet's choice, they do keep a long time without benefit of refrigeration.

• The same is true of Velveeta-brand products and Kraft's jars of snack-cheese spreads.

• Cheese products can be purchased in spray cans for easy cracker-decorating.

• Grated cheese keeps at boat temperature long enough to get through a shaker box (bulk buying not recommended).

• Cheeses with wax coatings are good keepers if the cover is not punctured or broken.

• A variety of canned cheeses are available from:

Washington State University Creamery
101 Food Quality Building
Pullman, WA 99164-6392
509-335-4014

• When you buy fresh cheese, like a chunk of cheddar, you can keep mold at bay by wrapping the cheese in cheesecloth that is periodically dampened with vinegar.

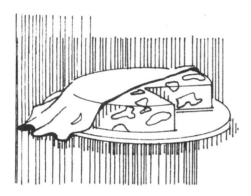

EGG SAVERS

• Eggs keep for weeks unrefrigerated. For storage purposes, it's better to start with really fresh eggs that have never been refrigerated, but the only way that's likely to happen is if you have farmers in the family.

• When you bring the eggs on board, coat them with vegetable shortening to seal the shells from the outside air. Use a solid type, like Crisco; vegetable oils are not heavy enough. (Some people use mineral oil or petroleum jelly for coating.)

• If you choose not to oil your eggs (or if you believe in redundancy), turn the eggs over each week. This keeps the yolk suspended in the white, rather than allowing it to settle against the shell, where it might deteriorate.

• Whichever method you choose, don't trust it completely. Always break eggs one by one into a small dish to check their freshness before adding them to the cook pot or baking bowl.

• When eggs start to lose freshness, they get thin; whites are watery and yolks appear flatter. At this stage, they're still fine for scrambling, baking, omelets, or egg sandwiches.

• You'll know when eggs are not okay. Sometimes the smell comes through the unbroken shell. Fortunately that's a rare occurrence.

• If you think the eggs are getting ready to spoil (the thin is getting thinner), hard-boil them and think of ways to use them up in a short time.

• To check eggs for freshness without cracking the shell, put them in a pan of water. If any float, don't waste time cracking or cooking them; throw them out. (As eggs get older, the air pocket at the large end gets larger; a noticeable upturn is a good indication of an aging egg).

• If a piece of eggshell goes into the bowl or pan with the egg, the best tool for retrieving it is a larger piece of shell.

SMOKED MEAT

• Dried hard salami, smoked summer sausage, and pepperoni sticks originally purchased unrefrigerated can be kept the same way. If they spoil (probably because the casing gets punctured), you'll know by the mold that is growing inside the casing.

• Country hams are dry-cured with salt, and can be stored on board without refrigeration.

• Real bacon bits will not keep well once opened. At boat temperature, they grow green fuzz in a week or two, depending on the weather. Fake bacon bits are a poor flavor substitute, but the only practical option.

FERMENTABLES

• Jams and jellies keep reasonably well unrefrigerated. Often, cheaper varieties keep better, perhaps because of added sugar preservatives. Buy smaller jars anyway, to finish them faster.

• In the rare circumstance that jam or fruit-based pancake syrups start to ferment, you'll recognize the fruity liqueur smell when you open the jar. If there's no mold, it's okay to eat. Serve it as a pudding-topping treat.

SANDWICH HELPERS

Even though you will never hear a food specialist say it's okay to keep certain items unrefrigerated, cruising people do it with no apparent ill effects.

• Sandwich helpers like mustard, pickle relish, and ketchup are kept in ordinary boat lockers all the time, as are pickles, bottled lemon juice, and many salad dressings. (Even some that look creamy are oil-and-vinegar based and require no refrigeration.)

• The biggest surprise of the nonrefrigerated items is everyone's greatest food-poisoning nightmare—mayonnaise. Each boat cook has a favorite brand, one that meets an acceptable reason-to-buy standard. One woman looks for cheaper brands that use vinegar and not lemon juice. Another wants "salad dressing" on the label, preferably one that does not use egg yolk. Another recommends buying only real mayonnaise. The only universal comment is a caution: always use a clean utensil when dipping into the jar so you don't contaminate the mayonnaise/salad dressing with bits of mustard or relish or bread crumbs. Whatever the "secret," it must have a lot of leeway, because whatever the brand, these products seem to keep long enough. (One woman buys only 16-ounce or smaller jars, since a 32-ounce size lasts too long for her peace of mind.)

• With two people on board full time, a 16-ounce jar of mayo/salad dressing is easily used within a month's time.

• Those who cannot get past the great mayo debate can buy the single-sandwich foil-wrapped packets used by restaurants and delis.

APPETIZERS WITHOUT ICE

If yours is one of the remaining cold-less boats, here's a list of things you can prepare for a snack party that easily becomes dinner. All ingredients are items usually stored in a cruising boat's pantry.

• Spread bottled snack cheese on individual slices of chipped beef or thinly sliced ham. Roll up, then slice into tiny pinwheel-shaped bite-size snacks.

• Cube salami or summer sausage and hard cheese or Velveeta, and alternate cubes on toothpicks. Vary color and taste with chunks of pickle served on the same tiny skewers.

• Put slices of sausage and cheese on crackers, and top with an olive slice.

• Dip chips or crackers into a cheese/mayo/spice mix: your choice for flavorings. (Use fresh veggie spears if they're available.)

• Serve "Tabby Treat": tuna, salmon, crabmeat, or sardines (or corned beef, ham, chicken, or turkey) mashed and mixed with mayo and/or pickle relish and spread on crackers or dipped with chips.

• Open cans of smoked clams or oysters or minishrimp and serve as is or with an appropriate dipping sauce.

• For hot additions, serve nachos (at least one nonrefrigerator cheese is already flavored with jalapeños) or corn chips to dip into refried beans.

• Heat cocktail sausages in barbecue sauce, or fold sausage halves in a wrap of biscuit dough and bake stovetop.

• If you're really ambitious, make miniature pizzas (see Chapter 4, page 39), but be prepared to supply seconds, thirds, and more for as long as you're willing.

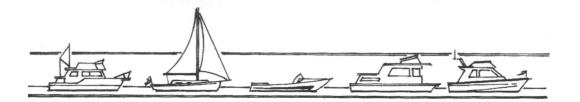

Inner Space

Few boats have enough storage. By some formula familiar to all boat folks, storables are always one or two stacks ahead of available space.

On a perfect boat, everything has a place and everyone on board puts things in their places. On a real boat, the places may be assigned, but the rest depends on each crewmember's definition of perfection. Neatness is not the sole reason for such attempts at organization; sometimes, it's important—even critical—to find things fast. Few boaters reach or maintain their ultimate goal regarding things and places, but each time you put a thing in its appropriate place you will be one step closer.

STORAGE HANG-UPS

• Temporary storage solutions in the form of net hammocks easily become per-manent installations, containing excess in many places. Larger hammocks hang over bunks for clean clothes or for not-quite-laundry (those items worn once but not yet ready for the official laundry bag). They're useful in the head for towels, shower kits, or plastic bottles. In the galley, hammocks keep fresh produce fresh; in the engine room, they hold a supply of extra fuel filters, keeping them safe, dry, and handy.

Hobby materials, children's games and toys, and pet paraphernalia all can find their place in the master organization plan.

• Look for net hammocks in craft shops. You may find different sizes and possibly different prices than in marine stores. Be sure to buy nylon; in a place prone to constant dampness, cotton eventually catches a case of mildew, and if the mold doesn't destroy the twine, an over-enthusiastic chlorine treatment might.

• Trios of metal mesh baskets in graduated sizes would ordinarily be rejected for boat storage because of the material, but the painted ones resist rust for quite a while. The baskets hang from one hook in a vertical row. Do not allow them to swing freely; among other problems, this causes a series of arch-shaped scratches on the nearest bulkhead. Attach the rim of the lowest basket to the bulkhead with a small screw. Cushion the wire mesh inside with colorful bandanas and use the baskets for fresh fruit or vegetables, potatoes and onions, pet toys, sewing yarn, and other odds and ends.

FLEXIBLE LOCKERS

For a more permanent add-on locker, fabric panels of canvas or boat acrylic can be fitted in many places, enclosing narrow but usable triangular spaces wherever the hull side curves upward, as, for example, in a V-berth or quarter berth.

To add such a locker, sew a basic curtain panel of canvas, with a hem pocket top and bottom. Attach the bottom hem to

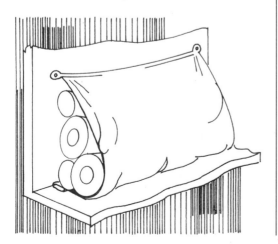

the boat with a dowel passed through the hem and snapped into brackets, or attach the fabric itself to the plywood base of the bunk using screws or fabric snaps. Shock cord through the upper hem pocket holds the panel up and the contents in, while allowing convenient access. (Put suitable fittings on bulkhead or hullside at the top ends, to hold the cord.)

DIVIDE TO CONQUER

Divide all lockers into manageable spaces; things are much more likely to stay where they're put when they're confined to a smaller area.

• Add separate shelves wherever possible, so items will not be stacked on top of each other, waiting for a chance to fall.

• Add vertical dividers to each shelf to prevent side slipping. Install them by attaching small wood strips to the shelf as braces for each side of the divider; or rout a groove in the shelf and glue the divider into the recess. The vertical separations don't need to extend to the top of the shelf space, just far enough to stop any sideways shifting.

• Hanging lockers may be a useful selling point from a manufacturer's view, but few boats carry a lot of clothes that need to stay on hangers. The space devoted to such lockers will hold a lot more, and a greater variety, if shelves are installed under, or instead of, the single hanger rod.

• Covered-wire home closet shelving is lightweight and simple to install, and the vinyl coating should prevent rusting for many years. Depending on the bracket installation, you may be able to hang the shelves upside down for a substantial built-in fid.

• Even lighter-weight shelf separators can be made of fabric. Sew shelf-size pieces of boat acrylic, and put a grommet in each corner. Inside the locker, put cup hooks or L-shaped brackets in each corner of each shelf level, and hang up the fabric squares.

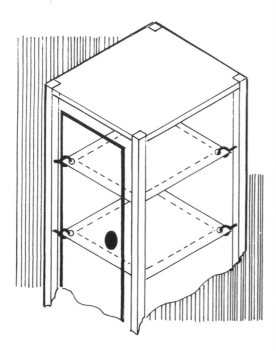

• Organize another few inches of space on the back of the locker door. Start with a door-size piece of canvas or other heavy backing material, and sew rows of mesh pockets to it. The pockets can hold socks, underwear, belts, shoes, whatever fits. (Attach the fabric panel to the door with screws, hooks, or a dowel—whatever you need to support the weight of the items you're storing.)

STACKING STORAGE

It's impractical to divide some spaces permanently. For example, the space under a galley sink may need to remain accessible and spacious enough for a person to crawl in to check on or repair plumbing. Engine rooms are already too confining in many boats, and the "floor" space of a hanging locker would be hard to clean if separated by permanent dividers. For these areas, the popular milk-crate storage boxes are perfect. Lined up side by side, they prevent sliding. Stacked, they separate, organize, and protect their contents. They don't add a lot of weight, they're easy to clean, and you can readily see what's inside.

HIDE AND STORE

Boatbuilders often close off potential storage space, either for aesthetics (hullsides may not be finished perfectly) or because they are not easily accessible.

• Boatowners can seek out these hidden places, then open them up so they can fill them up. Look under shelves, under and behind drawers, behind seat backs, and further behind locker backs. Beyond gaining the storage benefits, exposing hidden storage space should gain the approval of Coast Guard or U.S. Customs inspectors.

• Though not intentionally hidden, the space behind companionway or stateroom ladders is often overlooked. Since ladders are usually movable to allow access to compartments behind them, this is not a place for permanent build-ins, but the space can still be used. A toolbox of the right shape will often slide under the bottom step, and there may be room for a small hammock behind another step.

ADD-A-FID

• Sometimes lockers with doors don't have fids inside, and sometimes existing fids are not high enough to hold that locker's contents. Add whatever height fid is suitable. If you choose to install wood fids, leave an inch of space at each end of the locker to make cleaning easier (you can sweep out a spill of flour or oatmeal if the fid doesn't block the entire front of the shelf).

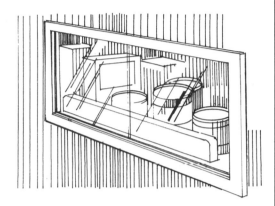

• Make removable fids. Drill holes vertically into each end of the bottom edge of the wood piece that will become the fid. Glue pieces of dowel into the holes, leaving ¼ inch to ½ inch of dowel extending beyond the fid bottom. Drill matching holes in the shelf so the fid can be put in or lifted out as necessary.

• Cup hooks and a length of shock cord stretched between them provide extra support for tall items on a shelf.

• A piece of ¼-inch line and two tiny cleats (or one cleat and one permanent fastener) might be a more nautically correct option.

• Even with extra fid support, there will be times when locker contents want to dance. To stop the clunking and the noise of shifting jars (prompted by a rolly anchorage or a rough sea), you will need to resort to the decidedly unnautical means of stuffing the shelves with pot

holders, dish towels, facecloths—anything to stop the motion.

SHELF HELPS

• On open shelves where items are free to slide side to side, use removable fids to capture books or boxes on a temporary basis, leaving the center of the shelf vacant so the cat can nap.

• Where a storage shelf is positioned directly under the cabintop or deck, the space may be noticeably warm when sun hits the outside surface and more prone to condensation than a shelf situated lower down in the boat. With that in mind, use the cooler, drier lower shelves to store instant coffee, creamer, lemonade crystals, and other items that could suffer from heat or dampness.

OPEN-AND-SHUT CASES

• Small door openings are good for most lockers; they prevent a massive fall-out if the boat takes an unexpected dip while the door is open. But for some lockers, a larger opening is desirable. To keep odd-shaped things accessible, hinge the entire front of the locker so it folds down. Long-handled frying pans or an electric saw or drill can slide in and out without a lot of turning to find the right angle to clear the door frame. With the door hinged down, you can hold it halfway up to stop things from falling out. When closed, a slide or drop bolt keeps the door securely shut.

• If you're adding a new locker or replacing a door, try using hinges that "spring" shut. Be sure the door stays shut and doesn't rattle by adding an inverted L of Velcro where the top of the door closes against the frame.

SHIFTING STORAGE

• Often, door latches are more decorative than functional. One bad wake roll and doors—and locker contents—start flying. Add a backup by installing turn-button closures on every locker.

   If the door fits flush into the frame, the turn-button will also fit neatly flush to both surfaces. However, if the locker door closes against and in front of the frame, you'll need to add a piece of wood as a spacer to bring the frame surface level to the door. A semicircle of teak makes a fancy base, but plain plywood painted to match the background works just as well.

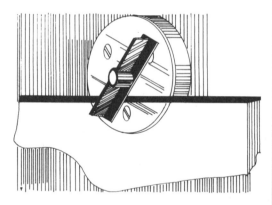

• For easier access to the contents of a galley locker, install a drawer base so you can pull the entire shelf out far enough to be visible. A locking pin holds the shelf/drawer in its closed position behind the locker door, so it cannot escape and take the door out.

• When drawers no longer slide open voluntarily, rub a bar of soap or a candle along the sides, or wherever they seem to be binding; a few push/pulls and they should start gliding again.

BIG STUFF

• Whenever you must store things that could break or spill—such as glass bottles of food items, gallon containers of engine oil, laundry or dish soap, and bleach—use plastic dishpans or other high-sided boxes or bins so accidents will be confined.

• No matter what you're storing, square containers are more practical than round. Side by side or stacked, they fit snugly, with no wasted space between them.

• Hardware items that are seldom used (grommet kit, hoses, C-clamps, fittings) can be put into heavy canvas bags. (Make your own in whatever sizes are useful.) The bags can conform to the hull side or to available locker space, so they take less room than boxes.

SMALL STUFF

• Zip-top bags can be used for everything—dry food, boat papers, clothing, books, letters, leftovers. They're relatively sturdy, moisture-proof, and reusable. The clear plastic allows instant identification of contents, and they can be made to fit almost anywhere.

• You can use the plastic canisters that hold 35-mm film cartridges to store many different items: a pocket pill supply or a purse coin supply, sewing accessories (buttons, needles, pins) and other craft supplies, small fasteners (washers, nuts, screws), or fishing things (hooks, weights, flies), cotter pins, keys.

   Label canisters with masking tape or mailing labels cut to size. Or buy Fuji-brand film—you can see what's inside their clear plastic cases, so labeling is unnecessary.

• Find a friend who drinks Crown Royal and ask him to save the trademark purple drawstring bags. Even spare lantern chimneys stow safely wrapped in a layer of bubble wrap encased in royal purple. Keep a few empties handy to hold and cushion those nautical knickknacks that are charming dockside but do not travel well.

HOLDUPS

• If you have an available bulkhead, hang up galley utensils where they can be easily reached when needed. Hooks on a board hold the items; snap brackets a few inches below keep them in position and quiet.

• If the same arrangement is used for an assortment of your most-used hand tools, there may be less searching and swearing when it's time to use them.

• A bulkhead-mounted box with a checkerboard of slots keeps spices where they are most accessible to the creative chef, and simultaneously protects them from direct sun and excess heat. The jars sit at an angle within the box, so they're not likely to fall out. Label the lids and/or color code those you use most often.

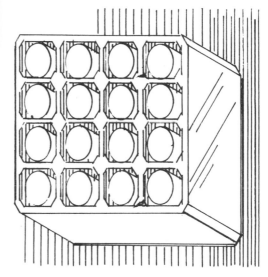

• Clothespins can be used to hold recipes during cooking time, clip to-do or to-buy lists to an obvious shelf, close snack bags, exchange family notes, and occasionally to attach clothes to clotheslines.

• With Plexiglas now available at picture-frame shops, boaters can stop worrying about breaking the glass covering the over-the-sofa artwork, but there is still the problem of the ever-tilting frame. Attach the painting to the bulkhead by screwing directly into the frame from the backside of the bulkhead. To establish the right location for the screws, put a thin screw through the bulkhead from front to back. Then, with the picture in position, use a larger screw for the back-to-front attachment of the frame.

• If that's too much trouble, use brackets that attach from the front of the frame. A plastic L-shape fits over the front; three brackets are enough to keep the frame in position.

• Everyone misplaces keys. A floating key ring is an obvious choice for boat keys, but a whole row of hooks can be assigned for boat keys, house keys, car keys.

• Everyone misplaces eyeglasses (prescription and sun). If an eyeglass case is screwed to a bulkhead, at least the case cannot get lost, and it may serve as a reminder to fill it with something.

MEDIA CENTER

• The television set can sit out on a shelf safely as long as it's tied in when the boat is underway. Attach a line to the bulkhead behind the set at about mid-TV height. Pull the line around and across the front of the set and secure it to a small cleat on the opposite side.

• Many boats carry a compact matched television set and video cassette player. Build them into a shelf with a substantial four-way fid around the bottom. If the shelf is at least partially rotatable, couch potatoes will be happy. You can also set the components into a locker to hide them behind a door when they're not in use. (Boats can have media walls too.)

TAPE DISPENSERS

• Build a simple, open-front box into a locker or onto a bulkhead. The dimen-

sions should be slightly larger than those of a videocassette tape. Slide the tapes in so an end label is readable; hold them in with a piece of shock cord stretched vertically down the front and secured on a cleat or with a hook and a U-shaped bracket.

• To make a different tape storage case, start with three rectangles of wood cut slightly larger than a tape's length and width. Two of the wood pieces become the top and the bottom of the case; the third is a midheight support. Use lengths of corner molding to frame the corners of the case. In each section (above and below the center support), notch a portion of the front molding on both sides, so one tape can slip through the notched opening. Stack as many tapes as will fit in each section. When you want to play one, lift and remove tapes one by one till you get to the chosen feature.

• Built-in slide-out racks for music cassettes or videotapes look neat and allow easy access, but on smaller boats, where tapes might be more exposed to damp air, it's safer to store them with a desiccant packet in a covered plastic container (unless you like the sound of New Warp music, the end result of a bad case of mildew growing on a tape of classical guitar studies).

BOOKCASES

• Book racks can often be fitted into small, open areas on bulkheads. If the space is too narrow for the books to sit in their usual binding-out row, line up groups of three or four deep with covers facing out.

• Keep books in place on their shelf with a ½-inch wooden dowel blocking the front

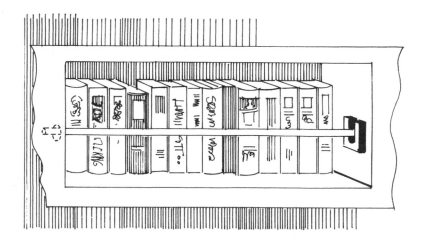

of the shelf. The dowel fits into wood brackets cut to the shape of an elongated U.

• The same dowel arrangement can be used with only one bracket. Drill a hole in the vertical side of the shelf space, midway up. Cut the dowel slightly longer than the shelf; insert the dowel into the hole on one side, and drop the other end into the U-shaped bracket.

CLOTHES KEEPERS

• Weekend boaters use large zip-top bags (or one plastic-lined beach bag) to keep all the wet swimsuits and beach towels together, and separated from the dry clothes, to avoid a soggy mess that demands immediate laundering.

• Use only vinyl-coated clothing hangers to avoid rust spots on those few boat clothes that require hanging. (But keep a few wire hangers around for fix-it uses.)

• If all the foul-weather gear on the boat is the same brand and color, try putting each set on a different-color hanger. Manufacturers have thoughtfully made the vinyl coatings in a variety of colors so you can make your own fashion statement.

• In all clothing lockers that suffer from dripping condensation, cover the stacks of clothes with old pillowcases or towels or fake chamois cloths. These are easy enough to wash from time to time, and they save the clothes from the musty smell that comes with a few unplanned wet-and-dry cycles.

• Simpler solution: keep clothes out of lockers that drip. Build shelves along the bulkhead at the foot ends of bunks, or use net hammocks or nylon mesh bags wherever they'll fit.

SWEET SMELLS

• To keep musty smells out of clothing or bedding lockers, use a bar of soap (wrapped in a plain napkin or facecloth, or covered with a charming and decorative crocheted turtle).

• Fabric-softener sheets will also combat a stale smell, but they tend to transfer their own distinctive scent to the clothes, so find one you like.

SHOE POCKETS

• A closet-organizer shoe bag—the kind that often hangs on the back of house closet doors—might fit behind a ladder in the stateroom, a perfectly acceptable place to keep shoes.

• The shoe pockets are a good size for storing other small clothing items, or perhaps craft supplies. If necessary, cut a large panel into sections, to hang wherever there's available space.

BUNK COVERS

• On stateroom beds, use a quilted cotton comforter as a bedspread, so nothing needs to be removed and stored elsewhere at bedtime. The quilted cotton is a comfortable fabric to sit on for daytime reading or lounging; it doesn't show wrinkles, and it washes easily.

• The dimensions of a comforter are usually smaller than an actual bedspread, but still large enough to fit boat beds, which often do not require the same amount of overhang as a house bed.

• Buy a larger-than-necessary spread, and cut off the excess to make pillow shams. (All you need is enough matching fabric for the front of the shams; a piece of complementary solid-color fabric will do for the backs.)

• Save the upholstery fabric in seating areas by covering it with woven cotton rug mats. They're sold in an array of attractive colors and patterns; the woven texture keeps the mats in place on the seat cushions, and it's much easier to toss them in a washer than to struggle with removing cushion covers. They are especially helpful if there is a shaggy beastie on board.

EASY-CARE BEDDING

• Many people like to use sleeping bags, finding them easier to handle than sheets and blankets, especially in bunks that are oddly shaped or difficult to get into.

• Nylon sleeping bags are light, air out easily, and can be stuffed into a pillow sham for neatness.

• It is possible to buy liners for sleeping bags. Top and bottom sheets are connected to form an inner bag, which can be washed weekly with the regular laundry, keeping the bulkier sleeping bag clean. Such liners would not be difficult to make, using the sleeping bag as a size guide and pattern.

SPARE ROOM

Few boats have guest rooms, but most boaters invite guests from time to time. Rather than fill valuable locker space with seldom-used extra blankets and pillows, make (or custom order) cushion covers, about pillow-sham size, in a fabric of your choice (boat acrylic is sturdy). Stuff the shams with the spare bedding, and use them for lounging pillows. If there's an artist in the family, have decorative designs painted on the shams for true decorator pillows. (Boat acrylic is a good painting canvas too.)

RESERVED SPACE

When planning general storage areas, remember to leave room for trash. No matter how much you crush or compact, you'll have bags full of condensed garbage to carry till you're back to a shoreside dumpster. Even if you're crossing an ocean, you're still required to stow your plastic trash. (See Chapter 27 for trash-handling tips.)

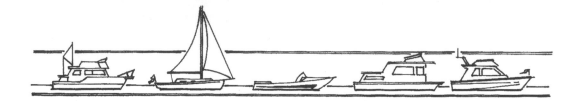

Inside Modified

Show boats look great, but most boats benefit from the kind of modification—often minor—that becomes evident only after real people spend some time on board. A shelf here, a locker there, a book rack in between; each seems relatively insignificant when viewed alone, but when a number of such changes are in place, the difference is obvious.

Whatever improves the functioning of your boat or enhances your enjoyment of boat time is more than "half so much worth doing": it must be regarded as a legitimate and necessary part of messing about.

HATCH HOLDUP

If you have an overhead hatch without a dependable holdup, make one. Start with a piece of 1-inch-by-2-inch pine or mahogany—something soft enough to cut easily. Cut it to an appropriate hatch-propping length—about 11 or 12 inches long. Notch one end with a 90-degree cut so it will fit securely against a square edge of the hatch frame when the weight of the hatch pushes it down. Trim the other end to a modified point so it will wedge into the inside frame of the raised hatch. With that as a basic shape, cut and/or carve the wood to suggest any design: a bird, a fish, possibly a dolphin. Dockwalkers and boaters in passing dinghies will stare with admiration and envy.

To prevent a wind gust from lifting the hatch wide open, attach a thin line to the center of the forward edge of the open hatch, then bring the line down to a cleat attached to the front of the inside frame. A taut line will keep the hatch support—and the hatch—in place.

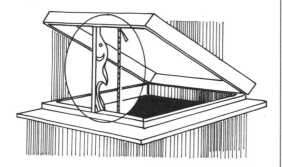

The contact cement is more likely to bond to a clean, new wood surface than to a sealer or finish that might repel the glue or resist proper adhesion.

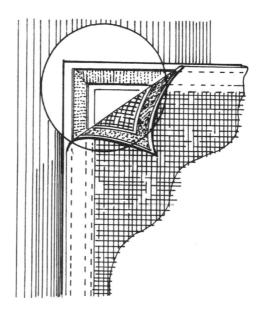

MOSQUITO CONTROL

• Make a framed screen for an overhead hatch. Use the same aluminum sections you find in house screens—the kind that hold the screening material in place with a rubber gasket that fits into a preformed groove. Or take the measurements to the nearest do-it-yourself builder's supply and ask them to do it themselves.

If you don't like aluminum, make a wood-framed sandwich and glue the screening material between the two skins.

To install, hinge one edge (probably the forward edge) and use a turn-button in the center of the opposite edge to hold it up.

• To make screened hatch boards, cut two pieces of doorskin sized to slide into the hatch opening. Cut a center opening, leaving 3 or 4 inches of wood frame on all four sides. Cut a piece of screen slightly larger than the cutout, and glue it into position. Then glue the two doorskins together.

• If you want to use Velcro to attach screening in a companionway opening, use a router to cut a groove into the wooden hatch frame. The groove must be wide enough for the Velcro strip to fit into the recess. When the Velcro is in place it will be flush with the frame, so there will be less chance of corners pulling up.

LIGHT SHOWS

• When it's too cold to leave the companionway hatch open, you close out light along with the cold air. Make replacement hatch boards of Lexan. Just cut to size and smooth the edges.

• If you already have screened hatch boards, put them in position and cover with a piece of clear plastic (such as the polyethylene sheeting sold for painter's drop cloths). Hardly as neat as Lexan, but the translucent plastic allows light in and does a good job of keeping cold out. Tuck the ends under the hatch boards if it's windy.

• If the overhead portion of a sliding hatch cover is solid fiberglass or wood, consider putting a Lexan insert into it, to bring more light into the boat. Carefully cut a square opening, and file and sand for a neat edge. Cut the Lexan piece ½ inch larger than the opening on all sides; screw it onto the outside of the hatch cover, using plenty of silicone caulking to ensure a complete seal.

• With ports that are just the right size, an interesting light pattern can be created by wedging a rattan plate holder into the window frame. While such an addition might not pass the standards of yacht decorators, it does serve the secondary purpose of assuring privacy.

• A similar diffused lighting effect can be accomplished by using pieces of woven caning material. Available in a number of different patterns, it can be inserted into any size frame to make a custom window insert.

DECK PRISMS

A few well-placed deck prisms can completely change the look of a boat's interior, and the welcome addition of light can, in turn, completely change the outlook of the crew. The only caution when installing them is to caulk, recaulk, and caulk some more.

HANDHOLDS

• Most production boats could use some extra handholds. These are available in traditional teak at marine stores, but a more reasonable alternative can be found in most building supply stores at a fraction of teak's cost. Plus, you'll be helping to save a teak tree.

Stainless steel "handicap" handholds are strong and easy to install anywhere. As purchased (curved at both ends), they're fine for horizontal placement. To use in a vertical installation, cut the curved portion off one end so the straight section can attach flush to overhead.

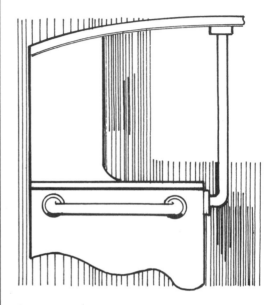

• Living areas in boat interiors are often separated by a half bulkhead—a waist-high divider that allows the important impression of openness. The top of such a bulkhead is a natural place for a handhold.

Rather than leave a plain white surface to collect fingerprints, put in a neat wood handle. For the simplest version, cut the corner of the bulkhead at a 45-degree angle, starting about 4 inches back on the top edge. Replace the cutaway portion with a triangle of wood, with an inner triangle cut out for easy grabbing. If you'd like to do some carving, design a fancier shape for the handle. In any case, round the edges of the wood so a hand will *want* to hold it.

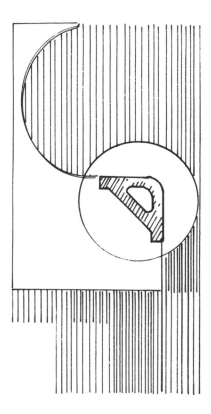

to the engine room. To keep the ladder itself portable, hardware on the ladder slides into brackets on the bulkhead. It may all look substantial, but these fittings eventually need help; constant, unavoidable ladder wiggle causes screw holes to strip and brackets to slide.

Add a stopper at the bottom. It may be a slide bolt dropped into the cabin sole, or wood braces on either side of the ladder legs—anything that effectively stops sideways motion.

KICK PLATE

The narrow section of bulkhead behind the top step of a ladder is open to a lot of foot contact. Rather than scrub scuff marks every week or repaint the area every few months, protect it with a thin stainless steel kick plate. Whenever you're washing ports or mirrors, give the plate a quick spritz and a fast wipe to keep it footprint-free.

LANTERN TIE-DOWNS

Trawler lamps are almost a nautical necessity. Beyond their lighting and heating functions, they *look* so right. But for safety's sake, sometimes they need to be constrained.

- If a lamp hangs over your dining table, tie thin lines to the side handles and knot them together at a center point about 5 to 6 inches under the lamp. Connect the lamp to the table using a metal spring with hooks at each end. (The top of the spring hooks into the knotted line under the lamp; the bottom hooks into an eye-fitting screwed into the tabletop.)

- Another way to connect lamp and table is to use shock cord and S hooks.

FINGERHOLDS

- Access hatches under seats or bunks are sometimes difficult to open, with fingerholds apparently designed for munchkins. Add more, or cut larger holes so you don't injure fingers and thumbs when lifting cover boards.

- If the boards are awkwardly long, cut them into two or three sections. If necessary, add 1-inch-by-2-inch support pieces inside the locker to hold the boards.

LADDER ANCHOR

Ladders often fit in front of bulkhead panels that must be removable to allow access

Drill a hole in the table to countersink a heavy brass shackle pin. (When the lantern is not attached, the pin sits flush with the tabletop.) To tie down the lantern, push up the pin high enough so the S hook on the end of the shock cord can be inserted into the top of the pin. (Drill a hole that is the right diameter for the S hook through the top of the pin.) A cotter pin inserted into the bottom of the shackle pin will prevent the shackle pin from pulling up through the tabletop.

• If the lamp fits in a spot where it can be hung more or less permanently, use traditional knotting for an attractive hold-down. Wrap two ⅛-inch lines around the lantern's side supports and connect them under the lantern into a knotted lanyard. Tie or snap the lanyard into a U-shaped bracket. (If you have a good knot book on board, look up and use a crown sennit.)

LAMPLIGHT

• In all oil lamps, pure mineral spirits are said to burn cleaner and, some insist, with a brighter flame than that of kerosene or sweet-smelling lamp oils.

• Whichever oil you burn, the cleaner the glass, the better the light.

• Check wicks regularly and trim them with scissors when they get too black and fuzzy (usually the result of a flare-up). When using the lamps, find a good light level and try to keep the wick in about the same place. Raising it too high raises the risk of the dreaded black smoke-out.

• Mix equal parts mineral spirits and scented lamp oil if you prefer a gentler scent of berries or pine. (Be sure mineral spirits are labeled 100 percent, or pure.)

• Put a small mirror on the bulkhead behind an oil lamp. The reflection will increase the lamp's lighting capability. (Glue the mirror glass directly to the bulkhead, or put it into a narrow frame to attach with screws or brackets.)

PORTALIGHT

For reading, fixing the engine, or looking for lost objects in small places, wire a movable clip-on light with a cigarette-lighter plug and a long cord.

KNIFE RACK

Loose knives are dangerous. Designer woodblock holders are both functional and attractive, but they're too bulky for many boats. Instead, make an in-counter storage place.

Get a length of wood about 1 inch wide, ¼ to ½ inch thick, and as long as you need. The wide side will be "up." From the top, cut slits through the wood to accommodate the blade widths of your knives. Find an appropriate place on the galley counter, next to a bulkhead and over a locker. Cut out a narrow slot in the countertop ½ inch away from the bulkhead and almost as long as the wood. Attach the knife holder over the slot; knives will slide in and fit safely under the counter. (If necessary, block off the area inside the locker so a hand reaching inside can't touch the blades.)

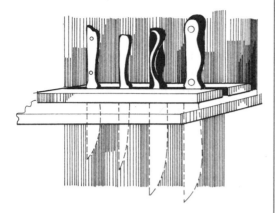

DINING IN OR OUT

• Small boats don't need big tables very often. Instead of a heavy, awkward fold-up, -down, and -away dining table, start with a small table for two for everyday use. When company comes, have a larger tabletop to fit over and attach to the small one. (You can store it in brackets against the overhead in V-berth or stateroom.) With a little ingenuity and a few more bracket attachments, the same larger table-top can be used in the cockpit or on the back deck for veranda dining.

• If the stove is gimbaled, make a tray to fit on top and use it as a work surface when preparing sandwiches or snacks underway. Put good fids on it and it doubles as a serving tray.

• Even without the tray, the self-leveling stovetop can be used to hold soup or coffee cups as you fill them. Set them into an empty frying pan on a spare burner. Any spills will be easy to clean.

TILE TIME

• Ceramic tiles are easy to install and make a safe backing behind a bulkhead-mounted cabin heater or around and under the cookstove cubicle. Don't skip the grout-sealing step. Though it's easy to postpone, you won't like the subsequent scrubbing and bleaching steps.

• With the leftover tiles, add a trivet-size section to the galley counter, as close to the stove as possible. It's a safe and handy place to park hot pots when all burners are busy. It can also be attractive; if you have mixed colors, make a border or a checkerboard. If you feel exception-ally creative, break the tiles into random shapes and do a mosaic.

CHANGE-A-SINK

• If you're redoing the galley, plan for a sink as big and as deep as will fit. For a large selection, look in home-plumbing supply stores and catalogs.

• Whether to use a larger single sink or two smaller ones is a question of personal preference. A double sink eliminates the need for an outside drainer, but if sinks are too small, you can't wash large pans easily. A deep sink is a convenient and safe workstation, especially for preparing food when the boat is moving.

HOT HOLDER

In rough weather, making and serving hot coffee or soup is a challenge for an unpre-

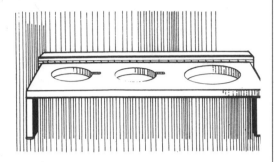

square, half round, or any shape you choose. The towel dowel can slide in and out in a routed groove, or it can be inserted through holes cut into each bracket. A screw holding a large washer will stop the dowel from sliding all the way through. At the other end, put a screw into the dowel; cut off the head, then use a finishing nut to keep the dowel in place.

pared galley. Pot holders—the metal rods that keep pots on the stove—solve half the problem; the serving half is made safer by using a small shelf with appropriate cutouts sized to hold cups or bowls. Use Plexiglas, Lexan, or wood; hinge the shelf to a vertical divider in the galley, where it can fold down over the counter. Foldout legs will add support when in use.

SILVERSAVER

Make a countertop box to hold silverware and cooking utensils vertically. Placed in a reachable spot in the galley, the stand-up organizer takes less room than the usual tray and makes things much more accessible.

Use wood that matches or contrasts with interior wood trim. Build a complete box, or do only front, sides, and partitions, letting the galley bulkhead function as the back. Three or four compartments will do the job, but size and number are your choice.

The box front should have U-shaped or scalloped cutouts so you can easily see the shapes of the items you're reaching for. If you've chosen an appropriately heavy wood, customize the box by adding a design to the front with a router bit or artist's chisels.

PAPER TOWEL ROLLER

Wood makes a sturdy holder for paper towel rolls. The side brackets can be

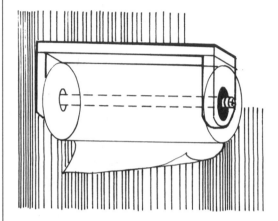

UPPER BERTH

When the height of a bunk mattress requires too much of a leap of faith, install a step. If the front of the bunk support needs to be open for access, make the step removable: put in small side brackets and glue some Velcro on the top surface of each bracket. Make the step and attach matching strips of Velcro to the underside of each end. Then pop the step on and off as needed.

BOTTOMING OUT

If you live aboard, assuming bunks have sufficient vertical space to allow it, replace standard mattresses with 6-inch foam of the highest density you can find. Not only will beds be more comfortable and provide better support, the foam won't bottom out after years of constant use.

For those with back problems, have innerspring mattresses custom made. Write to:

U.S. Mattress Company
2235 E. Barraud Avenue
Norfolk, VA 23504
804-626-1133

WET BOTTOMS

In cold weather, the inside of a fiberglass hull will sweat. In seat or bunk areas, condensation dripping down the hull side might be absorbed by the cushion bottom, creating cold, uncomfortable seating and a constant case of mildew. To prevent this problem, put squares or strips of air-conditioner filter material under the cushions. The thickness of the filter keeps the mattress or seat cushion raised up and away from draining water, while the material itself allows air to circulate, keeping the underside dry.

MATTRESS COVERS

If a boat bunk is a nonstandard size (aren't they all?), make custom-fitted mattress pads. Buy one size larger than the bunk. You can try tucking the excess underneath, but truly smooth sleeping will be found only if the pad stays flat. Cut the quilted top to the right shape, then reattach the elasticized sides. If that's too much trouble, hem the top pad and use pieces of elastic to hold the corners down.

SMALL-BOAT CURTAINS

• If you're an accomplished knotter (or an ambitious amateur), you can make beautiful curtains from off-white, natural-fiber yarns, following directions in macramé books.

• Make a whole set of small port curtains by cutting sections from one or two curtain or drapery valances. Hem the cut sides, leaving space at the top for rods to slide through. Instead of ordinary curtain rods, use shock cord or metal springs hung on cup hooks or L-shaped brackets. Add Velcro tabs to the bottom corners if the angle of the bulkhead is such that curtains would hang too far away from the port.

• Cloth napkins are another possible curtain source. If the width is an appropriate size, you will need to cut and sew only the top hem pocket. With a practically limitless choice of materials and colors, finding a suitable fabric should be simple.

CUSHIONED SEATBACKS

In some seating areas, a cushioned back is more desirable than movable pillows. You don't need to order seat cushions from a custom upholsterer; you can make them yourself, even if you don't know how to use a sewing machine.

Buy some suitable fabric (basic boat acrylic or a more formal textured nylon upholstery material) and soft foam rubber (2 to 3 inches thick). Cut a piece of plywood for backing. Then cut a piece of foam the same size as the plywood and glue it to the wood. Now cut a piece of fabric to a size that will allow it to wrap around the front and sides of the foam, and fold around to overlap the plywood backing by about 2 inches on all four sides.

Staple the fabric in place, pulling it snugly so the edges of the foam compress to a rounded shape. (If foam is especially dense, you may want to trim a bit from the front corners.) Finally, attach the seat backs to the bulkhead. Screw them directly into the wood, or use strategically placed Velcro tape.

These seat backs can be attached to hinged locker doors too; the lockers will remain accessible, but the seating area will have a more finished look and be much more comfortable.

VINYL REVIVAL

If vinyl cushions have lost their luster, or if you're just tired of the old color but can't justify the expense of re-covering while cushions are still serviceable, change them with vinyl spray paint. The paint is available in a limited number of colors, and it is advisable to switch to a darker one. (See Chapter 13 for brands.)

Vinyl paint is remarkably permanent. If occasional scratches expose the original color, you can retouch with more spray.

ANOTHER HOLDUP

Storage areas under bunks are often cavernous but accessible only through a checkerboard of hatches cleverly positioned under a heavy mattress. Rummaging around a dark locker while supporting a mattress on your head is nobody's idea of fun. To hold the mattress up and out of the way, sew a wide Velcro strap (adjustable) to the underside of the mattress and attach a sturdy O-ring to the cabin overhead. When it's time to rummage, pull the strap through the O-ring and fasten when the mattress lifts to a desired height.

AND A HOLDOUT

Velcro can also replace hook-and-eye hardware to hold a door open. Put a small square on the front of the door, at the top

corner opposite the hinges (with "front" defined as the surface facing out when the door is opened). Open the door so it rests flat against a bulkhead. Attach the matching Velcro to the bulkhead so a short length of tape reaches around the side or top thickness of the door to grab the square on the front.

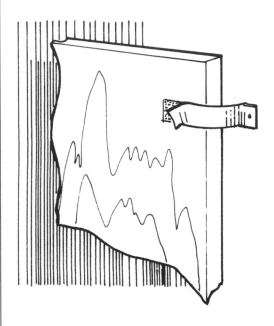

COVER-UP

Presumably sensitive electronic devices like depthsounders and engine gauges are often installed in such a way that their backsides are left exposed. Apart from the opportunity for dust and dampness to invade their innards, such an installation is messy-looking at best, ugly at worst.

To protect your gadgets, build an instrument-back covering box. If you use good wood, finish it bright and hang a decorative brass handle on the front. If you'd rather have it fade into the background, paint it to match the bulkhead.

Either way, hinge one side of the box and hook the other so it will open and close easily. Then make a long, thin, three-sided box to cover the wiring, or buy a suitably shaped piece of molding.

ADD-A-SHELF

Fold-down shelves can extend or supplement galley counters or desktops; add one wherever it would be functional (over a seating area, over a companionway ladder, as a temporary upper shelf over the counter itself). Attach the shelf with a full-length hinge; hold it in the "up" position with a slide bolt, or with nylon line over a small cleat.

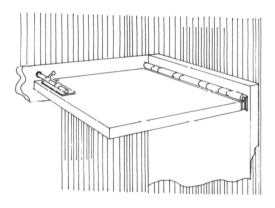

CHANGE OF PLACE

• If you don't need five or six or seven sleeping places, and you want a work surface, convert a bunk. A few possibilities: Bunk out, workbench in. Bunk out, storage locker with foldout desk in. Bunk out, tilt-top drafting table in. (If you're not comfortable with carpentry, hire someone to do the blocking in, then finish it yourself.)

• The storage locker/desk option replaces a single-size bunk. Build in the locker, with shelving and front-door access. It will be the same length as the original bunk, and the right height for a desk. Cut a desktop-size piece of wood and hinge it to the top of the locker so it can lay flat against the top when not in use. To set up the desk for working, fold it out and prop it up with a single leg. Use a sturdy dowel for the leg support; insert it into a countersunk hole in the underside of the desktop. Add a rubber pad to the leg bottom to keep it from slipping.

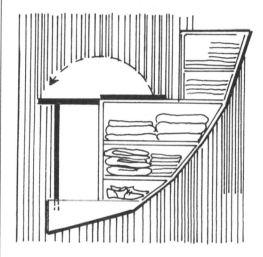

ROOM DIVIDERS

• For visual neatness, close off big storage areas such as a forward V-section or a quarter berth. Make a wood frame sized to fill the opening and put caning into it (perhaps a pattern that matches locker doors). The caning allows good ventilation; the divider is attractive as is, and it's sturdy enough to hang a picture on. Hinge the frame so it swings up and attaches to the overhead when you want to get to the storage space. (A wood bar installed athwartships gives you a straight edge for the hinge.) When the frame is up, fasten it with a line on a cleat. When down, use a drop bolt to keep it steady.

• For a different kind of divider, glue pieces of carpeting to the overhead or hull side, leaving excess fabric so it can reach down or across to cover the front of the storage area. Attach Velcro bands at the sides to hold the carpet door taut.

PENCIL HOLDER

Writing instruments like to hide. Keep them from rolling away into oblivion with a basic holder. Use two pieces of wood, each about 1 inch wide, ¼ inch thick, and whatever length is suitable for your use and available space. Drill a row of holes (plus a slot for dividers) through both pieces. Glue one to a countertop next to a bulkhead and attach the second one to the bulkhead a few inches above the first, lining up the holes properly for standing

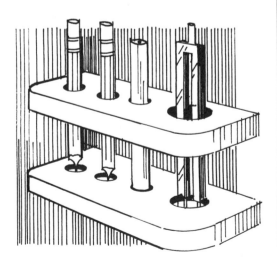

pencils. No guarantee the pencils won't continue to disappear, but it takes them longer to jump out of the holder.

FLIP-OUT SEAT

A handy seat at chart table or desk tips down out of a locker, much like an old-style bread bin, with a seat cushion filling the space where the bin's top would be.

ADD-A-RACK

• Buy or make storage racks or bins wherever there's a vacant spot on a bulkhead or in a corner. Fill them with magazines, charts, travel books, stationery.

• Make an in-and-out box to keep correspondence organized. If you're forced to look at the in bin every day, you'll be reminded of the letters you want to answer. And whoever is next off the boat should remember to check the out bin and head for the post office.

SOLE SURFACES

A new floor can change the whole atmosphere of a boat's interior. Though teak is traditional, with the protection of today's varnishes and polyurethanes, any wood can be used.

• A parquet floor can be real image enhancement. Installing it is not difficult, provided you are a perfectionist. Before you get to the fun part, you must create a level surface for the squares to sit on. If you're starting with a molded fiberglass cabin sole, the first step will be to put in a plywood subfloor, then level that with a belt sander. Add the checkerboard according to manufacturer's instructions, starting in the center of the sole and working out.

• Install a faux teak-and-holly cabin sole. Use real teak, traditional mahogany, or nontraditional oak (either red or white). Start with a bunch of 2-inch wood strips, about ½ inch thick, presealed with a coat of varnish. With 3/16-inch spacers between strips (get some at a tile store or make your own), epoxy the wood to your carefully leveled plywood subfloor.

After the epoxy has set, sand the strips level. (This could take days, depending on your definition of level.) When you're satisfied, prepare for the faux holly, also known as caulking. (BoatLIFE's Life Calk works; others may too.) Tape the wood surfaces with masking tape, then caulk the seams as neatly as the cartridge will allow. Next, use a popsicle stick to smooth each seam to the same level, which will be a slight dip in the caulking between the wood strips.

When the caulking dries, put a few coats of varnish over the whole cabin sole.

Important note: pretest the compatibility of caulking and varnish to be sure the varnish will set over the caulking.

• Cover the center walkway portion of the cabin sole with a strip of carpeting. A length of stair runner may be the perfect width, requiring only that the ends be finished. Though it's not available in a big variety of colors or patterns, you may find indoor/outdoor carpeting, which is easy to care for.

• For a more formal look, oriental rug clones can dress up saloon or stateroom. Made of nylon, they can go straight to the laundromat for spring (or any season) cleaning.

CUSTOMIZE

Ultimately, even stock production boats take on their owners' personalities, so encourage the process. Adopt the attitude of megayacht owners: customize, personalize, individualize. Make statements.

From underwater reef life to endangered wildlife to space exploration to Uncle Sam, themes can be expressed in murals, etched glass panels, painted fabrics, even galleyware. For the shell collector, the boat is one big display case. Intricate needlework can cover pillows or entire bunks. If the boat's name is *Dolphin*, happy Flippers may be everywhere. Decorating is fun, and it does say something about pride of ownership.

Airspace

Modify locker doors with decoration that also provides ventilation. Fit new door frames with caning, or use fancy carved-wood panels found at designer import shops. Or cut a design into existing doors. Anchors, fish, and dolphins are popular shapes; the boat's name or theme may suggest others.

Class Glass

A stained-glass panel adds an artistic touch to a boat's interior. It need not be large; it will be evident, no matter what the size. Look for a place where light will give the glass a proper display—perhaps the arched top of a doorway separating two cabins, or a round port anywhere. When you've established a place and a shape, go to a craft show or a local artist's co-op. You should be able to find a glass artist eager to be commissioned for such a project.

Copycat Glass

Plain Plexiglas, etched and painted, is a colorful alternative for a locker door. If you're artistic, draw your own design. If not, take an idea from a book.

Start by etching the dull side of the Plexiglas with a scribing tool (ask for one at a hardware store). Trace the outlines of your design; they will show up as white lines on the Plexiglas. Next, use artist's acrylic paints and add color wherever you want it, still on the dull side of the panel. When you turn the panel around and install it in your door frame, it will have a look similar to stained glass, without requiring back light to see the colors.

Plant Life

Flowers brighten any interior. If you establish permanent places for flowers, you'll be reminded to bring them aboard.

• A wall sconce with a small brass vase is one such reminder. A pewter vase can serve temporary duty as a pen holder. A wine bottle/rolling pin holds one red rose in graceful elegance.

• Plants do a lot to finish a room—even a boat room. Sailboats carry hanging planters to hold greenery safely and relatively out of the way. Powerboats sometimes have entire tropical gardens on the back-deck veranda.

• If you plan to country hop, leave the plants at home. Though not always enforced, the laws of most countries prohibit the transfer of plants, to prevent an invasion of plant pests or an attack of killer exotics.

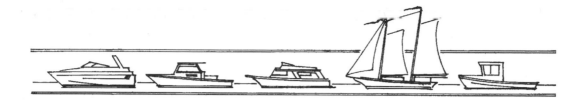

Bucket Brigade

A house usually gets a standard cleanup once a week, with some extra days devoted seasonally to more extensive efforts. Except for giant yachts, boats have different cleaning problems requiring different methods and schedules.

With their smaller space, boats cannot absorb much dust or disorder; everything is immediately noticeable. Under constant threat from mold and mildew, boat surfaces must be watched and washed often. Despite constant dousing from rainwater, boat exteriors need regular scrubbing, mopping, and waxing.

Neatness counts, and cleanliness counts even more.

THINK CLEAN

• Boring though the task may be, make a list of all the chores that need to be done on a regular basis. (That "regular" is now your schedule.) Writing the list will force you to think about all those things that are not self-cleaning.

• Establish a cleaning system that seems most efficient, and be consistent; that way, you won't accidentally leave an eight-week accumulation of dust on the trawler lamp. With weekend boating, it is (or should be) a given that you clean up before you close up. But for long-term cruising or live-aboard crews, distractions are everywhere.

DELEGATE

Delegate specific jobs to specified individuals. If only two people are involved, the question of who will be the delegator (and, by elimination, who the delegatee) might require outside arbitration.

If children are involved, it may be necessary to appoint an enforcer as well. If nothing else, the delegating arrangement leaves no doubt as to who is to blame for undone jobs. On the optimistic side, children will learn responsibility and pride of ownership. Maybe adults will too.

DIVIDE

Split, share, or somehow divide timely maintenance chores. These differ from regular chores in terms of more time, more effort. If these tasks are not assigned, everyone will sit around waiting (hoping) someone else will tackle the varnish, the teak, the stainless, or the bottom yuck.

One way to assign jobs is by drawing up a priority list: whatever's on top gets done first. Exceptions, such as "I don't change oil" or "I don't do ports," can be established early on.

To ensure that all crew devote equal time to the list, determine the number of hours allotted to boatwork per week, and have the enforcer keep track.

CLEANING KIT

Depending on the size of your boat, it may be practical to make up a cleaning kit. Fill a tote bag or bucket with general-purpose cleaners, window cleaner, powdered cleanser, scrub pads, rags—all the tools of the trade. Carry the kit from galley to head to stateroom to saloon, keeping all your dirt fighters close at hand.

LINT FIGHTERS

Some fabrics not only attract dirt, they refuse to give it up, whether it's cookie crumbs or cat hair.

• Gadgets to the rescue include a hand-size version of a manual carpet sweeper. Its small, rotating brush loosens tenacious particles and flips them into a holding compartment.

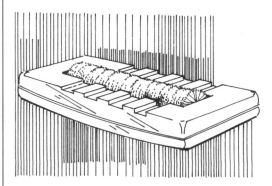

• Another hand-size picker-upper is ergonomically shaped into an oval. A velourlike fabric covering a cushioned pad persuades the dirt to stick to it instead of to the cushion cover.

• Yet another invention is a roll of sticky stuff on a stick (a medium-tech version of wrapping masking tape around your hand, sticky side out). These helpers are intended for use on clothing as well, though boat clothing may not be what the manufacturer had in mind.

• If the resident dog or cat leaves a lot of hair on the upholstery, try rubbing across the fabric with a damp sponge or cloth, a piece of rubberized nonskid material, or a rubber glove.

• A sweater defuzzing gadget (a battery-operated razor for clothing) will help smooth out nubby fabrics, making them easier to keep lint-free.

CLEAN SWEEPS

• Keep a tiny whisk broom/dustpan set everywhere you might use one. If you don't find them with the supermarket cleaning supplies, look in automotive sections of family department stores.

• Bigger sweeping jobs can be accomplished with a child's broom, which still stows easier than a full-size one.

• For quick pickups on upholstery or carpeting, use a 12-volt hand vacuum, especially good for chasing dust mice in small places.

• If the boat has the storage space (and the need), get a 12-volt wet/dry vacuum cleaner, a smaller version of the home/shop model. The concept is perhaps better suited to a boat, with or without a shop.

• A poodle owner recommends using Resolve carpet cleaner. It removes stains with a minimum of washing and doesn't leave an ever-growing ring. It works on carpeting or scatter rugs. According to the manufacturer, it not only cleans the spots, it also leaves a soil-and-stain repellent on the carpeting.

• For temporary carpet cleanups, try dry granules (sold in supermarkets or hardware stores). Shake them on, brush in with a soft nylon brush, then vacuum.

• Trusty baking soda will help deodorize a carpet: sprinkle it on and leave it for about 15 minutes before vacuuming.

DUST GRABBERS

To dust moldings, caning, or carved wood panels, use a small feather duster, a synthetic feather duster (the kind that resembles a multicolored, elongated tube of cotton candy), or a soft-bristled paintbrush (possibly an artist's brush, if you can't find anything suitable in housewares or hardware). All are fairly flexible or self-adjusting so they'll fit odd surfaces. All can be sprayed with dust attractors.

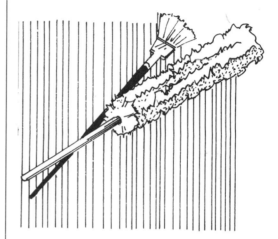

RAGS

Keep the leftover sock (after the washer has eaten its mate) for a low-lint dustcloth, polishing cloth, tack rag, or wiping-the-varnish-with-alcohol cloth.

DIRT REPELLENT

Keep surface dirt on the surface. Use carpet samples (or remnants, if they're bound), and shake the dirt out often. Keep a mat at each boarding site, one by sink or stove, and one in each high-traffic area in the boat. Indoor/outdoor mats catch dock or dinghy dirt before it gets inside.

DOUBLE DUTY

Hardly used paper napkins or towels can be filed in a plastic bag under the galley sink, ready to serve secondary duty—mopping up floor spills or outdoor messes involving oil, gas, or paint.

AIR CLEANERS

• Give bedding a big breath of fresh air and sunshine now and again. Hang blankets, comforters, sleeping bags; prop pillows on deck or a seat, clipped to something stationary if there's a good breeze.

• Give the boat interior some new air too. Instead of a fresh air–scented commercial air freshener, try tossing a handful of orange or lemon peels into a pot of boiling water for some citrus steam.

FUZZ FIGHTERS

• Use a chlorine solution (¼ cup in a gallon of water) to clean mildew from painted surfaces and discourage its return. Wear gloves, and be sure the boat is well ventilated when you're cleaning.

• Baking soda will clean most surfaces, and is easier on hands and nose.

• Use an enamel with mildew inhibitor. (Interlux #223 Eggshell enamel is one.) Read label precautions to be sure your selection is okay for interior use.

• Add your own mildew inhibitor to any oil-, alkyd,- or latex-based paint.

For information on M-1 Additive, contact:

Boatek
P.O. Box B
Havre de Grace, MD 21078
800-336-9320

• One boat uses deck prisms to bring sunlight into locker areas as well as into the cabin, thereby discouraging the growth of black fuzz.

• Where copper tubing is led through clothing lockers, cover it with foam rubber pipe insulation so condensation doesn't drip from metal to fabric, creating a favorable environment for mold and mildew and causing hard-to-remove stains.

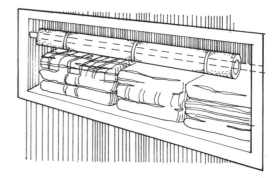

CAPTIVE CONDENSATION

While you're on the boat, you can control excess dampness by using dehumidifier crystals. These draw moisture out of the air, then deposit it into a plastic container. Eventually, a person must do something about the accumulated water. While this may seem an exercise in futility, given the usual moisture content of air in a boat, it apparently helps to keep things dry in hanging lockers and other closed-in spaces.

Kept in lockers near a bunk, these mildew crystals are credited with capturing hull condensation; the bunk stays dry as long as the water is emptied regularly.

FUNCTIONAL CONDENSATION

Occasionally, spray the air (and/or wipe down surfaces) with a deodorizing, disinfecting cleaner that coincidentally hates mildew and mold.

PLATE PAINT

Straw paper-plate holders, especially those with the natural look, have too many surfaces that can trap moisture and spills. They grow mildew, and attract bugs. Scrub them with a chlorine solution, dry them in sunlight, and spray paint them with a gloss enamel that matches your galley decor. The slick surface repels water; no moisture, no mildew, no bugs. (One can will cover eight plate holders, though the backs will not be completely covered; two cans will leave you some extra paint for a matching bread basket.)

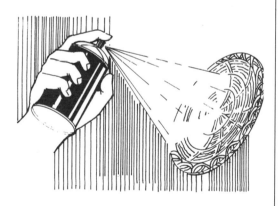

DISHWASHING

A boat without a fixed galley still accumulates dirty dishes (unless your boating style and your budget tend toward restauranting).

• If you have no sink, arrange a dishwashing system that will work in the smallest possible space. Start with a covered plastic bowl or box, and a bucket. The bowl or box is your sink; the lid, your drainboard; the bucket, your drain.

Before washing, wipe off excess stuff from dishes and pots with paper towels. Heat some water and pour it in the bowl. Wash the dishes and set them on the lid. Rinse by pouring water over the dishes and letting it drain into the bucket. Set the dishes back on the lid to drain.

• Not all meals create a mess that requires hotwater washing. Dish soaps work well in cold water, except after meals like barbecued ribs or fried anything.

• Try to clean up cookware as you cook. There is no room to stack dirty dishes or pots in a typical galley.

DISH RINSING

• Excess suds require excess water to rinse. You could use inexpensive dish detergents; they are not usually super sudsers. Unfortunately, they may not be super washers either. Better idea: buy a known brand and dilute the liquid with water. Start with a two-to-one mix, or equal parts of each. You can always add more soap as you need it, but if you overpour a concentrated liquid, you're stuck with the bubbles.

• A folding dish rack is easy to use and stow, but a rack that fits inside a dishpan is a much better idea if the boat doesn't have a convenient place for a drainboard. (Also, the hard-plastic drainboards sold with folding racks tend to crack.)

• If you opt for the dishpan drainer, put small fids on the galley counter to keep the pan in position when anchored or underway. Remember to pour out the drained water every day, or you may start breeding mosquitoes and mold.

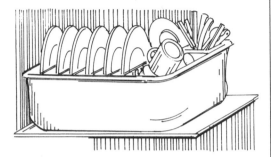

WONDER CLEANERS

In case anyone has missed any of the wonders of baking soda, boat cleaning provides many opportunities to learn.

• Use a baking soda solution to wipe sinks, countertops, fiberglass or painted surfaces, chrome fixtures, a tile or fiberglass shower stall, or a bathtub.

• Use a paste made of baking soda and water to scrub tile grout and clean stainless steel.

• When vacuum bottles or plastic containers take on the color or smell of the last food or drink they held, fill them with warm water, add baking soda, shake, rinse, and repeat if necessary.

• Put coffeepots through a cycle using baking soda and water instead of coffee and water. Then do a water-only rinse cycle.

• Use baking soda paste to soak off spills that have burned onto stove or pans, and to clean and deodorize cutting boards.

• Clean the stainless steel teapot with a baking soda solution.

• Whether you're leaving the boat for a week or for six months, clean out the cooler and wipe it down with baking soda. If you forget to empty and dry it, you may find unwelcome things growing inside when you return.

• Baking soda absorbs odors and helps prevent a transfer of smells and flavors in fridge or freezer. Leave an open box inside, and replace it every couple of months.

• When it has done its job in the refrigerator, pour the baking soda down the sink drains in the galley and head.

WINDOW AND OTHER WASHER

A spritz of glass cleaner works in a lot of places: on windows and mirrors and for fast cleanups on fiberglass or painted surfaces, on porcelain, or on stainless steel. (If you're out of your usual cleaner, add ¼ cup of denatured alcohol to a quart of water.)

Newspapers work best for glass polishing; paper towels are okay. Old pantyhose have been recommended, but who has those on a boat?

SHOWER SHINE

If a fiberglass shower wall has a bad case of hardwater deposit, pour vinegar on paper towels and "glue" them to the vertical surfaces. After soaking/sticking this way for a few hours, you'll be able to rub the stain off with a bit of elbow effort.

HEAD ATTACKS

To clean a stained toilet bowl, try these (one at a time): Soft Scrub with chlorine bleach. Rust stain removers made for porcelain. Denture cleaner. Vinegar, for hardwater deposits. (Muriatic acid has been suggested, but check with the head manufacturer before trying it, to avoid possible damage to the system.)

CLEANER CAUTION

You probably know that products containing ammonia must not be mixed with products containing chlorine, because the two react and produce harmful fumes. Heed this reminder, because in small spaces, vapors become concentrated, perhaps with disastrous results. (Ammonia alone in a small space is hard on eyes, nose, and throat.)

STAIN LIFTERS

• Clean tea stains from drinking cups with a readily available alternative to bleach: toothpaste.

• Add hydrogen peroxide to a baking soda paste to clean stains from porcelain.

• To clean rust stains from fiberglass surfaces, try Fantastik, Zud, Bar Keepers Friend, Bon Ami, or Soft Scrub with Bleach. Many other products can probably do the job; try cream of tartar and ordinary cola.

• Naval Jelly, a favorite of many boat cleaners, is described as a rust dissolver.

BILGE CLEANERS

• Keep shower water out of the bilge. Otherwise, whenever the bilge water is stirred up you will think some unfortunate creature has drowned; the odor ranks right next to rotten potato, but is considerably amplified by the area it covers. To prevent the problem, install a shower sump. (See Chapter 10, page 101.)

• To mop up small drips low down in the bilge, tape a sponge or absorbent rag to one end of a long stick.

• Use a retired deck mop for bilge cleaning until it disintegrates completely.

• Simple Green and Dawn dish detergent are both good grease busters. Simple Green is popular to clean almost anything. It's concentrated: you use less, you carry less. It's also nontoxic and biodegradable, two more favored green words.

• Oil-soaking pads (to lay in pans) or cylinders (to hang in the bilge) are a great help in keeping oil out of the bilge.

ECOCLEANERS

Many people are looking for "natural," or nature-friendly, cleaning products. The Shaklee Company manufactures Basic-L (for laundry), Basic-H (for household), and Basic-I (industrial). All are ecologically safe and sold in concentrated form. The line is handled through individual sales representatives. Local sources can be found in white-page listings under "Shaklee."

Jacques Cousteau used Shaklee products on board all ships and in offices.

OUTSIDE SHOWER

If you carry lots of water, run a hose from a water tank to the cockpit or swim platform. Attach a kitchen-sink spray hose for a handy and efficient way to rinse the dive gear, take a shower, wash the dog, or clean whatever needs cleaning.

DECK SWABBING

• When the boat's at anchor, use salt water when scrubbing the deck. Then mop it as dry as possible, rather than letting it air dry.

• Morning dew will lift a lot of surface dirt; a thorough mopping each morning will keep excess dirt from grinding in.

• The morning dew will help save the exterior varnished surfaces too. Wipe them down with a soft pseudochamois.

OUTSIDE CLEANERS

• Many good products are made specifically to clean fiberglass, but eventually everyone seems to resort to kitchen-type cleansers. Naturally, the less abrasive, the better. Two of the finer powdered cleaners are Bar Keepers Friend and Bon Ami. Both have good bleaching qualities and can rid a boat of "ICW mustache," the telltale brown stain caused by 1,000 miles of bow wave.

• Both products are excellent teak cleaners. (Bar Keepers Friend contains oxalic acid, a wood bleach.) Easier to use than two-part products, they can bring long-silvered teak back to a golden glow. Use a lot of water when you scrub.

• Toilet bowl cleaners are also recommended for removing stains from fiberglass.

• Multipurpose products are practical on a boat, but with so much research done on special-purpose products, you may benefit by buying those that are formulated for specific jobs (whether cleaner, degreaser, bleaching agent, deodorant, disinfectant, mildew retardant, or combinations of any of the foregoing) and for use on particular finishes.

SHINERS

• Stainless steel isn't stainless. Clean it with a gentle cleanser (the two that work on fiberglass—Bar Keepers Friend and Bon Ami—will also do metals). Use a damp cloth or a nylon scrubber, *not* a heavy-duty scrub pad. Finish with a good metal polish.

• If you can be satisfied with one polish to do all metals, it is an advantage in the stowing department. Nevr-Dull metal wadding polish is a standard; it does a great job, but some people object to handling the wadding. Flitz is also popular for multi-metal use.

- Chrome hardware can be shined with rubbing alcohol or an alcohol-based window cleaner on a lint-free cloth.

- Copper and brass can be cleaned with a vinegar-and-salt mix. It takes some hard rubbing (it's easier on the brass), but it will eventually remove even the cooked-on blackness from a copper-bottomed pan.

BUG BODIES

If you have the misfortune to suffer a bug attack, wherein the boat is covered with great numbers of dead bodies (lovebugs, blind mosquitoes, no-see-ums, or Lake Erie's bugpourri), clean them off as quickly as possible. Gelcoat will stain and painted surfaces will really suffer.

SCRUBBERS

- For cleaning fiberglass surfaces, use nonscratching materials: plastic or nylon net scrubbers, nylon scrub brushes, terry-cloth rags.

- Heavier scrub pads can be used to clean cooking pans, boat bottoms, boot-top, scuff marks. (Don't use them on chrome or fiberglass, and be very careful on stainless.)

FABRIC CARE

When the bimini top or other boat acrylic needs washing, use a solution of mild soap (not a detergent), such as Ivory, and water. Add ½ cup Clorox to kill any clinging mildew. (If washing white fabric, use Clorox 2.) Rinse with cold water. After washing, the fabric will need waterproofing. (Sunbrella's manufacturer recommends the product Aquaseal #3.)

VINYL CARE

- To clean vinyl-coated lifelines or vinyl fenders, use Soft Scrub with bleach.

- Vinyl cushions can be cleaned with baking soda or any mild soap or detergent. If they're badly mildewed, try cleaning with a mixture of ¾ cup distilled water, ¼ cup hydrogen peroxide, and 1 teaspoon ammonia. Abrasive cleansers or scrubbies may damage the surface. Be careful with solvents too; they may melt the vinyl itself, or remove a printed pattern.

- Many commercial cleaners also leave a protective coating. Or apply your own protection with a paste car wax, baby oil, or vinyl wax.

PLASTIC CLEANERS

- To clean soft-plastic ports, use Lemon Pledge furniture wax.

- Remove surface scratches from soft plastic with liquid car wax. Try it on Lexan and Plexiglas too.

- Use Brasso on scratched or solvent-etched Plexiglas. You may need more than one application, but you'll be able to see through the ports again.

- Rain-X and other water-beading coatings work amazingly well. Glass remains clear of steam and allows some visibility even in heavy rain. It can be used on plastic windshields too.

NONSMEAR GLASS

When you're washing a windshield, wipe one side with a circular motion and the other with straight strokes. Then the pattern of the smears will tell you which side needs more work.

HULL SHINE

Wax the hull, whether the finish is original gelcoat or one of the new miracle paints. (Starbrite's Premium Marine Polish with Teflon actually resists the Intracoastal Waterway bow stain.)

BOTTOM CLEANERS

Between haulouts, clean the bottom from time to time. Do it yourself, or hire a diver. If you choose the former, use a suction-grip handle, or hold onto a line attached to the boat, or hold onto the dinghy, moving it around the boat as you scrub.

• To clean moss and slime off the waterline, mix water and bleaching peroxide, about 4 to 1; spray it on and wipe off.

• Paint over the waterline with bottom paint; you'll have an easier scrubbing job (presuming the bottom paint is doing its job).

• If the water is shallow enough so you can brace your feet against the bottom, that helps get some weight behind your scrubbing efforts. Scrub with a soft-bristle brush with a stick handle. Use a putty knife or plastic scraper to remove barnacles and other gook.

• Keep a few wire coat hangers on board. Among other uses, they're handy for cleaning out through-hulls.

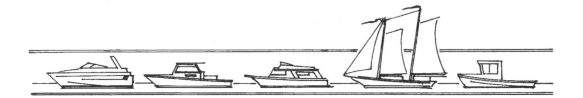

Clothes Lines

In a transition from house living to boat life, laundry may be one of the more noticeable differences. In a house, laundry doesn't require a lot of planning, except for putting soap on the grocery list. On a boat, there are many options.

Sometimes, the choice will depend on which marina has a washer, which town a convenient laundromat, or which resort a laundry service. Other times, in other places, a laundry decision is based on the immediate availability of rainwater.

It's unlikely you'll stick to any particular schedule, but like everything else on a small boat, visual space is too limited for overflowing laundry bags and the air too close for their mustiness.

MACHINE OR MANUAL

Until reverse osmosis desalinators were sized for boat use, only megayachts could handle the water demands of a washing machine. With a constant water supply now available via these watermakers, more boats have the luxury of an onboard washer, though "more" is still limited to those boats with ample space for both the washer and the watermaker, as well as the power capability to operate both.

The majority of cruisers are still dependent on shoreside laundromats, a friend's home washer, or any of a number of variations on the handwash theme.

CLEAN MACHINES

The almost universally favorite laundry tip: Find a laundromat.

• Carrying a gallon jug of detergent to the local wash house is hard on the arm muscles. Use a 1-liter soda bottle or a

1-quart dishsoap bottle with a pull-top dispenser. Mark the bottles emphatically to prevent mistaken identity.

• If you're using powder, carry it in small, covered jars or containers (premeasured, if you're very organized).

• Quarters fit neatly in a 35-mm film canister, or in a sandwich bag in your pocket.

• Try to remember to count socks before you go to the laundromat so you needn't waste time searching for a sock the washer did not eat.

• Never throw away the unmatched socks that come back from the laundromat. Cotton ones are handy rags for a number of cleaning and polishing applications. Unnatural fibers can still be used to wrap liquor or other bottles so they don't clank together in a locker.

LIQUID OR POWDER?

• Liquid detergent has some advantages over powder. Sometimes, even at the shore laundry place, the water is not hot enough to completely dissolve powder, especially if it is lumpy already. Also, when you're handwashing clothes on board, you don't bother with hot water at all. A liquid cannot harden into chunky cakes that resemble blue sandstone but are not as soft. On the downside, spilled detergent likes its freedom and resists attempts at mop-up.

• If you have a favorite brand of powder and prefer to continue using it, repackage it in watertight containers; don't leave it in a cardboard box, even if the box is kept in a plastic bag.

• Whether you choose liquid or powder, look for concentrated brands. The less you use, the less you must stock on board.

• Especially for hand laundering, but also useful with machines if you don't usually measure: dilute liquid soap with water, as much as half and half. You'll be less likely to oversoap, which forces you to use extra water for rinsing or to watch helplessly while sudsy foam floods the laundromat floor. You can always add *more* soap if necessary.

CLOTHES HOLDERS

• Use a mesh bag to hold laundry, and hang it, if possible. Circulating air will discourage mildew from settling in before you have a chance to wash.

• A wicker basket without an inner liner (so the clothes will get the advantage of all the air spaces) is a second choice, admittedly more attractive than a hanging bag.

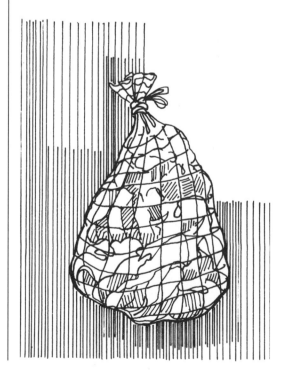

CLOTHES CONTROL

The amount of laundry in the bag or basket can be controlled by washing a few things every few days, rather than waiting until a giant load has accumulated.

TOWEL CONTROL

You can also keep a laundry pile down by buying the smaller-size bath towels, and by choosing thinner terrycloth fabric for *all* towels.

BEDDING CONTROL

Instead of washing all the sheets every week, try this method of making up bunks: The first week, make the beds using two flat sheets. At the start of the second week, the bottom sheet goes into the laundry; the top sheet moves down to bottom-sheet duty, and a new sheet goes on top. This simple rotation cuts sheet-washing in half: one sheet per bunk per week.

It's possible to extend the time between washings even more by flipping the bottom sheet over for the second week, and continuing that routine, but that leaves each sheet in some kind of use for a month, which is probably pushing it, especially in warm climates. Plus, you might require a flip chart to keep track of each sheet's status.

STAIN ALERT

• You could keep a list of stain removers handy, but unless you plan ahead, you may not have the ingredients on board. For example, ballpoint ink can be removed from fabrics with hairspray or nail polish remover, but these are not must-carry items on a lot of boats.

(Acetone would probably be a good substitute.)

• For a more common boat stain of grease or oil, ordinary presoaking may be impractical, but the gooey stain-sticks work well on engine-oil spots. Lard is also credited with spot-removing capability, but that is another item seldom found in seat lockers.

• WD-40, the boatowner's favorite metal protector and fastener loosener, is also a laundry aid. Spray it on grease and oil stains; rub it in, then wash as usual.

• A heavy-duty hand cleaner can also function as a prewash stain dissolver. (Goop brand works well.)

• Apply stain remover to the back of the fabric to try to push the stain out the same way it went in.

• For a fresh bloodstain, try a cold-water rinse followed by an application of plain meat tenderizer. Let it sit for about 10 minutes before washing.

• Make a paste of the old standbys—vinegar and baking soda—to rub into grungy shirt collars. Keep an old toothbrush to use for spot scrubbing.

ODOR ALERT

Toss some baking soda into the wash water whenever you need a little extra cleaning or deodorizing boost. In a washing machine, add ½ cup of baking soda. If hand washing, guess accordingly.

MILDEW CONTROL

• For mildew stains on clothing or other fabric, try some lemon juice (or baking soda in water) followed by a few hours of sunshine.

• On fabrics that can be bleached, try soaking in a solution of chlorine bleach, or oxygen bleach, or hydrogen peroxide.

WATER DEBATE

Clothes that are wet from salt water will never dry properly. They fool you by *feeling* dry after a few hours of flapping in wind and sun, but as soon as you fold them and file them in a locker, their true character returns. A penetrating dampness that carries the distinctive odor of salt eventually evolves into an equally distinctive look of mold.

• Some people wash clothes with salt water, then rinse with fresh. Others think you use more fresh water to get rid of the salt than you would if you used fresh from the start, presuming it takes more water to remove salt and suds than to remove suds alone.

• Some saltwater advocates recommend using a fabric softener in the freshwater rinse, claiming this will remove the salt from the clothes. Again, others disagree, explaining they are left with stiff clothes. Experiment to find what works for you.

HAND WASHERS

In some countries, having the laundry done may be an affordable option. This is not the case in Europe, where it may cost $10 to $15 per load. Wherever you travel, have a handwash plan and the tools on board.

• If the boat has room to store big buckets, take a couple of 5-gallon containers (perhaps left over from a home drywall mudding or painting project) to use as wash and rinse tubs. Of course, uniform containers are not necessary; use ordinary

buckets, cooking pots, large bowls, the dishpan, a cooler—anything big enough to hold a suitable amount of water.

• To wash, pour small amounts of water into a succession of containers. Wash in the first bucket until the water is gone or gets too dirty. Dump it, and transfer the water from the first rinse container into the washing bucket, because by now it is too sudsy for rinsing anyway. The number two rinse water moves to the number one position, and clear water refills the second container. Rotate the water as often as necessary.

• Carry a toilet plunger (new, and definitely dedicated to laundry use) to agitate clothes in the washing bucket.

• Find an old-fashioned washboard (the small size: about 1 foot by 2 feet). New ones are sold at hardware stores, old ones at flea markets. A dishpan makes a good washtub for the board.

NATURAL LAUNDERING

Some boats seem ideally designed for doing laundry in the midst of a rainstorm. If possible, plug up deck scuppers (after an initial rinse from the first cloudburst). A sufficient amount of water will soon be sloshing back and forth in a shallow puddle on each deck. Wash on one side (the nonskid pattern will be your washboard), then transfer to the rinse puddle.

NOT-QUITE-AUTOMATIC DRYERS

A clothes wringer will cut drying time by getting rid of more water than your hands can. Look for new ones in sports or marine stores, or used ones in junque shops. Mount one permanently on a pulpit rail or, for nautical correctness, keep it portable.

• One camper catalog offers a plastic version that clamps in place "anywhere." Write to:

Camping World
653 Three Springs Road
P.O. Box 90018
Bowling Green, KY 42102-9018
502-781-2718

• For hanging laundry on lifelines or shrouds, use old-style wooden clothespins rather than the plastic type with the metal spring/hinge. The old ones hold better, so you won't lose the laundry. They don't rust, so you won't have stains to remove. They're less likely to break, so you'll use them longer.

• Put up a couple of sturdy hooks so you can string an actual clothesline in a wheelhouse or across a back deck. Put washed clothes on hangers and clip the hangers to the line; you'll fit a lot of

clothes into a narrow space, but they'll still benefit from the breeze.

• Put up a tension curtain rod over the tub or shower, then hang an umbrella-spoked dryer from the rod. Dry laundry inside, or move the whole thing out when it's practical.

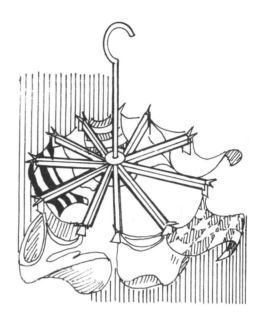

FOLDING TRIVIA

• Former military persons insist that folded-and-rolled towels stow in less room than those that are folded only. If those who so insist are willing to fold and roll and stow, let them.

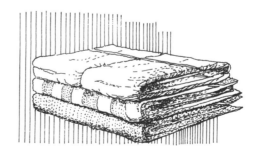

• Eliminate some folding by putting the same sheets back onto bunks until the day they come out of the washer in pieces. The same applies to towels; use the same few till they are demoted, first to boat-drying cloths, then to boat-washing rags.

THINKING GREEN

Increased environmental awareness has increased people's scrutiny of the ingredients used in laundry products. Chlorine has taken on a split personality; hailed for its cleaning, disinfecting, and bleaching properties, it is also criticized for its potentially harmful effect on the environment. Similarly, an overdose of phosphates has been cited as one cause of the algae blooms that suffocate fish and aquatic plants. Nonphosphate, low-phosphate, and biodegradable products remain strong marketing boosters for laundry and general-purpose cleaners.

Baking soda, vinegar, and borax are familiar "natural" cleaning agents. Oxygen or peroxide bleaches can be used in place of chlorine for laundry. Seventh Generation markets a line of environmentally friendly products. (For example, their concentrated laundry liquid uses stain-removing enzymes in a vegetable-based cleaner, and it works in cold water.) For a catalog, write:

Seventh Generation
Products for a Healthy Planet
Colchester, VT 05446-1672
800-456-1177

These products are also sold at natural foods supermarkets.

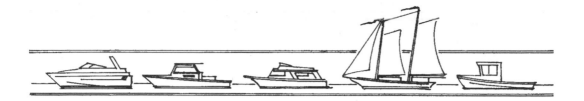

Head and Bath

The nautical version of the "necessary room" can be a portable toilet not very discreetly hidden under a dinette seat or bunk, or it can be the megayacht's interpretation of master bath suites for him, her, and them. Similarly, bathing facilities can run a gamut from a bucket or bag of water with gravity-fed pressure to the steaming swirl of a full-size spa. Somewhere between the extremes, the average cruising boat is equipped with adequate facilities, if not actual amenities. With an occasional reminder of boating's back-to-basics philosophy, boaters adjust to their version of necessary.

TOUCH-BUTTON TOILETS

Owners of boats with ample electric power are most fortunate in being able to choose push-button toilet technology. (Guests are especially grateful.) Efficient macerator/deodorizer/disintegrator heads are the closest thing to familiar home toilets, where people seldom concern themselves with questions of where the discharge hose goes.

HEAD ACHES

Those who must deal with manual heads look back with envy at the magic of one-touch flush. In an age of runaway technology, the marine head remains a continuing source of annoyance and frustration. Theoretically, operation is a fairly simple process of moving water into one hose and out another, but it is amazing how many snags can develop along the water's way.

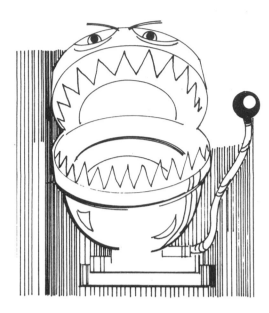

HOW-TO INSTRUCTIONS

• Boat rule number one often refers to instructions for proper use of the head. This could be viewed as a disappointing comment on the romance of yachting, but considering that boats sink when heads are used improperly, the significance of "handle down" or "valve off" becomes immediately clear.

• Post how-to instructions in the most obvious place, such as the back of the head door.

• Explain operating procedures verbally to all newcomers as soon as they board. Repeat often.

LID DOWN

Not usually part of basic instructions, but important nevertheless, is a reminder to keep the lid closed. The reason for this caution goes beyond the typical gender-prompted seat debate. Small items accidentally falling into the bowl may be relocated elsewhere in the plumbing system and will not be easily retrieved. Large items falling into the bowl will not be cheerfully retrieved.

OIL TREATMENT

Feed the head on a regular basis. A splash of vegetable oil (cooled post-deep-fry oil is fine) poured into the bowl and pumped through the system will keep the pumping mechanism working smoothly.

VINEGAR TREATMENT

• A larger amount of vinegar, also pumped through, will help control the formation of mineral deposits.

• An overnight soaking with a strong vinegar solution will help remove waterline marks from the bowl.

• Repeated overnight soakings will clear much of a bad case of scale, which you may have inherited when buying a used boat.

SPECIAL SCALE REMOVER

Eventually, the discharge hose will need to be cleaned or replaced. To clear out the hose, remove it (much easier said than done). If you're dockside, hit the dock with the hose a few times; if at anchor, knock the hose against the toerail and hope the hardened scale will break away from the inside wall. If that doesn't work, replace the hose.

FIX-IT KIT

• Don't leave the dock without a head repair kit on board. Usually, the only part that needs to be replaced is the joker valve (a curious and ironic name for the toilet part that keeps water from flowing back into the bowl). You will probably need to buy an entire repair kit in order to get a new valve, so if you must change it, change the rest of the kit parts at the same time. Nobody wants to go through the repair routine any more often than absolutely necessary.

• One solution to the head repair problem is to get rid of the entire head *before* it needs to be fixed. Some people find the complete replacement option far more desirable than rebuilding. Recycling advocates will frown on the philosophy, but if the idea appeals to you, remember that timing is everything.

COMFORT ZONE

The seats on some marine heads are not the same size as standard house toilet seats. Not everyone notices the difference, but those who do will be pleased to know they can replace the seat with a full-size model.

An off-the-shelf seat will not attach "as is," but it's easy to adapt. Notch the back of the seat so it can slide back around and past the hinges; then use some boater's ingenuity to hinge the new seat to the head.

PORTABLE POTS

• If the boat has a portable toilet, build in some kind of tray under it, not only to hold it in position, but also to catch leaks. If it's not practical to build in a base, keep the pot wedged, strapped, or fastened so it can't slide around.

• A portable toilet should be cleaned thoroughly after each weekend use. Hose it out and soak it with a bleach or baking soda solution until it rinses clean.

TANK TREATMENT

• For holding tanks, trial and error is the best way to find a treatment you can live with. Good results have been reported with natural, enzyme-based digesters. Appealing from the environmental perspective, it should also be an advantage to the apparently overworked sewage treatment facilities that ultimately are expected to re-treat pumped-out waste.

• Holding tank treatments are available in different forms. Liquid seems the most logical mixer for the tank, but if it spills in the boat it is a smelly mess. Powder can cake in the envelopes if stored too long. Whichever you choose, stow it with prevention in mind.

• One unusual but sensible approach is to treat all the water flowing through the system long before anything gets to the holding tank. To accomplish this, you install a treatment-dispensing unit near the head intake. As water enters, the treatment product (a plant extract) is added automatically with each pump, to stop odor and prevent the damaging buildup of deposits in the lines. In areas where harbor water is polluted, this is the only way to eliminate the problem of foul odors entering the boat with the intake water. For information about the Tank-ette Head-O-Matic system, write:

Alex Milne Associates Ltd.
376 Orenda Road East
Brampton, Ontario L6T 1G1
800-563-5947

DOCKSIDE SOLUTION

If you're living dockside and have room for yet another water tank, put in a fresh-water tank the same size as the holding tank and connect the head intake hose to this tank. With a controlled water supply, saltwater deposits and river sludge can't leave a buildup in head or hoses. Each time you pump out the holding tank, refill the freshwater tank.

ONE PLY OR TWO?

• Buy a brand of toilet tissue that is compatible with your head system.

• One-ply paper deteriorates quicker than two-ply; it lasts longer, because it has more sheets per roll; and you don't have to store as many rolls, so you save storage space. Still, manufacturers do produce two-ply tissue specified for use in marine heads, a probable response to the Mr. Whipple influence.

• Tissue made from recycled paper disintegrates faster than ordinary tissue.

POWER SHOWERS

• On boats with large water supplies or watermakers, it's easy to ignore water conservation habits. Nevertheless, it's good discipline to shower by the start-and-stop method, rather than allowing the water to run constantly. As populations grow and water supplies shrink, such conservation techniques will become increasingly useful in land homes too.

• A 2-gallon bug-sprayer holds plenty of water for one shower and ample water for two showers, if it's used very conservatively. Start and stop is essential, with stop the dominant mode.

• For hot showers, coat the bug-sprayer with flat black paint, and leave it out in the sun for a few hours.

• Stored on a corner bracket in the head, the portable shower is out of the way; with the bracket set at a convenient height, the hose can be used to rinse

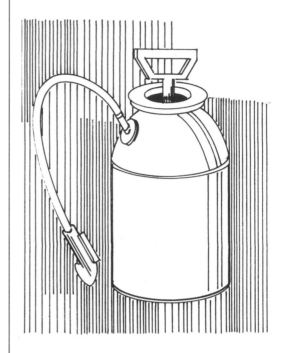

into the sink after shampooing. Secure the tank with a line and cleat, or a strap on a U-fitting.

• For a more efficient shower mechanism, attach a kitchen-sink sprayer hose to the bug-sprayer. The sink hose is longer, so it's easier to use. However, it allows more water through the spray nozzle, so you must be more careful when using it. Heat some water on the stove to mix with the cooler water in the tank until you find an acceptable temperature for bathwater.

SUN SHOWER

• The black plastic water tank with a gravity-feed hose is a very popular shower setup, with good reason. Sunshine provides a hot shower; the bag holds a good amount of water for a one-person shower and shampoo; and it stores flat when not in use.

• To keep the bathwater hot if you prefer an evening shower, get an insulated bag about the same size as the Sun Shower. (Ice cream stores use them for transporting ice cream cakes; Dairy Queen offers them for sale.) Make a boat-acrylic bag the same size and sew the insulated bag inside. Heat the Sun Shower during the sunniest part of the day; put the shower bag inside the insulated bag and it will stay warm for your bath. (Leave a hole in the bottom seam of the fabric bag for the shower hose to come through.) The bag is also useful for carrying ice to the boat.

• Take a cue from the black bag and heat water with sunshine. Wrap a dark, heat-absorbing fabric or plastic bag around any water container.

SHOWER DRAIN

Shower water should not drain into the bilge. Sour soap scum stinks. Install a sump to pump the water out of the boat.

Buy the components to put together a sump system. Build a box, and fiberglass it to make it rot resistant. Run a hose from the shower drain to the box. Put a small bilge pump with a float switch inside the box. Connect the pump discharge hose into an overboard fitting or hose, and connect the pump to the 12-volt system. The sump works automatically while you shower; when the water reaches a certain level, the float switch turns on the pump.

Alternate plan: buy a self-contained shower sump system.

SHOWER WALLS

• If your boat has the luxury of a built-in shower, care or maintenance will be the same as in a home bathroom. For fiberglass shower walls, a regular wipedown with baking soda will keep them clean and shiny. If you inherited a shower with bad water spots, try the vinegar-on-paper-towel spot remover described in Chapter 8. (See "Shower Shine," page 86.)

• To stop water spots from settling in, keep an old towel or a fake chamois to wipe down the shower walls after each use. (While this no doubt works, it's unlikely that everyone who uses the shower will be equally conscientious about drying it.)

SHAVE AND A SHAMPOO

• If you run out of shaving cream, or you didn't stock it in the first place, shampoo is a usable substitute.

• For an occasional hair wash, a 2-liter soda bottle holds enough water and serves as a handy dispenser. If you can convince someone else to do the pouring, you'll have both hands free to catch the water and hold it close to your head so your hair will saturate quickly.

• To prevent excess suds, dilute the shampoo in the bottle before you start.

BOAT SOAP

Boaters have used Joy dish detergent (as well as assorted shampoos) for both bathing and shampooing, because they will suds even in salt water. Now, liquid shower soaps are made specifically for the purpose; one is Sun Shower Soap and the other is Aqua Lather from Davis Instruments. Both are concentrated and biodegradable, for use in fresh or salt water, hot or cold.

SALTWATER BATH

If there is a secret to nonsticky skin following a saltwater bath, it is to towel off vigorously. By removing most of the water, you minimize the formation of little salt crystals that make skin so itchy. It's also been suggested that if you rinse hair with fabric softener, salt residue will not be a problem and hair will be soft and lustrous. However, people with very fine hair find that a salt wash adds a fullness and body they appreciate, even if they must sacrifice their hair's usual sheen.

SHORE SHOWERS

• For marina showers, take a large tote bag so you can hang it from the lone hook that some showers provide. (You may need to use the doorknob in some marinas.) Clothing, towel, and shower kit can all stay inside the tote bag, clean and dry.

• Wear flip-flops to and in the shower. Don't save old ones for this purpose; once the soles have gotten smooth, they are a danger in a wet shower room.

• A Soap Caddy is a simple but clever shower aid. It's a covered soap dish with a line attached, so it can hang from a shower head, a faucet handle, or your neck. Holes in the bottom of the dish let water drain so soap doesn't turn to mush in its case. Plus, it won't pick up mystery dirt from shower or bathroom surfaces.

Use one caddy for its intended purpose, and take a second one to hold a small shampoo bottle and a razor.

FOOT PADS

• Snap-together squares of plastic grating are a good solution for nonskid safety on the shower floor. In boats without separate tub/shower stalls, the movable squares provide the same safe footbase on a temporary basis. Snapped apart and

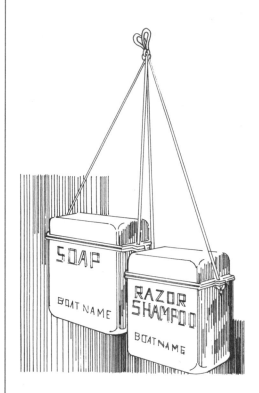

strapped in, they stow vertically against a bulkhead in a few inches of space.

• A small wood platform sold as a portable floor for campground showers will fit in many boat heads as a permanent shower floor. Made of redwood decking strips tacked onto two backing strips, it measures about 2 feet long by 16 inches wide and is hinged in the middle to fold for smaller stowing. It would be easy to build a similar footbase using teak.

• Make a flexible head floormat of cedar (or teak) strips. Measure the floor surface you want to cover. Use wood strips 1 to 1½ inches wide and about ⅜ inch thick. Determine how many you'll need to cover the desired length, allowing about a ½-inch space between strips.

Lay the wood upside down, properly positioned and spaced. Take two plastic or canvas bands, each about 2 inches wide, and lay them on top of the wood pieces, perpendicular to the wood and about 1 inch in from each side. Use nonrusting staples or brads to attach the bands to the wood. Turn it over and you have a shower mat. Roll it up, band side in, for storing.

FOOT PEDAL

Using a foot pedal to pump water at the head sink is most practical. Both hands are left free to wash hair, to shave, or to wash each other while a dancing foot controls water flow.

SOAP PUMP

Liquid hand soap in a pump dispenser bottle is much more practical than bar soap in a boat head. It is neater and less wasteful than bar soap, which is alternately mushy from too much water or gritty from dirt and sand. Bar soap spends as much time on the floor as it does in its dish. Instead of using it just to wash yourself, you must wash it and the floor too.

• Make a wood bracket for the soap bottle to keep it confined to head quarters.

WET TOWELS

• Towels that are folded and hung neatly on towel rods do not dry very well. Better to stretch them out across a bulkhead. Hold them up by inserting top corners into stick-on "grabbers" bought from a kitchen gadget store.

• In a larger head, put up a tensioned curtain rod over the shower, and hang towels on the arms of an umbrella-spoked dryer. The towels will get much better air circulation than they get hanging on a rod.

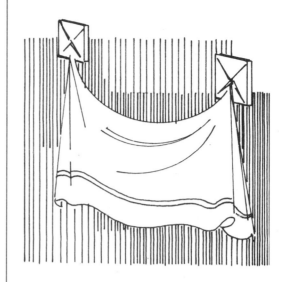

The whole unit unhooks and folds away when the shower's in use.

SKINNY TERRY

• Jumbo, thick and fluffy bath sheets are a luxury to be confined to house bathrooms. On a small boat, two sheets could fill all the locker space allotted to towels. They could fill an entire laundry bag. If you had no access to a dryer, they might never dry outside in a typically humid boat atmosphere. And who would want to wring them out by hand, if ever you managed to wash them by hand?

Instead, buy thin towels in the smallest size you can be comfortable using. Crewmembers who don't have long hair that requires heavy-duty toweling can make do with a larger hand towel instead of any size bath towel.

• A good many boat folks eventually forget about using terrycloth facecloths. They're impossible to rinse well without using an inordinate amount of water, and they start to smell musty before they ever dry. Not practical for the one use you get.

• When buying towels, remember that they will probably spend a lot of time hanging outside the boat, so pick colors that go well with the boat's exterior color scheme.

• Instead of limiting towel colors to one or two, as is customary in home decorator baths, buy sets of different shades of the same family (four different blues, or six different greens). That way, everyone can keep track of his or her own towels.

HEAD AND BATH STORAGE

• Arrange the towel locker so you can keep same-size items in individual stacks: bath towels, hand towels, dish towels. It's easier to see at a glance what's clean so you can schedule a laundry trip. Plus, it probably takes less room if each group is in a uniform, space-saving stack.

• A small shelf in the head can hold the liquid soap bottle, toothbrushes and glasses, shaving cream and brush: whatever items are used daily.

• To prevent noise, spills, and breakage—and help you find things—use plastic drawer dividers or boxes or trays to organize and separate the assortment of bottles and jars usually stored in a head locker.

• Put a bunch of glue-on grabber holders on the head bulkhead to grab and hold toothbrushes, razors, hairbrushes.

• Keep a can of moist towelettes around for a quick, refreshing face or hand wash. Also try dry shampoo for a fast hair treatment.

• A mild, lemon-scented stick-on deodorizer stuck to a head bulkhead freshens the air without an overpowering phony floral smell.

• If the head has a circular shower curtain to confine the shower spray, be sure the toilet tissue is either well covered or removed. It doesn't dry well.

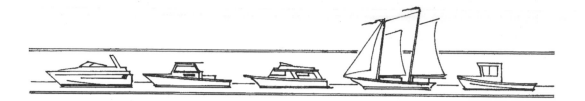

Mechanical Maintenance

Engine and electronics manufacturers spend considerable time and money preparing model-specific instruction manuals. For some products, owners can watch videotapes to literally see how to handle maintenance, troubleshooting, or basic operation.

Problems with specific products are best resolved with help from the people who know the most about them, so contact the company when you have big questions. But just as some little ideas make boating time more comfortable, similar suggestions can make regular maintenance and small repair projects easier, neater, or safer. Traditionally this has been men's domain, but lately more women are assuming responsibility for basic engine care: changing oil, charging batteries, remembering fuel additives. For everyone on board, a little knowledge—and practical experience—can be a good thing.

OUNCES OF PREVENTION

• Keep the engine as dry as possible to prevent rust and corrosion. Spray it with WD-40 at the start and end of each day's running. It displaces the moisture and protects the metal.

• If you're out of a favorite marine lubricant or anticorrosion product, use plain old petroleum jelly on engine parts, water pumps, any metal. It's efficient and inexpensive, but it's not exactly neat.

• Use heavy-duty waterpump grease on any metal parts that don't get hot. It will prevent corrosion on the water strainer, on the shaft between engine and stuffing box, and on seacocks. It's messy, but it keeps the green away.

• For a versatile metal-protecting, lubricating, penetrating wonder product, Corrosion X (Corrosion Block in an earlier formula) has gained many fans. Use it to stop corrosion on everything from engine to fishing reel (electric circuits included).

• Boeshield T-9, developed by Boeing, is another multipurpose corrosion preventer and moisture displacer that delivers what its advertising promises. People who use it swear by it.

GALLONS OF PREVENTION

Engines equipped with freshwater cooling systems should use distilled water in the heat exchanger to eliminate any possibility of mineral-deposit buildup. Antifreeze is often recommended also, but unless you do your boating in an area where freezing is a possibility, don't bother. The engine will probably run cooler without the antifreeze. You can add the rust inhibitors and pump lubricants separately, rather than use antifreeze for the benefit of those additives.

ENGINE CHECK

• Keep at least an informal log of fuel and oil consumption and expenses, as well as all regular maintenance or special repair projects. Beyond the financial record, a notable difference in fuel or oil consumption can indicate a problem, or it can show if an already completed repair brought the desired result.

• Engine access hatches are often big and clumsy. If it's practical, put small access hatches into the big one, and use them when checking oil, switching batteries, or checking the fuel and water strainers.

OIL STORAGE

• Buy engine oil in gallon containers, and save the empties to catch the dirty oil from the next oil change. They're the safest containers in which to hold used oil until you find a place for recycling or disposal.

• Store the bottles of new or used oil in plastic crates. They'll keep the oil safely confined.

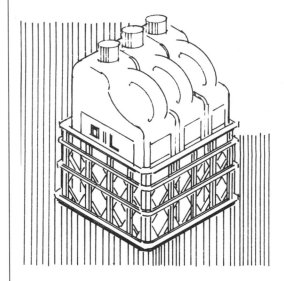

OIL POURER

For neater oil changes, get a Spill Saver, a pour spout that can be turned on and off while it's attached to the oil container and while it's upside down in midpour. One end of the spout screws onto the oil container just like a lid. Close to the pouring end, another twistable section of the spout can be opened or closed to control the oil flow.

OIL CATCHER

Get a rectangle of heavy-gauge wire screen, set into a frame if necessary, to fit underneath the full length of the engine. Keep an oil-absorbing pad on this screen to catch drips and spills and keep them out of the bilge.

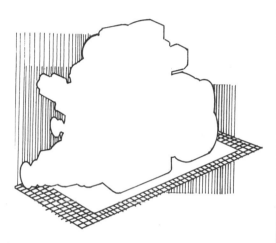

OIL PUMP

• A good brass hand pump is useful for taking out engine oil; it works well, it's much simpler to use than an electric pump, and it gives you more control. (If you're pumping and the container of used oil fills, you can stop a hand pump immediately.)

• After using a hand pump to change oil, avoid messy drips by connecting the two hoses together. Pump out as much oil as possible. Then take the metal tube that fits into the engine's oil fill and insert it into the end of the pump's discharge hose. Now any drips will be locked into the pump hoses.

• Find a convenient spot in the engine room to attach a snap bracket for hanging the hand pump.

OIL PLUS

From the owner of a 65-hp Perkins diesel with 14,000 hours' service and no over-haul comes this tip: for a 10-quart-oil-capacity engine, add one pint of STP with each oil change. Consumption goes down, viscosity stays up.

FUEL FILTERS

• Putting fuel filters in a hammock in the engine room keeps them handy, and the heat from the engine keeps them dry. The high visibility should give you more than fair warning when you need to add them to the buy list.

• Keep a container of diesel fuel to use when changing the fuel filter (a gallon will do). Don't let it get stale by keeping it too long; pour it into the tank and refill the container with clean fuel each time you fill the tank.

FUEL ADDITIVES

At first glance, many fuel additives seem to do the same thing for the fuel. Read the labels more carefully, and choose the one most specifically formulated for your particular problem; one product may be useful to prevent a problem, another to treat it after the fact.

• If fuel tanks have developed a sludge problem, use Sludge & Slime Control to break it up. To prevent the growth of microorganisms in clean fuel, use Biobor. Be careful when using these products; measure precisely, and don't splash.

• Use Sta-Bil in gasoline tanks to prevent gum and varnish from forming in the fuel system. Long recommended as a stabilizer when storing a motor, it is also helpful for ordinary use, especially in warm climates.

• Marvel Mystery Oil is a popular additive, perhaps because of its multiple uses. Added to diesel or gas, it cleans and lubricates the fuel system. Added to crankcase oil, it prevents gum and sludge. It loosens sticky valves and cleans internal parts. And it smells good, too.

FILL-UPS

• You will often hear it said that if you keep fuel tanks filled, there is less chance of their developing slime or condensation problems. But after a long storage period, especially in a hot climate, it may be necessary to pump out diesel tanks and start over with clean fuel. If sediment gets out of the tank and into the engine, you won't have a happy engine. If it starts gasping for fuel after a bouncy day on the water, sludgy fuel could be the problem.

• From an American couple cruising in the Mediterranean: Try to buy diesel from pumps that are used a lot. Those that are used less are much more likely to dispense bad fuel.

• From an English couple on a world cruise: Carry a funnel that is fitted with a nylon-screen filter. Then use a finer nylon mesh (from a stocking or pantyhose) as a second filter for any fuel you take on.

FUEL TANKS

If you're repowering the boat and changing from gas to diesel, you may have to change fuel tanks too. You should not use galvanized tanks for diesel; the galvanizing will flake off and mess up the engine.

TOOL SETS

Any small boat should have its own set of tools stored on board, in a plastic box or a canvas bag. This applies to dinghies as well as runabouts.

TOOL SET-UPS

• Keep a few often-used tools near the engine so they'll be immediately available for surprise engine checks. Hang them from hooks set into a wood support, and snap the midsections into clamp brackets so they can't vibrate loose.

• If there's a convenient place in a larger engine room, put up a tool rack. Use a single shelf or two or three tiers. Make shelf and side supports of wood. On the front of each shelf, use ¼-inch-thick acrylic to make a wide fid, about 3 or 4 inches high. This holds the tools in place while keeping them clearly visible and reachable.

To hang screwdrivers, attach a short piece of square wood horizontally near the top of each side support. Drill a row of holes through each piece, sized to accommodate the screwdrivers—regular on one side, Phillips head on the other.

Storing tools this way has an advantage beyond accessibility: heat from the

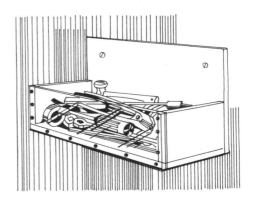

engine will keep them dry, and dry metal doesn't rust.

• Use a plastic tray to hold only those tools you're using on a particular project. It saves constant rummaging through the big toolbox, it keeps messy tools from spreading their dirt, and it could prevent a massive fallout if the big box tips over.

• Buy extra screwdrivers and keep them available everywhere you might need one quickly. Keep many sizes; stripped screw heads are more than an irritation when you're at sea and cannot replace them even if you *could* remove them.

WORKSHOPS

• The ideal situation for the active mess-about boater is to have a walk-in workshop, complete with bench vise and table saw and as many hand tools as will hang on a bulkhead. When the engine room is actually room size, there may be a place for a narrow bench along one side.

In an average-size cruising boat, a shop can be set up in a converted bunk space, a forward V-section, or in place of a second head or shower. Be sure to include good lighting (fluorescent will give the most light for the amps) and convenient outlets. Establish a place for every tool, and keep every tool in its place.

• Small boats often carry a wide board that will fit across cockpit seats or on a back deck to use as a solid work surface— one that can take bumps and nicks and glue spots and paint spatters.

HELPERS

• To free rusted fasteners, try spraying with Liquid Wrench, smearing with Naval Jelly, soaking with vinegar, and swearing loudly as you apply brute strength. Scrub

with a wire brush; try an impact wrench. (Be sure to use a tight-fitting wrench when trying to remove a rusted nut; if you round the edges, you may never get a grip on it again.)

• Use children's play dough or florist's putty to hold a screw onto the end of a screwdriver until you can start turning it in (especially useful in awkward places where you cannot hold it in place). In a pinch, chewing gum might serve the same purpose.

• Carry Liquid Steel for emergency repairs. An easy-to-use one-part putty, it dries quickly, allowing you to get to port for permanent repair. (A separate product is sold for repairs to aluminum.)

• If the alternator or refrigeration belt starts to squeak, a quick spritz with WD-40 should stop the noise.

• Keep Rubba Weld tape on board to wrap around and repair a failed water hose. Even when wet, the tape will seal, making a fast emergency repair.

SPECIAL HELPERS

• To help with an overhaul on an Atomic 4 (or other small gas engine), go to your nearest bike shop and buy a motorcycle valve lifter. It will save hours of frustration.

• If you're planning a long cruise, especially one where you may be away from help, ask the engine manufacturer for an extensive troubleshooting guide, or hire a mechanic to lead you through imaginary repair situations. It would be well worth the mechanic's fee to go through all the what-ifs he can think of. For starters, if the exhaust smoke is white, blue, or black, what's wrong and how can you fix it?

• In some cities, you may find a short course in engine repair offered by a local manufacturer or perhaps a community college. If you can take the time, take the course.

• Mechanics, plumbers, and other such specialists are well paid for their knowledge and expertise. One friendly refrigeration mechanic shared an important bit of wisdom regarding a memory aid to use when working on some project where you may be upside down or otherwise disoriented by your position in a tiny engine room. Remember: Lefty, loosey. Righty, tighty.

BILGE CHECK

Mount the bilge pump on a long stick; when you want to check the pump, just pull up the stick. Or mount both the pump and a switch on a piece of Lexan; when

you need to check either, use the hose to pull up the Lexan.

SAFETY CHECKS

• You may want to add some handholds in the engine room. They're very useful when you must reach some nearly unreachable section of the engine and find nothing to hold onto when you get there.

• If the engine room is a walk-in—or at least a step-in or brace-your-feet-on—put some nonskid strips in those places where your feet are most likely to stay awhile when you're working. You might appreciate the extra bracing effect to help turn a stubborn bolt or hose fitting.

• Keep a small fire extinguisher in the engine room, even if you have an automatic system in place. If a spark should start a small fire while you're working, you may be able to put it out quickly if the extinguisher is within reach.

• If the engine-room light is a hanging bare bulb, put a cage over it. It's too easy to bump anything that is so vulnerable, and it's too hard to clean broken glass from engine parts or bilge.

LIGHT SOLUTION

• A fluorescent light in the engine room will spread light over a larger area than the lone bulb.

• A flashlight attached to flexible tubing (sold at hardware stores) helps you see in awkward places, but it doesn't hold itself in place if you need to fix something after you've seen it. A small clip-on utility light with a flexible neck might solve that problem. If not, you can always hold a flashlight in your teeth; not very high-tech, but it does leave both hands free for the job.

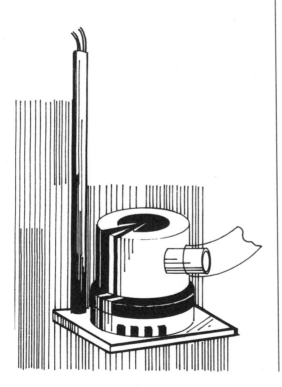

FINDERS KEEPERS

• Keep a good-size magnet on board to locate metal objects that fall into the bilge, or into the water outside the boat, if it's shallow enough to warrant a search. The magnet should have enough pull to pick up your largest wrench. You might want to keep a smaller horseshoe magnet also, for searching in small places.

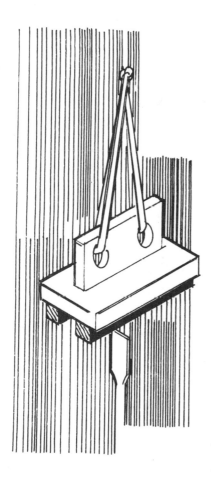

• A shrimp casting net can also be used to retrieve some fall-ins from the sea bottom. For larger objects, try a grappling hook.

NEATNESS COUNTS

• Plastic bins are especially helpful in the engine room. Any goo that spills will stay confined and out of the bilge water.

• Cans can rust, leaving rings on clean paint. Use a plastic battery box to store them.

• The same plastic grabbers that hold towels in the galley can be useful in the engine room to hold shop rags while you're working on a maintenance or fix-it project. But don't leave them there when you're through. Oily rags in a warm engine room could be a fire hazard, and there's a chance—however slim—the rags might get loose.

CLEANING TOOLS

• Make a small shovel-shaped tool to retrieve small things from the bilge. Use thin-gauge aluminum sheeting (or something soft enough to bend, but stiff enough to hold its shape when scooping through bilge water). Screw the shovel to a wood dowel at a 90-degree angle so it can be

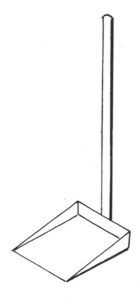

positioned flat against hull sides or bottom as you move it along.

• Keep a toothbrush-size stainless steel brush for scrubbing corrosion off small metal things, such as tools or engine parts.

• After fixing greasy stuff, degrease yourself with a waterless soap. It not only cleans the hands, but it soothes all the cuts and bruises and blisters you acquired during a day of boat play.

GAUGE MARKS

Put a line of thin, colored tape on the front of engine gauges (temperature and oil pressure) to indicate what each gauge usually shows at the also-marked normal cruising speed or rpm. Anyone running the boat will know immediately if something is obviously wrong. Even owners who know what to watch for might otherwise miss something if they're tired.

GAUGE COVER

Protect engine gauges from potential damage from flying hardware, flying feet, or flying salt by covering the instrument panel with Lexan. If the panel is not inset, frame it with a piece of thin wood so the Lexan will be raised enough to clear the front of the gauges. Attach the frame (from the back, if convenient), then attach Lexan to the frame front.

KEY COVER

If the ignition switch is located in a vulnerable spot, protect the key against Bigfoot with a Lexan shield that covers the top and sides of the switch.

INTAKE PROTECTION

• Short pieces of monofilament or polypropylene line can work their way up into the Cutless bearing, and that could stop water from getting through to lubricate the shaft. Check this underwater, if you're in a place where you can do so. (A donut zinc attached just outside the Cutless bearing could prevent the line getting inside.)

• In the northeast, wedge-shaped eelgrass is a constant problem for boats; it is bad enough that some owners put a strainer on the outside of the hull. Use a commercially designed prevention device, not a makeshift contraption.

IT WORKS FOR SOME

Rub STP gasoline treatment on the bare metal of your prop—it will keep barnacles off.

PROP PROTECTION

If you'll be staying in an area for awhile, check the local knowledge about location-specific cautions. In Maine, for another

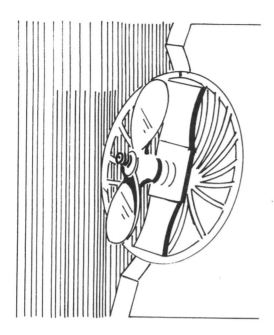

example, many boaters use a prop basket, which is a cage attachment that prevents lobster-pot lines from wrapping around the prop.

POWER-GENERATING OPTIONS

AC House Power

• Away from shore, boats can access standard 110-volt household power by plugging into the onboard 110-volt generating motor, which can be anything from a suitcase-size gasoline generator to a diesel model as big as a boat's main engine. You could also use an inverter, which takes in the boat's 12-volt DC power and sends out 110-volt AC.

• Inverters are available in many sizes, from a cigarette-lighter plug-in that powers a small TV or typewriter to a unit that can handle a microwave or a washing machine. Battery capacity is the limiting factor. Before you choose an inverter, check the power requirements of the 110-volt items you want to use and the holding capacity of your battery system.

• Chief advantage of inverter over generator: no generator noise, no generator fuel consumption (though the battery power will need to be replaced with the main engine or shore-powered charger eventually). Possible disadvantage: away from the dock, it depends on power provided by the propulsion engine, which will be the boat's *sole* power source.

• A separate generator can provide the occasional AC power and it can be a comforting backup as well. Even on a smaller cruising boat, the suitcase-size model can power an electric drill or run a small battery charger to recharge a starting battery that has somehow lost its startability. At this size, generators are relatively quiet to operate. Remember to add stabilizer to the fuel, since you probably won't be using it often.

DC Boat Power

Solar power would seem the perfect solution for generating DC power on board. The source is free (after the initial expenditure for components). It's quiet, and it has no moving parts that might stop moving.

Solar power can provide a constant trickle charge to a starting battery or it can maintain power for all onboard equipment. Determine the number of amps you use on average each day, then get a professional opinion on how much sun power is feasible for your boat or application.

• On a typical 35-foot sailboat, a 10-watt solar panel will keep the typical 100-amp-hour starting battery charged.

• On the same boat, a single 3-amp panel (charging all week) could replace the approximately 100 amps used each week-end (two days' usage of lights, VHF radio, TV/VCR, but *not* refrigeration).

• "Three-amp" describes the panel's peak hourly output, presuming the perfect conditions of high noon, no cloud cover, and the panel at 90° to the sun. Real conditions don't allow the simple math of 3 amps multiplied by the number of hours of daylight.

• If the typical 35-foot sailboat is used on a full-time basis, a solar power system might need more panels than the boat has appropriate space for; power product companies may then suggest a combination of charging methods.

For specifics regarding your boat, write to Hamilton Ferris Company, P.O. Box 126, Ashland, MA 01721, and request information about their Ferris Power Survey.

Or, ask Jack Rabbit Marine, 425 Fairfield Avenue, Stamford, CT 06902, for information about their packaged energy systems with D-I-Y installation instructions.

• Wind-powered generators are naturally popular with cruising sailors. You can buy a complete package or put together your own. The propeller and the generator itself can be purchased individually. You will need to make a housing (use a section of large-diameter PVC pipe) and arrange for mounting and wiring. Lead wiring directly to the batteries, or bring wires through a deck plug fitting to run them inside.

• A components kit is also available.

• Slow boats can keep batteries charged with a water-powered system. With this generator, power comes from the action of a spinner as it moves through the water, trolled behind a sailing boat. An Atlantic crosser found the system supplied all the 12-volt power the boat required.

BATTERY CARE

• Don't let batteries get so low the cabin lights dim; it's detrimental to their continuing ability to hold a full charge. If your batteries are not equipped with a visual charge indicator, get and use a battery charge tester.

• Keeping batteries properly charged will extend their useful life. Determine how much power you normally use so you can estimate how often you must recharge and how long it will take, whether you are running the engine to charge or you're using a battery charger plugged into shore power.

• Deep-cycle batteries should give better service (longer life) than ordinary batteries, but try not to discharge any battery beyond half its rated capacity.

• To test if a battery has a bad cell, remove the covers so you can look into each cell and watch the water. Put a load on the battery (it must be a substantial power drain, like turning on a refrigerator or starting the motor). If any cell bubbles, it's bad. (You'll see it in a few seconds.)

• A small, thin flashlight is perfect for checking the water level in batteries. You can hold it in your mouth if need be, so you have both hands free.

DUAL BATTERIES

• Using a dual battery system is common practice; one battery powers the boat's accessories, so the starting battery is always maintained at the fully charged level. True believers in backups may want to carry a spare battery as well; keep it charged with a small solar panel or switch it with the working accessory battery from time to time.

• Install a battery linking system that automatically puts the charge into the battery that needs it most. (No more dead batteries because someone forgot to turn a switch.)

• Build a two-battery box of wood, and line the interior with fiberglass. On the sides, attach brackets that extend upward beyond the top rim. Attach a box lid to these brackets, positioned slightly above the side edges, to allow air circulation around the batteries. (A slight cutaway portion on the front of the box adds more ventilation.) Drill holes through the upper ends of the brackets and pass a metal rod through the holes. (The bar is an added top support to ensure that batteries will stay in the box if the boat should suffer a knockdown.) Bend one end of the bar to stop it from slipping through; secure the other end by threading the bar and using a wing nut.

• If the batteries have a sight gauge to show their condition, cut a hole in the top of the box so you can check the gauge without removing the top.

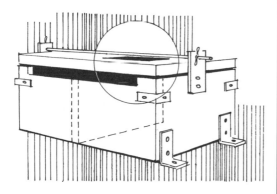

SPARK SMARTS

"Keep them dry" is the favorite hint offered by electronics experts. Then they smile, or not, depending on the kind of day they had.

• When sensitive electronics do get wet with salt water, rinse with fresh water. If possible, remove covers and dry them out (a hair dryer can help). You can try spraying with a moisture-displacing product, such as Boeshield T-9 or Corrosion X, but check with the manufacturer first; some do not recommend any spray.

(In our experience, such a treatment worked for one drowned VHF radio. After we poured the water out of the case, we used a few applications of spray, which helped dry it out; the radio functioned for another eight years. And this was before the age of superdisplacers.)

• Today's electronics hold more technology in smaller packages, making them available to more boaters. If you don't have much room, look for compact units and mounting brackets. One such stacking bracket for Ross Electronics can fit a VHF and a loran, in matching cases, into a space smaller than an 8-inch cube.

• If you buy a portable GPS, buy the mounting bracket too, not only for the protection of the unit, but to allow you to read it easily. If you don't like the manufacturer's bracket, make a teak box.

• Make a box or bracket for the handheld VHF to keep it safe, dry, and handy to the helm. Keep another box inside the boat and bring the radio in at night.

• Before looking for the troubleshooting hints, remember that fluorescent fixtures often cause interference with electronics.

• To jog your memory and help you stay on the good side of the FCC, post a list of VHF channel numbers and their assigned use. Update it as necessary.

LIGHTNING PROTECTION

According to the American Boat and Yacht Council (ABYC), the most widely accepted approach to lightning protection is a grounding system, where large metal objects on the boat are bonded and led to a grounding point, often a ground plate. Ideally, the lightning will travel the path of least resistance to ground (in this case, to the water), neatly following along the grounding system's conductors to exit into the water via the ground plate.

• The phrase "cone of protection" is often used in connection with a grounding system. It sounds reassuring, but it doesn't mean you are surrounded by some Star Trekian shield.

On a sailboat with a proper grounding system, a lightning strike would seek the easiest path to ground. Within the cone-shaped "shadow" area beneath the masthead, the lightning is not likely to side flash. As long as it follows the path of least resistance, and as long as people don't touch the metal parts that may be conducting the strike, they will most likely be safe.

Powerboats can put up a similar, if temporary, protection system. Call the Coast Guard Boating Safety Hotline—800-368-5647—and ask for Boating Safety Circular 66 on lightning protection.

LIGHTNING CAUTION

• A ground plate attached to a boat hull does not necessarily mean the boat is protected against lightning. The plate might be part of a lightning grounding system, or it could be in use as part of an anticorrosion setup. If in doubt, hire a competent surveyor or grounding systems installer.

• From time to time, a different form of lightning protector is promoted as a de-ionization rod, or lightning dissipater. The premise—that a specially pointed rod would deflect lightning away from the boat—seems the best possible protection. If it worked. Unfortunately, while studies have shown promising results on land-based radio towers, success in transferring the idea to boats has yet to be proved.

• Another school of lightning thought advocates the find-a-taller-boat philosophy, for no good reason except that it makes people feel better.

• If thunderstorms are grumbling, disconnect radios and other electronics. Go below and stay away from large metal objects.

• The very good news is that lightning strikes are relatively rare.

WIRING

• Always make a schematic of any wiring you put into the boat. You won't remember all the routes and connections.

• Tape and label wires at the box end (backside of the panel), and wherever a question might someday arise.

• Tape a minischematic to the panel door.

• If a number of wires are led into a conduit, it's helpful to label them where they enter and where they exit.

• A soldering iron requires electric power to operate. Keep a small butane-operated soldering kit for quick repairs.

• Protect wiring by sealing connections with a liquid electrical tape that melts. A liquid's advantage over standard electrical tape is obvious: it can seep in to fill gaps you might not see, yet it will peel off when you need to remove it.

• When living dockside, be sure to have a ground-fault device installed on the main 110-power plug-in. It breaks the current if anything unusual happens to the power.

PLUMBING ASSIST

Flexible PVC pipe is useful for all hose installations: water line, sump, drains. PVC can be glued quickly for easy assemblies in odd-shaped areas.

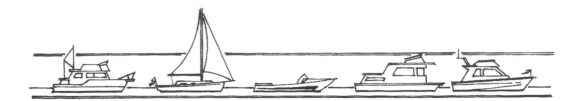

 Conditioned Air

---

Boating is such an outdoor activity, it might seem foolish to think in terms of conditioned air. But for true liveaboard comfort—even in three-day or three-week intervals—it's almost a necessity. A Michigan autumn can offer some of the finest cruising time to be found, but not if your fingers are as blue as the water. And Virginia in mid-July could stifle the enthusiasm of the most ardent boater without the relief of cool sleeping. Whether you heat it, cool it, or just move it around, controlling the air in your boat can have an amazing effect on the mood of the crew.

JUST-LIKE-HOME REVERSE CYCLE

Big-boat owners take for granted the familiar convenience of air conditioning or heat accessed with the turn of a dial. The system works on shore power or with onboard generator.

COOL CHOICES

• Smaller boats can cool their interiors with a portable air conditioner that comes to the boat with the rest of the weekend supplies. The Carry-On sits over an open overhead hatch to cool the boat while you have access to shore power. When you want to go boating, you store it in the car or dock box, or do what most people do: wedge it into a bunk for the day.

• BC (Before Carry-On), some live-aboard boatowners chose the cooling option of an appropriate-size RV rooftop air conditioner positioned over an open overhead hatch and modified as necessary for a good seal. These units do an efficient cooling job, but they are not easy to transport. However, since they have a low profile, such units can be left in place for occasional weekend boating if covered to protect against most of the salt spray.

• On a smaller liveaboard boat with a smaller budget, you can use the smallest home window air conditioner. These can be installed in the companionway hatch of a sailboat, but a better alternative for any boat is to install the unit over the overhead hatch opening.

Remove the hatch cover and make a wood frame to fit the opening. On the forward edge, attach a square piece of plywood (standing upright) with a cutout where the air conditioner will fit. On each side of the frame, attach a piece of plywood cut like quarter-round molding (two sides stay square; the rest is arched).

Buy some Plexiglas that is flexible enough to bend easily, and bend it over the rounded wood until it touches the back edge of the hatch frame. Caulk all seams. Secure the framework to the hatch with C-clamps or whatever fasteners can be adapted to the installation. (As a simpler alternative, an inverted plywood box shape would work; the reason for the curved Plexiglas is to allow light inside.)

Slide the air conditioner into the cutout; attach a drain hose to direct condensation off the boat.

• If you can tie a small tarp over any air conditioner, the cooler temperature of the shaded area will allow it to work more efficiently.

HOT OPTIONS

AC Power
When you have access to shore power, a small electric heater is the best choice; it will warm a small boat cabin quickly with clean, dry heat. The compact units take very little storage space when they're not needed.

Coal Power
• "Fatsco" Brown designed and built a line of charcoal-burning heaters. A man of refreshing principle, he would not sell a stove unless the buyer promised most emphatically to install it within a few inches of the cabin sole so the heat could do its job while following its expected path of ascent. If that meant adding 6 feet of 3-inch stainless stove pipe, so be it.

Of course, Fatsco was right, but few heaters are installed following his recommendation. Most are situated about mid-cabin height; the bulk of the heat they generate goes straight to the overhead, where it hangs around warming the light fixtures. To counter such self-defeating foolishness, install a small oscillating 12-volt fan to blow the hot air back down and around the cabin.

• Charcoal-burning heaters may create minor cleanup problems, but they win the prize for charm: a real flame, glowing coals, and an occasional red-hot chimney.

Note: When using a charming charcoal heater, or any cabin heater or cookstove with an open flame, maintain adequate ventilation. The presence of an outside venting pipe on a heater does not mean you can ignore this precaution. Fire uses oxygen; in a completely closed boat, it will use *your* oxygen, and the result could be fatal.

Kerosene Power

• Kerosene cabin heaters work well. Fuel can be purchased almost anywhere, and it's not expensive. It should not follow that fewer kerosene heaters are being made, but that's the case. Spare burners will be around for a long time, so if you find a heater, don't be afraid to buy it on the basis of its being a discontinued model.

• When running copper tubing from the kerosene tank to the cabin heater, enclose the copper in a PVC conduit (white or gray, depending on your decor). The conduit protects the pipe, and it keeps bulkhead or cabin sole green-free.

Propane Power

• If the boat uses propane for cooking, you can "T" into the same tank to use a propane cabin heater.

• A propane heater will create moisture in the cabin, but when you're cold, you probably won't mind.

• Traditionally shaped cabin heaters that once burned kerosene can now burn propane. These bulkhead-mounted heaters are vented through the cabin roof. Besides the usual safety precautions associated with propane installations, look for an oxygen depletion sensor that will extinguish the flame and shut off the gas supply if the oxygen level in the cabin gets too low. (The message is plain: open something enough to let in fresh air from time to time.)

• Any gas heater should be equipped with a device that shuts off the fuel automatically if the flame is extinguished (by a stray breeze, perhaps).

• See Chapter 1, pages 3 and 4, for precautions regarding propane installations.

Diesel Power

Diesel heaters have a few obvious advantages: Other heaters increase humidity in the boat; diesel does not. The fuel is probably already on board. Diesel fuel is safer than propane. Diesel heaters are efficient, and in large boats a forced-air system can carry heat throughout the boat.

Alcohol Power

For small boats, or small staterooms on bigger boats, a bucket-type cabin heater operates just like a nonpressurized alcohol stove. Pour alcohol onto absorbent material in the bucket and light it. The bucket gives off considerable heat; you don't have to cut a vent hole in the cabin roof, but you will want some fresh air coming in when you use it.

Special Power

Simple but effective, a heat-transferring unit takes heat from the engine's freshwater cooling system and sends it into the boat interior. The heater/fan is installed in the bulkhead that separates engine room and interior. Besides the heat advantage, it gets rid of the excess moisture that condensation brings.

Flower Power

Turning a clay flower pot upside down over a stove burner is supposed to send heat into a boat cabin. (Why a boater would have a terra-cotta pot on board in order to discover this secondary function is an interesting question.) Nevertheless, the pot does get warm, and it will stay warm as long as the burner stays lit, and for a short time thereafter. (Put a flame tamer over a low flame for the same effect, though neither arrangement is recommended from a safety standpoint. If you do it anyway, don't forget to crack open the hatch or a port for some change of air.)

Other Power

• The trawler lamp and other kerosene- or oil-burning lamps radiate heat as well as light, a welcome supplement to the cabin heater on a cold night.

• One way to solve the problem of no boat heater: when it's cold in the boat, bake a cake.

• When it's cold outside, the fresh-air advantage of nonclosing louvered panels is greatly diminished. To keep out drafts, tuck a few thicknesses of newspaper into the top and the bottom louver so the paper covers all the openings. The visual

effect may not pass a Bristol inspection, but your toes won't care.

HEAT WARNINGS

• On a cold November evening, you'll be tempted to leave the cabin heater on while you go visit the neighbor's boat; it will be so nice to come home to heat. *Don't do it.* Murphy waits for such opportunities.

• If the air outside is cold but still, the cabin will usually retain whatever heat is generated, and even a small heater will suffice. The real test comes when the outside air is cold and windy. Wind not only affects the boat's heat-holding ability; a downdraft can push flame or ashes where neither belong.

HEAT SHIELD

Make a shield around the cabin heater. Use a stainless steel or brass rod or a 1-inch-wide flat and bendable strap. Bend the strap

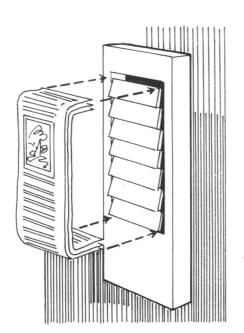

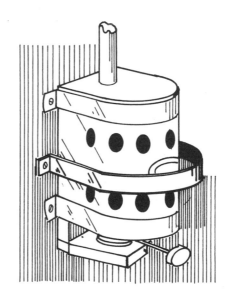

around the stove's circular shape so it stands about 3 or 4 inches away from the stove body, and fasten it to the bulkhead at both sides. (A single strap is more a reminder than a protective shield, but it does help keep hands away from the hot metal.)

HEAT HELPER

Though cabin heaters are usually cozy and charming, sometimes they are not able to handle their heating job. You may not be able to add more heat, but you can shrink the space to be heated.

Hang a piece of fabric (a folded sheet will do) as a curtain between the V-berth and the main saloon, or to block off a side galley area. The separator keeps more heat confined to the now smaller space. Do the same thing with a quarter berth and raise the saloon temperature by a few more degrees.

AIRFLOW

Windscoops have moved air through sailboat cabins for years, their colorful nylon scoops catching even the lightest breeze and funneling it down the hatch. Powerboats with the right superstructure could fabricate a way to suspend a scoop, though powerboaters' peers might take advantage of the association to make life mildly intolerable for the scooper.

AIR CATCHER

Instead of the spinnaker-shaped air scoop, make one that will catch air from any direction without changing its position.

Cut two rectangular panels of lightweight nylon. The short side of the panels will be determined by the size of the hatch opening, measured diagonally. The after-hemming dimension should be a few inches

longer than the diagonal measure. Make the long side of the rectangle as tall as you want the air catcher to be—probably about 3 feet.

Finish all sides, leaving only the top hem open at the sides. With the two panels positioned long side up, stitch them together with a vertical seam at their centers. (If the fabric is stiff, it can be opened into the shape of an X when viewed from the top.)

Near the top center, where the panels join, cut slits into the hem so two dowel rods can slide from one panel to the other to hold the X shape. Cut a small opening at the top center to allow access to the dowels, screw the two together, and attach a fitting for hanging. (Where to cut the assorted slits will become obvious as you assemble the air catcher.)

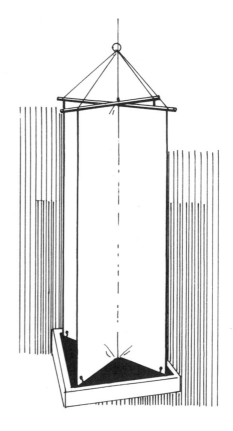

Put a grommet into the bottom hem at each corner, to slip over turn-button fasteners attached to the hatch frame. Hang it with a halyard, secure the bottom corners, and you can catch air from any quadrant. (You might prefer to rig a bridle hanger by tying lines to the ends of the dowels and bringing them all together on a central ring or hook.)

WIND TUNNEL

Both powerboats and sailboats can use a low-profile hatch hood that funnels fresh air into the boat.

Make a pattern for a canvas cover, shaped like a wedge to fit over an open hatch. Use PVC pipe and corner fittings to make a square frame for the front of the wedge. Make a duplicate PVC frame and move it forward of the hatch about 2 feet. Continue the pattern by adding a rectangular box shape (open on the underside) connecting the two frames.

Now sew the canvas cover to fit. When in use, the canvas box will catch the breeze, sending it back and down the hatch. In an ordinary rain shower, the hood stays in place, still allowing air to circulate.

The wind tunnel is easy to stow. Leave one corner of each frame area open so you can remove the PVC. The canvas itself can be tossed into a washer when necessary.

AIR MOVERS

• Solar vents can be used to bring air in or send it out. Sunlight powers the fan in these vents; the day/night models store the energy in a rechargeable battery for night use.

• A mushroom vent will keep air moving enough to discourage mildew and its accompanying musty odors.

• Watch the natural path breezes follow when they come through the boat. Then install strategically placed 12-volt fans to send air into the forgotten corners.

• Moving air has a cooling effect disproportionate to fan size.

SUN BLOCKS

• The color of boat curtains can make a difference in the inside temperature. White curtains will reflect heat back outside, keeping the interior cooler, while dark fabrics will absorb the heat and bring it inside.

• When the boat is sitting under a scorching sun on a windless day, any shade outside will keep the inside a bit cooler. Put up tarps over as much surface as you can, whether you use solid fabric or a light-diffusing screen.

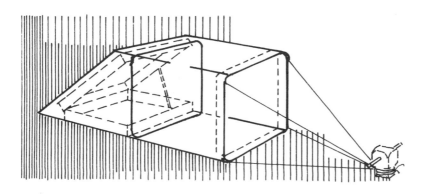

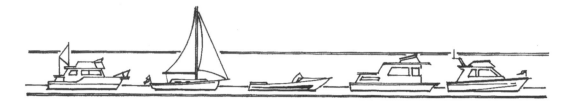

 Outer Space

Exterior spaces don't need—and probably shouldn't take—nearly as much reshaping as interior places. A boat should retain the lines its architect envisioned, whether the look is straight and substantial or graceful and uncluttered. At least that's the ideal.

If you want to make a significant change, try to consider it long and objectively. Will it trigger an immediate impression of afterthought? Or worse yet, sore thumb? Better to confine exterior modification to basics, just enough to turn not quite into just right. More accessible, more attractive, better arranged. More comfortable, more usable, better protected.

SUNSHADES

If you're in the tropics in winter, you need protection from the sun. If you're in the Chesapeake in summer, you need relief from the heat, even if it's only the few degrees' difference shade will bring.

For sailboats, the simplest cover is the rectangular boom tent tied onto lifelines to provide shade (and its cooling effect) and some privacy. Powerboats have many configurations, and their sun covers follow suit, though the first choice is usually a basic bimini.

ADD-A-ROOM

Canvas shops have found a niche in custom designing sophisticated dodgers, wheelhouse extensions, and complete cockpit or flybridge enclosures, for the obvious reason that they create whole new living spaces.

• If your boat could use an add-on, plan it carefully. If it will be permanent, it must allow easy access and have opening options, possibly with screened sections.

• For some enclosures, you can solve the port-or-screen problem by having separate panels: for cold-weather boating, use fabric panels with ports; when it's warm enough for mosquitoes, put up screen panels.

• Use a boltrope and track for the tops of such panels. They'll be much less likely to allow water drops to find their way inside.

CUSTOM COVERS

• Help the varnisher by extending the time between recoating. Ultraviolet is varnish's worst enemy; if you can't keep the boat under a roof, make minicovers for all the varnished surfaces. The squares and circles and tubes of matched fabric tell the world this boat is really loved.

• Make neat boat-acrylic covers for cowl vents that are not totally leakproof. Small white-plastic garbage bags will do until you get around to the fabric covers, though they may send a questionable message. Tie a piece of shock cord around the neck of the vent, and they'll hold through most squally winds.

• Put an overhead port into a bimini top. On a sailboat, it lets you look at the sail. On any boat, it lets some light into the cockpit/steering station. Make a fabric panel to cover the port during the noon hours of high sun. Velcro the edges for easy attachment.

• When buying Velcro for outside use, be sure to buy it from a marine supplier. Velcro is made with either nylon or polyester. Though it may not be labeled, those products intended for marine use are polyester, and will hold up to ultraviolet exposure better than nylon.

• If you do your own canvaswork, use a HotKnife. It fuses cut edges so they can't unravel. (It's especially useful if you want to cut out letters to add the boat name to weather cloths.) This tool is available from Sailrite Kits, 800-348-2769.

CLASSIC COLOR

The original blue acrylic seems to retain color and strength longer than some of the newer colors. White, of course, reflects light and heat best, but it also shows stains the worst.

HARDWARE

Snaps hold well, but if you'll be removing panels often, the constant pulling weakens the fabric around the snaps. If a grommet/turn-button fastener can be substituted, the fabric will probably last longer. (These pose a potential toe-stubbing problem, however; consider all aspects when installing.)

CANVAS CARE

Check all canvas often for the beginnings of mildew, not only because cleaning will be easier at this stage, but also because the longer you ignore mildew, the more damage it will do to the fabric itself. The manufacturer of Sunbrella acrylic recommends washing covers with a bleach solution. Curiously, chlorine bleach is fine for all but the white fabric, for which you should use nonchlorine Clorox 2.

After it's dry, waterproof the fabric with Aquaseal 3. (Look for it in marine stores or canvas shops.)

ACRYLIC ALTERNATIVES

• For liveaboard or long-term cruising, the sun awning should be made of the relatively permanent, standard boat-acrylic fabric. For weekend cruising, you can get by with an awning made from an ordinary sheet, since its primary function will be as a sunshade on a windless day. Put an extra-wide hem on all four sides; use snap-on plastic grommets to attach shock cord for tie-downs. (Snap-on grommets fit over fabric; no need to put holes into the material.)

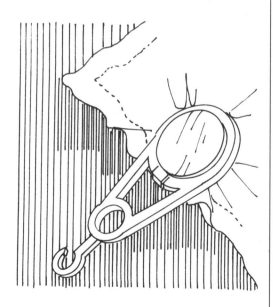

• A nylon parachute acquired from military surplus makes an odd-looking but functional sunshade, with its multiple folds of white swaying in the breeze like a giant ghost.

• Most unusual alternative: a portion of a retired hot-air balloon—a graceful drape of yellow and green.

TEMPORARY TARP

• Keep a square of sun-screening fabric on board to put up as a temporary shield when the sun is too low for the usual shade to block. Use it for a side extension on the sailboat's boom tent, or drape it wherever it's needed to keep out the sun's heat. On a powerboat, rig a way to attach it to the upper-deck overhang to keep afternoon sun off the sliding-door cabin entry. The fabric is available in an assortment of colors from the garden section of larger discount stores.

• Or go to a plant nursery and try to buy some of the black screening material they use to protect young plants from direct sun.

• Solartex brand is sold with locking clips or a lacing line that attaches to whatever line you may put up. (Use snap-on grommets for these temporary tie-downs too.)

RAIN COVER

Sew (or buy) a square of boat acrylic to tie over a forward hatch. It should be big enough to extend well beyond hatch borders, so when it's raining a gentle, straight-down rain, you can keep the hatch open and enjoy the air and the sound. Hold the fabric in place by tying it to lifelines or rail.

RATTLE STOPS

Sliding ports in a wheelhouse are great for pulling in fresh air, but when the wind gets up or the anchorage develops a surge, they can start a clanking rhythm as annoying as a faucet drip.

• An easy antirattle device for Plexi ports: At the aft end of the inner port, drill a hole about halfway up. Thread the hole, then use a thumbscrew and tighten the screw against the outer port, thus keeping the two ports from touching. (Glue a small piece of wood or a rubber tip to the place where the screw touches the back port.)

• Temporary fix: wedge pads of sponge or neoprene material between the two ports.

• For glass ports, buy a fitting that clamps around the edge of one glass panel and pushes against the other.

WATERPROOF PORTS

If you're tired of caulking leaky ports and you don't need them to open for ventilation, replace them with plain plastic. Remove the offending port. Clean up the opening, patching and sanding edges as necessary. Cut a piece of plastic about ½ inch larger than the opening on all sides. Sand edges smooth. Caulk the outer ¼ inch of plastic, using silicone caulking, and fasten the port in position, screwing in from the outside. Plexiglas will work; Lexan is stronger.

WATER-RESISTANT PORTS

• Eyelids over ports are not a complete antileak solution; they work fine at anchor

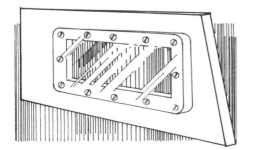

with a gentle rain, but they can't help much when the rain blows sideways or waves send saltwater spray splashing upward.

• A drip rail will be only a part-time help too. Water running off the top of the cabin will be redirected to flow off to the sides of the port, so it cannot sit in the bottom lip.

BUGS AWAY

• Make a screen to replace wood hatch boards when you want air but no flying friends. Use doorskin. Measure for a single screened panel, not separate boards, and cut two doorskins to size. Cut out the centers, leaving a wood frame a few inches wide on all sides. Glue a piece of nylon screening onto the inner surface of one doorskin, then glue the sandwich together.

• Screen panels that attach to the boat with Velcro are practical: a folded fabric is so much easier to stow than a rigid frame. But if you are to use them successfully, the Velcro strips must be well attached to the boat. A good contact cement is the correct adhesive, but it must be applied to a surface that is not only clean but also free of paint, varnish, and any other sealer. If you're attaching to wood, remove finish coating and rough-sand the surface before applying glue. If you're attaching to fiberglass, clean thoroughly and sand enough to remove gloss.

• For overhead hatches, make screens that attach on the outside; then you can open or close the hatch from the inside without affecting the screen. Open the hatch to full height and make a paper pattern to fit over it. The screen will be a triangular wedge shape. Leaving enough material for a hem at the bottom, cut and sew nylon screening to the shape of your pattern. Put shock cord through the bottom hem to hold the screen snug against the hatch frame.

At the center of the forward edge, add a snap (reinforce the screen fabric with a vinyl tab) so the screen can be secured to the hatch frame. It's far too much work to risk letting the screen blow away.

• Make a screen for an opening windshield panel. Use a boltrope to hold the top, and attach Velcro to snug both sides, reaching over and around opening brackets. The bottom can be held in place with another Velcro strip or tucked under a piece of wood pushed against the windshield base.

HELM SEAT

Certain items end up in the cockpit even if that is not their place in the master storage plan. Binoculars, horn, sunglasses, sunscreen: these items are used in the cockpit, so why not keep them there?

• A helm seat/storage box serves a dual purpose. Build an appropriate-size box with a hinged top. If you use doorskin and fiberglass, this top can be shaped to accommodate the heeling position on sailboats. A custom-made cushion makes it comfortable, though an ordinary throw-type seat cushion works fine.

• Easier solution: use a hinged-top ice chest to keep cockpit miscellany dry and handy.

• A different helm seat: put a swivel-based boat seat (with molded back support) atop a storage box, raising comfort level along with eye level.

PASSENGER SEATS

Teak seats attached to bow or stern pulpit are probably not a do-it-yourself project, but they are an add-on worth considering. People like to spend time on the bow or at the stern, watching the water (or the dolphins), escaping the engine noise, having some alone time. Built-in seats made of curved teak slats are perfect for such times, adding comfort and a measure of safety; the space they take usually isn't used for anything else. Plus, they're attractive.

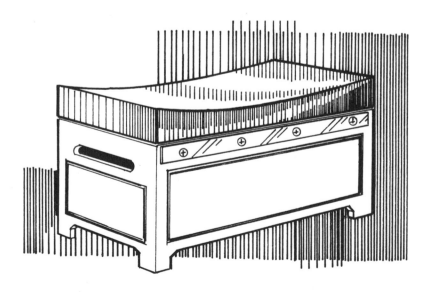

COCKPIT CHAIRS

For extra seating on a back deck, get the smallest folding camp chairs you can find. The most basic aluminum-tubing-and-canvas models fold flat to fit behind a door in a few inches of space. Their compact, no-arm design allows more people to fit into less back-deck space.

PICNIC TABLES

• A tray made from teak grating becomes a snack table when perched on top of a cooler or box.

• A simple plank becomes an elongated table when placed athwartships on cockpit seats. (Put wood crosspieces on the underside near each end to prevent side-slipping.)

• Kits are sold to turn a pedestal into a temporary table support.

• Most cockpits have a bulkhead where a shelf could be hinged to fold up or down and hold serving dishes or pass-around snacks.

PORTABLE LIGHT

• A traditional anchor light with light-refracting glass attractively illuminates evening get-togethers in the cockpit.

• Keep a portable 12-volt fluorescent light to clamp to a railing. It provides a low-drain sidelight for any outdoor need: cocktails on the flybridge, dessert on the back deck, or a quick caulking on a leaky port.

RED LIGHT

If your compass does not have a built-in red shield for the light, fit a small piece of see-through red plastic between the light

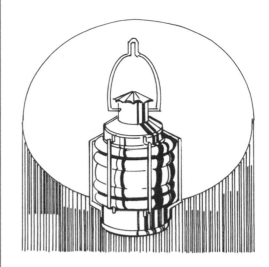

and the compass card. It shouldn't touch the light, or it might melt away. The plastic might come from a reclosable can lid or a bottle cap.

NEW COLOR

Vinyl cushions can take just so much abuse, be it weather or overzealous scrubbing. When the surface finally refuses to clean up, you can revive its appearance with a can of spray paint. If you choose a color close to the original, you'll use less paint and future scratches will be less noticeable. The paint seems to bond well, so you won't be finding little paint chips to clean up later.

Plasti-Kote is sold by Kmart, and VinylKote may be found in marine stores or catalogs; it can also be used on leather, PVC, ABS, or polycarbonate. It penetrates into vinyl, so the grain is retained.

NEW CUSHIONS

If you're going to replace cockpit cushions, make them or have them made of vinyl-covered closed-cell foam; they can't get water-logged.

• C Cushions has patterns for hundreds of boat cushion designs; if yours is special, send them a tracing on brown Kraft paper and they will custom-make cushions to fit your boat:

C Cushions
206 Highway 35 South
Rockport, TX 78382
800-531-1014

• Temperature affects cushions, so if they seem slightly off-size, you'll know why.

BACK CUSHIONS

Extra PFDs (the Coast Guard–approved, rectangular bargain variety) frequently get pushed into corners of lockers, surfacing only if it becomes necessary to count them. Instead of filing them in mildew-land, make a boat-canvas "bag" or cover for each PFD, and use them for back cushions on the cockpit or flybridge seats. (The covers can be designed to close with Velcro for easy access.)

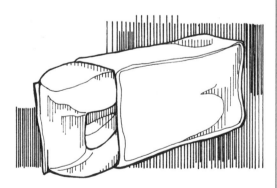

HOW HIGH ARE YOU?

• Know how much vertical clearance the boat really needs. On a powerboat, if you have no spec sheet, measure boat

height in sections: cabin or wheelhouse top to deck, deck to water, then the "up" dimensions of any fixed superstructure. Add whatever extra makes you feel comfortable.

• On a sailboat, if you have no sail plan or published specs, tie a line to that end of the main halyard that usually hoists the sail. (Use a large knot.) Raise the knot to the masthead till it stops at the sheave. Mark the line where it touches the deck, then drop it and measure knot-to-mark for an approximate mast length. Include some for the antenna or other masthead fittings; add the total to your cabin-to-deck-to-water figures.

• Or use the hoisted line to measure the boat's full height. When the knot is at the sheave, cleat the halyard and drop the end of the tied-on line into the water. From the dinghy, you can pull the line fairly taut. Use a twist-tie to mark the place where the line enters the water. The knot-to-twist-tie measurement, plus extra for masthead extensions, will be close to your true height. Any variance for the slight angle would give you a safety margin.

HOW LOW CAN YOU GO?

• If your trawler has a steadying sail, put the mast on a tabernacle. You'll be able to lower the mast to clear more bridges, and this arrangement will open new cruising grounds to you.

• Establish a convenient way to lower antennas, outriggers, and flagstaff so you can get under more bridges. Bridgetenders can refuse to open if you don't comply with their lowering requirements.

LADDER ADD-ON

• Add wood treads or nonskid tape strips to an aluminum boarding ladder. A nonskid patch may also be useful on the caprail, where you ordinarily board the boat from the dinghy.

• A swim ladder that hooks into brackets and folds down to water level is sturdy enough, but be sure it is also long enough so you could climb onto the boat from the water, not only from the dinghy. You can probably add a step, if necessary, rather than buy a whole new ladder. Even a rope stirrup may solve the problem.

PAD A PLATFORM

Cushion the edge of a swim platform with canvas dock padding. Put grommets into the turned edge of the padding, then lace it onto the platform (assuming the platform has a wood or metal grid to lace into).

in. (In strong winds, it would send messages all by itself.)

A brass fog bell almost *asks* to have the boat name engraved along the rim.

OUTBOARD HOIST

Make some arrangement to hoist the outboard from the dinghy to its stern rail bracket. Sailors can use the boom vang; sailors or powerboaters can buy a hoisting bracket system that mounts to stern rail when needed and stows in its own storage bag.

SOLAR PANELS

Make up some simple brackets to attach solar panels where they are most likely to get maximum light but least likely to be bumped or stepped on. Put them on the cabintop, but keep them tiltable to take full advantage of different angles. Clamp them to pulpit or rails, again allowing for angle adjustment. Sailboats might hang a panel from a boom gallows or frame it on a lazarette lid.

BELL BRACKETS

Hang a bracket for the fog bell fairly close to the helm so you can send signals when necessary. Try to find a spot where it won't be bumped constantly, or you'll send more signals than you intend. Put another bracket inside so the bell has its assigned place when you want to bring it

DECK DRAINS

To help decks drain faster, add extra drains. Drill holes through toerail or gunwales so the bottom of each hole is level with the deck. Cut a short length of 1-inch copper tubing (or a short section of 1-inch PVC pipe); put it into the hole, extending out about ½ inch to 1 inch, and glue it in place with epoxy putty. The water will drain through the tube, but because the tube sections extend past the hull side, water doesn't drain directly down the hull, so it cannot leave water stains.

TRANSOM CLEANER

Cut a short piece of PVC pipe and put it into the exhaust exit with epoxy putty or polyurethane caulking. Exhaust smoke and water will now come out past the transom instead of dripping down the surface of the transom. No more black smoke stain on the fiberglass.

PROTECT A DECK

• Put a patch of vinyl nonskid material (the kind made to be glued over old decks) on the forward deck where anchoring activity takes place. It can take the dings and knocks and scratches much better than a fiberglass surface can.

• A flemished line makes a good temporary cushion for heavy tools when you're working on a deck project, keeping the fiberglass free of scrapes and gouges.

COOL PAINT

White is the best boat color if you're planning to cruise in a hot climate. Even beige or the palest gray will absorb enough heat to make a difference between your being able to walk barefoot on deck or not. While you may not care about bare feet, the heat absorbed by tinted paint will affect the temperature inside the boat too. (Exterior varnish will make the inner surface noticeably warm to the touch.)

PERSONALIZE

• Find someone who can sandblast a design into an acrylic hatch cover to simulate the look of etched glass. Do the boat name, or a design element that echoes your decorating theme.

• A propane tank is not a thing of beauty, but the safest place to carry one is on deck, where it is most visible. Make (or have made) a canvas cover. Color coordinate it with your boat's canvas, or make it white or gray to be unobtrusive and fade into the deck or cabin color. You might also paint the boat name on the canvas in lettering to match the transom.

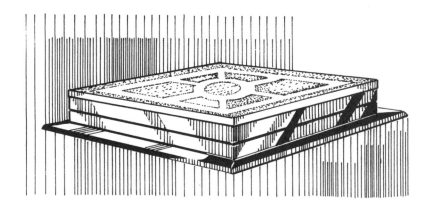

- Another way to personalize: have a bronze nameplate made; use it for a boarding step.

STORAGE BOXES

- Whether in cockpit, wheelhouse, or flybridge, find a corner or a recess to build in separate boxes for binoculars and a flashlight so you can find them even in the dark. (A glasses case could hold spare eyeglasses or sunglasses.)

- On some sailboats, a covered cooler fits between the side cockpit seats just inside the transom to function as a lazarette. The space is never missed; the tiller fits over it.

- A covered cooler positioned on deck provides protected storage for PFDs, docklines, anything. Put some wood braces on the deck to hold the cooler in place.

- Another outside storage option: truck toolboxes. Keep fishing gear, snorkeling gear, any kind of gear on deck accessible but protected. It's a budget-loving substitute for the marine deck box. A cushion on its top can double as a seat while camouflaging the box.

- Square plastic wastebaskets separate and hold stuff safely inside seat lockers, engine rooms, and deck boxes. They confine spillables, protect breakables, and organize messables.

CAPTIVE HATCH BOARDS

- Hatch boards slip and slide a lot when loose. Give them a place when they're not in their primary place. A bracket or two can be attached to a convenient vertical surface (perhaps right next to the hatch). The bracket opening will be

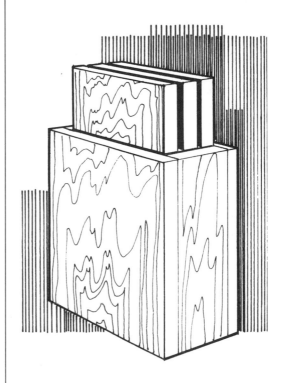

just wide and deep enough to hold all boards; stand them on edge vertically to take the least room against the cabin side.

- If the boards are finished bright you have even more reason to prevent them from knocking about. Make individual slots in a narrow box; line each slot with felt for super protection. The box may fit in a seat locker or just inside the hatch opening.

SEAT-LOCKER SPAGHETTI

If lockers are deep, hang as many items as possible: docklines, winch handles, spare blocks, fenders. When they are easy to see and remove, lines generally emerge still wound in their neat coils rather than pulled out in a tangle of knots.

EXTRA STORAGE

Weekend boats can organize weekend stuff (and cruising boats, day stuff) in a backpack designed for boat seats. The compartmented pack hangs on the back of most cushioned seats. Sun lotion, sunglasses, keys, and the like are securely held in fabric or mesh pockets.

PATRIOTIC PROTECTION

Make a tube of boat acrylic to slip over the flag when it is neatly rolled up on the flagstaff each night. Or take the flag in and cover it with a less attractive but equally efficient case made from a retired pant leg.

HANDLE HOLDERS

• To keep a boat hook stowed safely but still handy, put a length of PVC pipe on a stanchion or shroud (use a hose clamp to hold it in place) and drop the hook through the PVC. Or snap the hook into a pair of round clips mounted in the wheelhouse or under a cabin overhang.

• The deck mop can also be stowed in a PVC holder. It may not be exactly Bristol, but you won't trip over the mop, it won't fall overboard, and it *will* dry after use.

• You may want to shorten the mop handle for more convenient storage. If you cut the handle, drill a hole near the end and tie a line through it so you won't lose the mop when you dip it into the water.

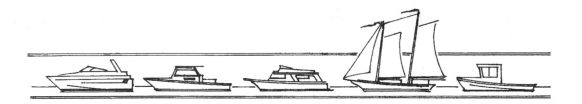

Hook, Line, and Fender

A good sign of competence in boat handling is dexterity in line handling. Watch somebody roll or throw a bow line, wherein the person holds a piece of line loosely, then shakes and wiggles and flips it a few times and voilà: instant knot. It makes you wonder where your dextrous went.

While enviable, such theatrics and super speed aren't essential, but a certain measure of ability is. Sometime, you'll need to dock quickly before the current takes you downstream backward. Other times, you'll want to be comfortable with anchoring gear, or the getaway dream will turn into an insomniac misadventure. Anytime, you'll like the self-confidence of knowing "I can do that."

ANCHOR SIZE

Recommendations for anchor size relative to boat length and/or weight can be only the most general of approximations. "The largest you can carry" is a common answer to questions about anchor size. Some overkill in this department may draw a few condescending smiles, but you'll sleep best.

ANCHOR STYLES

• Most boaters quickly adopt a favorite anchor, but a cruising boat should carry at least two different types, preferably three. A Danforth design is reliable in many bottoms, but in a current-switching situation, it could pull out. Plow types are designed to reset in such a circumstance, but in some bottoms, they plow right through. Really hard, scoured bottoms laugh at all anchors; here, simple weight, and a prayer for no wind, are your best hope.

• A Bahamian fisherman found a way to alter one anchor design for a specific purpose: if you sharpen the pointed ends of a Danforth-type anchor, it will dig into grassy bottoms better.

RODE TALK

• Use nylon for its stretchability.

• Mark anchor rode so you can keep track of scope. With line, attach the brightly colored tabs with feet numbers printed on each. Or use different colors of tape or paint to put a narrow ring around the line at regular intervals—color tells you the number of feet. At night, a small flashlight will show you how much scope is out.

• Mark chain by attaching plastic cable ties around links at regular intervals—one tie at 25 feet, two ties at 50 feet, three ties at 75 feet; then start over. At night you can feel the number of ties to know how much chain is out.

CHAIN TALK

• Add some chain to anchor rode. It helps maintain a horizontal pull on the anchor; if you're anchored in coral or other rocky area, it could prevent loss of the anchor because of a chafed line.

• If you're using all-chain rode, use a chain stop so you can safely prevent the chain from continuing to feed out after it has reached the desired scope. Install the stop far enough behind the bow roller so that when the anchor is raised, there will be a few links of chain between the end of the anchor and the stop. The chain-stop pin pops into one of these links to keep the chain (and the anchor) from accidentally moving forward.

• With all-chain rode, use a snubbing line to secure rode to a cleat, rather than leave chain on the windlass. When you have let out almost as much chain as you want, tie a short length of nylon line into a link. Let out another 15 feet or so, then cleat the line off, leaving a bit of slack in the chain before stopping it. Now the pull will be on a flexible line, rather than on an inflexible chain. This also prevents the noise of chain shifting and/or rubbing on the bow roller.

SCOPE

When calculating appropriate scope, a common mistake is to use water depth as the multiplier. When scope is figured at 5 to 1 or 7 to 1, the 1 is not the depth of the water, but the total distance between anchor chock and bottom—water depth *plus* distance from bow at deck level to water surface. While it may not be a critical difference for small boats, it does change the ratio for boats with high bows.

ATTENTION-GETTER

Unless you like attracting attention to your anchoring efforts, and also don't mind disrupting the quietude of an anchorage and its occupants, establish some communication system between helmsperson and anchorperson. In the daytime, hand signals are easy: pointing for direction, plus a way to request forward, neutral, or reverse power. At night you'll need a little more ingenuity. A deck light would allow the helmsperson to see the anchorer, but would affect night vision beyond the boat. A flashlight can point directions—and possibly *up* for forward power, down for reverse—but the flashing could disrupt another anchorer. Battery-operated voice transmitters (the old-fashioned walkie-talkie) should be most clear.

BAHAMIAN MOOR

This two-anchor system is useful wherever strong tidal flow reverses current direction at regular intervals. The sought-after result is for two anchors to be led from the bow of the boat—one set forward, one set aft—on a general line with that of the current flow. The boat swings in the small area of its own radius, shifting direction with each tide change, hanging first on one anchor, then on the other.

TRIP LINE/FLOAT LINE

Use an anchor float to mark the place you drop the anchor. The float line should be a bit longer than the water depth, and tied to the anchor in such a way that you could use it to haul up the anchor by a fluke or the lower part of the shank rather than from the shackle where rode is attached. (If you do use the float line to break out a stubborn anchor, it becomes a trip line.)

The float itself can be a Styrofoam ball from a fish trap, a plastic bottle, or a small fender. Or you can personalize one with whatever shape/color/marker you choose. Mannequin heads and hats may be too frightening, but an inverted ducktail is fun. Dinghy drivers who know only full-speed-ahead are not fond of floats, since they add one more line to the maze of hazards to avoid.

UNSETTING ANCHORS

Sometimes wind and waves may be too much for your anchor. Learn to recognize signs of a possible pull-out.

Most cruising boats use chain as all or part of rode. As the anchor starts to pull out or move, the chain bounces along the bottom; inside the boat, you may feel an unusual motion—a slight shudder, as though the boat has bumped something. If the anchor starts dragging in earnest, the boat will swing to a beam-to-wind position, and that difference in motion should get you on deck immediately.

First Remedy

If there's room in the anchorage, let out more scope, snugging rode occasionally to see if the anchor is digging in.

Second Try

Have a second anchor and rode on the bow, ready to drop, especially when weather is iffy or downright threatening. If the first anchor starts to drag, you can drop the second one immediately. Even if it doesn't set right away, it should help slow the boat's backward motion till you have time to organize for reanchoring.

WINDLASS CONTROL

• Most manual windlasses come with a short metal handle; this makes for very bad purchase, and therefore more work. It also sinks like a stone if it goes overboard.

Make a new handle. Use a full-size oak ax handle with a slit in the butt to take a ¼-inch stainless/Monel plate that fits the windlass slot. Through-bolt the plate into the butt (you'll need a good drill and bit to drill the plate). Fit the handle with a lanyard to keep it from going overboard. (Put a screw-eye on the handle end

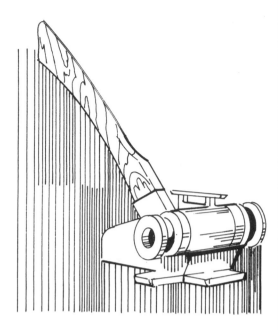

and a snaphook tied into the other end, for attachment to a lifeline.)

• A very low profile Anchorman manual windlass from Simpson-Lawrence brings in line or chain rode with a continuous circular motion, much quicker than the lever-handle models.

• Remember to grease manual windlasses once or twice a year, or as often as the manufacturer recommends.

• Instead of using a toe switch for an electric windlass, wire-in a hand switch and hang it from the pulpit or lifeline. You won't be confined to the foot-switch area; you can watch what's happening as you operate the windlass with your hand.

RODE CLEANERS

• When traveling on the waterway, or whenever you're likely to be moving every day, keep the anchor rode stowed on deck

to keep the mess out of the anchor locker. Coil it on the foredeck and/or cover it with a bag or tarp to keep sun exposure to a minimum.

• To keep the clutter off the deck completely, put up two stainless steel lifering brackets around which to coil the lines.

• When there are no rocky bottoms that require the protection of chain-anchor rode, take off the chain portion and avoid the daily demudding bath that dirty chain necessitates.

• Tie two scrub brushes bristle to bristle and attach them to the boat at the bow, where the anchor chain comes on board. As the chain moves between the brushes, mud and goo will be removed, so (in a perfect world) only clean chain will come aboard.

FRESH FINISH

• When anchor and chain start to show their age, give them a new start by having them regalvanized. A new coating provides the antirust protection that effectively maintains the strength of the metal.

• If you can't get to a commercial zinc hot-dipper, get some short-term help with a can of spray galvanizer coating such as CRC Instant Galvanize. It will add some protection against corrosion and slow down any rust spots in progress.

ANCHOR STOWAGE

• For anchors without a permanent home on the bow platform, install a set of chocks to keep them safely confined on deck.

• To stow a Danforth-style anchor, attach a section of PVC pipe to a stanchion and slide the stock of the anchor into the tube. Use line wrapping to secure the PVC to the stanchion. Hose clamps would work, but their sharp edges can catch fingers or lines.

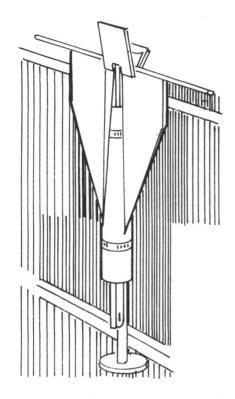

• In weekend boats and dinghies, stow the anchor in a canvas bag. The boat will stay cleaner and the anchor will be less prone to rust; if you tie the bag into a permanent storage locker, you'll be less likely to leave the dock without an anchor.

ON AND OFF

• First and best anchor hint: tie the bitter end of anchor rode to the boat.

• At the same time, always be prepared to let the line go—under controlled conditions. The control is that something float-able is tied to the line. Keep a small fender or some kind of float handy at the bow. If you must leave an anchor, you can come back later to retrieve it.

OFF AND ON

Situations that might require a temporary anchor abandonment:

1. You have two anchors down; one is dragging, and you don't want to risk running over an unseen line.

2. A fast-approaching squall line will turn you around too close to a shore.

3. Another boat has wrapped your rode around his prop and you're forced to cut the line.

Are we having fun yet?

LIGHT SUPPLEMENT

• A 12-volt fluorescent light draws little current but adds considerable light to a cockpit area. If you're in an area with a lot of traffic, a bright light at deck level is much more visible to nearby boats than a high anchor light, making it a sensible supplement. Plus, you can read by it.

• A small solar-powered yard walkway light is another option, not as a substitute for the anchor light, but for additional light during busier evening hours, especially when you're away from the boat and no cabin lights are on.

LINE KINDS

Ultraviolet light bothers synthetic line to varying degrees. Polypropylene is most susceptible to deterioration, Dacron probably the least, with nylon somewhere between. But UV sensitivity is not the only reason to choose one type of line over another.

- Polypropylene is lightweight and it floats—a plus for ski tow ropes and dinghy painters.

- Dacron is low-stretch: good for sheets and halyards.

- Nylon is strong and allows the most stretch; it's used for anchor lines, mooring lines, and docklines.

KNOT KNOW-HOW

- A figure-eight knot should look like its name. Tie it into the end of a line so the eight stops the line from escaping through a block or fitting. It is an easy knot to untie; you can push as well as pull the line.

- The bowline is not a complicated knot, but it is most versatile and should be on your must-tie list. Remember the scout camp instructions: the rabbit comes out of his hole, runs around the tree, and dives back into the hole. Nobody needs to know this is your method of marlinspikemanship.

NEAT CLEAT

A cleated line should show a continuous eight-shape too. Many people start out right, but the last turn points the wrong way. Take a complete turn around the base of the cleat before you start the S-turns around the ends. To secure the line, turn the bitter end under the last loop.

PROPER COILS

- Practice coiling line so it doesn't kink into a tangle. As you practice coiling (usually clockwise), roll each turn over as you

coil, so the line lays in flat circles, with no bends or eights.

- Secure coiled lines with a quick-release twist rather than a wraparound with the bitter end. Pull the bight of the standing part of the line through the coil, twist it once, and place the loop over a cleat.

- If you want to collect points for neatness, flemish the ends of your docklines (or any other lines you leave on deck or dock). Lay the line on deck in flat ever-widening circles that will look like a round mat when you're through.

CUT LINES

To cut synthetic lines, put tape around the spot; cut in the middle of the tape, then melt the cut ends with a lighted match (or dip them into "liquid tape") to prevent unraveling.

LINE CARE

- Extend the useful life of anchor lines and docklines by turning them end-for-end occasionally to change the wear spots on each line. Rotate whichever docklines are the same length, for the same reason.

- Check all lines often for signs of damage or fraying, and change them before anything snaps.

- Wash lines occasionally. Put them in a bucket (if it's a large bucket or you're washing small lines) or a cooler, or perhaps the dinghy after a good rain has filled it with soft washwater. If the sun's out, the water will even be warm. Add some mild soap and let the lines soak for the afternoon.

- An overnight soaking with fabric

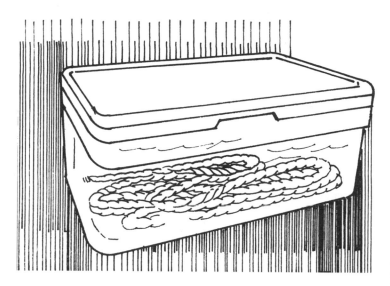

softener in the water should relax some of the stiffness in older lines. Use about ½ cup to 3 gallons of water.

CHAFING GEAR

Chafe not only weakens a line, it also makes an annoying noise as line runs back and forth through chocks.

• Pieces of plastic or rubber hose are good chafe preventers. You can split the hose lengthwise to slip it around the line, or leave it intact and put it on lines before splicing, whether you're attaching to an anchor shackle or looping for docklines.

• For docklines, an 18-inch length of hose is plenty; for anchor line, use as much as is needed to clear any bow fittings.

• Plastic hose is better than rubber; it cannot mar the boat. Rubber breaks down with long exposure to sunlight, and it might start to leave messy colored shreds on the line and the boat.

• Small pieces of leather are strong chafe-resisters too. Tie them in position onto

anchor or dock lines with a thin nylon line. If you're not into leather, any cloth wrapped around the line a few times and tied in place will cushion the line.

• For long-term use, using hose may be better than tying anything to the line. With hose, the line moves quietly back and forth through the smooth surface of the plastic. With leather or cloth, the line is still rubbing back and forth across chocks; though chafing is prevented, noise is not.

FENDER COVERS

• If your fenders are small and oblong in shape, you can sew covers from retired khaki or denim pants. For each cover, cut a pant leg to the appropriate length. Sew the bottom end shut; install grommets and a drawstring cord at the top.

• When fenders get too grimy to clean, paint them. Use spray vinyl, or experiment with whatever kind of enamel you have on board. (Good results have reportedly been achieved with a brush-on acrylic-urethane enamel.)

UNCOVERED FENDERS

Big round fenders do a great job, but where will you store them? Anything left out all the time will suffer from UV exposure, and colors absorb more sun rays than does white.

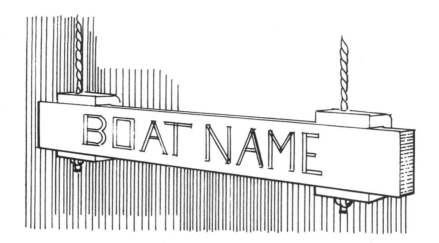

FENDERBOARDS

• Personalize your fenderboard. With a router, etch the boat name into the wood. For emphasis, paint the letter grooves black and the board background white. Or use whatever colors coordinate with the boat's exterior decor.

• If your fenderboard is large enough, use it as a workbench too, by propping it across seats in the cockpit or flybridge or laying it on the back deck.

RAFTUPS

Boats raft for the fun of a community cook-in, the convenience of regatta entries, or of necessity when they outnumber available dock space.

• When rafted at anchor, they should be tied tight to each other, so that when they move with wind or current, they move as a unit.

• Sailboats must watch spreader location in relation to the neighbors.

• And don't go spinnaker flying.

• When you're rafted dockside, if you're not actually friends with the other rafters, *don't* walk through your neighbor's cockpit in the middle of cocktail hour (or any other hour). Walk around the bow or stern and pretend you're invisible so the other boaters can do the same.

IT'S WORTH A TRY

Good docking technique depends on many variables. A reversing prop may push the boat one way when current is pushing it another. Wind compounds the problem. Springline docking is the frequent solution, but here's a variation.

The first tie-up line is one, short, tight line positioned amidships. Once this temporary line is secure, all others can be added. The boat can't go very far forward or back; if it's snug to the dock, neither bow nor stern can swing very far sideways either (in a perfect docking situation).

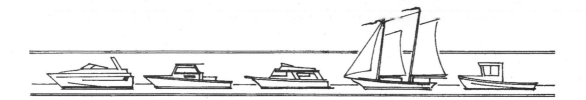

15 Water Everywhere

Boating teaches you to use water wisely, right after it has taught you to conserve it cleverly.

In a house, one shower or a few toilet flushes could easily take the equivalent of a boat's water allotment for a week. "Running water" as a concept should be forgotten on a boat, even if the faucet handles can provide it, and even when it's easily obtainable. "Think stingy" is the best plan. (That thinking translates to dollar signs for the cruising boater: in other countries, water is one more commodity, and it costs more in relation to its scarcity.)

Start and stop. On and off. Challenge the crew to lengthen the time between tank fill-ups. (But not necessarily at the expense of Saturday's bath.)

WATERMAKING

• High on many an accessory dream list is a watermaker. While a reverse-osmosis desalinator does not actually make water in the same sense that The Rainmaker can, it does make salt water drinkable, and that potential is seen as the ultimate in self-sufficiency. All it takes is the right components, a lot of electric power, lots of filters, and an ironclad guarantee that nothing will ever break.

• Like anything that depends on perfect function, when it's good, it's very, very good, and when it's bad, it's a disaster. Always keep your boat's water tanks filled in preparation for just-in-case scenarios.

RAIN CATCHERS

As much as boaters might want an unlimited water supply, the average cruising boat can't meet the power requirements for a desalinator; it's essential to devise a water-catching system.

Any catching system must be simple (quick) to set up, and its components must be simple (small) to stow. Since rain usually comes along with wind—often shifting—the system must be weighted or tied in such a way that it can withstand the wind's attempts to foil its purpose; it must function reasonably well whatever the weather.

The basic idea is to find or create a good-size surface, usually in a close-to-horizontal position, and direct water draining from that surface straight into a water tank, or if necessary, into a bottle fill for later transfer to tank.

Tarp Catcher

For a simple rain-catching system, make a square or rectangle of boat acrylic and sew grommets in each corner. Establish a place and a way to hang the square in a more-or-less horizontal position. Cut a hole in the center of the fabric to insert a hose fitting. When it rains, connect a hose between the tarp and your water tank fill. If the weight of the hose does not pull the center down enough for the water to drain quickly, tie it down enough to make a dent.

Neo-Faucet

In a real downpour, you can fill the spare water bottles by holding them under a rainwater spigot. If the deck drain is led through the toerail or gunwale, water will pour off the boat in a steady stream; the harder the rain, the more horizontal the stream.

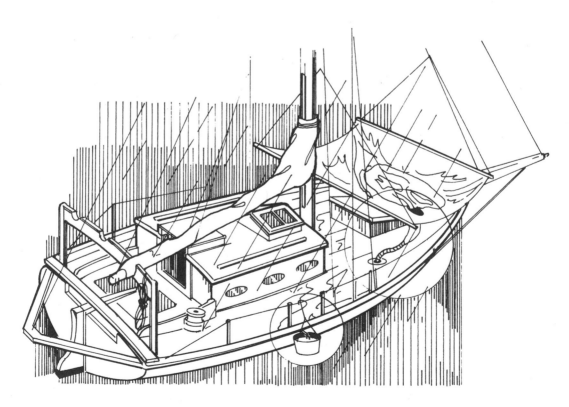

Cabin Catcher

The cabintop has plenty of horizontal catching surface and may be adaptable to a collection method that can ignore wind. Block off water exit areas under handrails with towels or canvas pieces made for the purpose. Fit a hose at the aft, or "drain," end to catch the water trying to leave; feed the other end of the hose into a collection jug or directly into the tank fill.

Deck Catcher

Boats with a deck fill plate have a ready-made water catcher. After the first good downpour washes off the deck, put plugs into scuppers so rainwater flows back into the water tank fill. Encourage the straightest flow by placing sponges or mounding rags to form a berm to direct water to the fill site.

Sailcover Catcher

In the right conditions (a howling storm would not be right) sailors can try to catch water running off the mainsail by hanging the sail cover upside down under the boom. Cut a hole at the bottom of the pocket (top of the sail cover) where the most water collects, and add a fitting for the hose that will lead to the tank fill.

• Fill all available containers. After the permanent tanks and bottles are full, start on coolers, ice buckets, regular buckets, and anything else that will hold water temporarily. If everything that can be filled *is* filled and it's still raining, wash yourself and/or a load of laundry. (See Chapter 9.)

WATER TANKS

If the boat has more than one water tank, be sure each one can be separated or isolated from the rest. If one springs a leak, you don't want the others feeding into it, causing you to lose your entire water supply as it runs happily down to the bilge.

WATER HOSES

• If you're filling water tanks at a marina's fuel dock, try to use your own hose. Marina hoses that lie around a dock for months have a terrible smell of stale, mildewed rubber, which they transfer to all water flowing through them.

• For the boat hose, white ones are best; they impart the most neutral taste, if any. The fold-flat roll-ups look like a good idea but prove to be a nuisance after the first unroll, due to their unwillingness to reflatten. (If space is really a problem, then you'll take the time to fight with the hose.)

• Keep hoses neatly coiled in perfect, kinkless circles. Tie the coils together in two places with short pieces of line so they'll stay coiled in seat locker or deck box. If practical, hang the hose from a permanent bracket inside.

WATER FILTERS

• To keep water tanks clean and ensure a good water supply, put a filter right on the hose to clean the water as it's coming into the boat.

• If the boat has multiple tanks, keep one tank exclusively for drinking water. Filter that one tank as much as you want, using in-line filters.

• Charcoal filters are good, but they are also expensive. Try using a double filtering system: use a cheaper filter in front of the charcoal; water runs through that first and is partially clean before it gets to the charcoal.

• A slight lessening of water pressure may be an indication that you need to replace the filter.

WATER PRESSURE

Water pressure is a house convenience most people never think about unless the system breaks down, or until they buy a boat.

• Boat pressure systems are self-contained and easy to install. A 12-volt pump moves water through the system, and an accumulator tank situated between pump and faucet holds pressure (so the pump doesn't work constantly) and smooths out fluctuations in water flow.

• The 12-volt system uses either just-like-home handled faucets or boat-convenient foot switches. You can put pressure water in most cruising boats if you want to use amps that way.

• A foot switch is a practical way to control water flow, leaving both hands free for whatever you're doing. (Don't use too small a button; even though it's cushioned with rubber, it can hurt your toes.)

• If the boat is set up with electric water pumps, put in at least one manual pump so you'll have a way to get the water out of the tanks if something goes wrong with either the pump or the power.

MANUAL PUMPS

• Many people think manual (hand *or* foot) pumps give them better control over the amount of water they use. With hand pumps, one hand moves the handle (back and forth or up and down) while the other practices one-hand washing. With practice, it is possible to pump a lot or a little water with one stroke, depending on your enthusiasm for the job.

• A foot pedal for pump operation in head or galley is a supplement for the 12-volt system, and you'll get a lot more exercise when you are the power source. If possible, install it under a cabinet or inside a recessed spot in the locker. If the pedal is too exposed, it's an easy target for toes, and accidental stubbings hurt the stubber much more than the stubbed.

• If the undersink locker door opens all the way down to the floor, install the foot pedal inside the locker. When you want to use it, just leave the door open; when not in use, it's closed away from passing traffic.

• A small foot pump encased in a small, round, fairly flat case is available, and it's much easier on stray toes.

HOT WATER

Hot water is a welcome amenity, especially for showers.

• Hotwater tanks are available in capacities of about 6 gallons and up to as large as you'd want. They're heated with AC shore power or by utilizing the engine's heat exchanger; if you're running the boat by day, you'll have hot water that night.

• No separate hotwater tank is needed with a "demand" heater that works on propane or CNG, because water is not stored. When you turn the faucet on, water is heated instantly as it flows. Turn off the faucet, and the burner shuts off automatically.

LOW-TECH HEATER

Paint a water container black (whatever size fits your boat and suits your purpose) and leave it on deck all the time. The sun will keep the water hot.

Position the water tank close to a hatch or port near the head; a hose can then gravity-feed your shower water.

WATER DIRECTOR

If the faucet is so far above the sink that water splatters outside it, or you if you want to direct the spray differently, put a short piece of plastic hose on the end of the faucet. It helps with rinsing big dishes, pot lids, cutting boards, and other large objects.

PORTABLE WATER

If you vacation on a boat without installed water tanks (whether motel-

hopping or beach-camping), you'll probably stop often to refill gas tanks, so you'll be able to refill water bottles as well. The square 2½-gallon bottles are easy to handle, yet they're heavy enough not to slide around readily. Don't fill them completely; if one goes overboard, the air at the top will keep the bottle afloat so you can retrieve it.

• One 2½-gallon jug is probably all you really need, although two may be more convenient—one for cooking, one for washing. (And don't forget to refill the bug-spray shower tank.)

• If you freeze your own ice blocks in refillable plastic containers, the melted ice provides drinking water for the second day.

WATER CARRIERS

Carry as much water as you can. Most boats can be easily fitted to carry more water.

• Flexible bladder-type tanks wedge into all kinds of odd spaces, and you need no special skills to install them.

• Building a fiberglass tank would be good practice for later projects.

• Carry a bunch of 2-liter plastic soda bottles, refilled with water; they'll fill vacant spaces in engine room or lockers or deck box. This "spare" water also postpones a potential emergency if the water tanks run dry, whether from normal use or a sudden leak.

WATER FERRIERS

• In your master water-storage plan, leave space for a couple of jerry jugs. You'll need them occasionally to ferry water from shore. The 2½-gallon size is easiest to handle, since you may be transporting them in the dinghy; you may have to make more trips, but your back will be glad about not hoisting 5-gallon bottles from dink to boat.

• White plastic containers hold up *much* better than red or blue, and usually look better longer too. Which is probably why it is nearly impossible to find them.

• Collapsible plastic water jugs can help you make fewer ferry trips. They really do fold down to stow in a small space. Buy them in 2½- or 5-gallon sizes.

• Canvas buckets are a practical choice; they can't crack like plastic or scratch like metal. Eventually, they'll rot like fabric, but in the meantime they solve a storage problem for a small boat.

WATER PURIFIERS

• If your water source is questionable (as in a well or cistern or rain), treat it with purifiers. These products, sold in tablet or liquid form, are formulated specifically for their job and are measured to add in correct proportion; they kill bacteria and other contaminants.

• If you don't have any purification tablets, chlorine bleach is a substitute. Interestingly, the Clorox Company does not give specific recommendations for this use, because they are not in the water purification business. A Red Cross worker suggested that 8 drops in a gallon of water should do the job. (Since nobody likes the flavor of chlorine, this would not be a first choice anyway.)

• If you do resort to using chlorine, remove the cap from the water bottle and leave it open overnight; some of the chlorine taste/smell will fade.

• You can always boil water to make it safe to drink.

TANK CLEANERS

• Install inspection ports in your water tanks, if possible, not only so you can see the water level, but so you can get your arm inside to clean the tank as well. Cut a hole with a saber saw and put in a port with a screw-on lid or snap-on cover.

• Even with regular use, tanks, hoses, and pipes start growing mold and mildew and mystery fungus, which bring with them their attendant unpleasant smells. Clean everything periodically with baking soda, chlorine, or other mold-killing solutions made for the purpose.

• If you use the chlorine solution to clean the tanks, be prepared to rinse and pump two to three times. Excess chlorine is persistent.

LESS-WATER COOKING

To conserve water when cooking:

• Prepare one-pot pasta or rice meals where the cooking liquid is all absorbed by the pasta or rice.

• If you're offshore, use seawater to cook pasta or potatoes.

• If you're heating a boil-in-bag meal, use seawater.

• If you're preparing macaroni or potato salad, boil the eggs in the same water as the macaroni or potatoes.

• If you steam vegetables or shellfish instead of boiling them, you not only save water, you also save more of the flavor and nutrition in the food. Use an actual steamer, or just simmer at low heat in small amounts of water.

• Use whatever water is left from steaming vegetables to water your onboard garden.

LESS-WATER WASHING

To conserve water when washing:

• It isn't necessary to fill a whole sink with hot sudsy water. All you need is a small pan or bowl filled with warm, soapy water. Dip a cloth or sponge and wash everything. Then stack it all in the sink to rinse together; water from glasses and cups helps rinse the plates and silver underneath. You'll eventually develop ways to spin a small amount of water around a cup so it rinses clean with one flick of the wrist.

• Many dishwashers eliminate rinsing altogether and dry everything immediately, which is fine if you don't mind a few extra dish towels in the laundry.

• Prevent the overrinsing that oversudsing causes by diluting the dish soap. It's easier to control the amount of soap you use if it's already partly controlled in the bottle. The proportion of soap to water depends on the sudsability of the brand. Experiment with a half-and-half mix; you can always add more soap.

• Save water by washing fewer items. Leave spoons or scoops in sugar, flour, instant coffee, instant creamer. Those may be only one or two fewer items to wash for a given meal, but the idea starts a mindset of "minimal"—whether you want to conserve the water or save the washing effort.

Another example: At breakfast, stir hot cereal with a spoon and use that spoon to eat the cereal (don't use a giant stir-spoon). You might also use the cooking pot instead of a separate serving dish. Also, squeeze orange juice into a pitcher that becomes a drinking glass. (Juice boxes save glassware too, but they add trash.)

• When making hot cereal or rice, measure the rice and transfer it to a dish you will later use as a dinner plate. Then measure the water; slosh it around as you pour it into the pan, and the cup will be sufficiently rinsed so that you need not wash it.

• Using paper plates for meals and paper towels for sandwiches saves the water you'd use to wash real dishes. Determining whether your water is more valuable than the plates' percentage of a tree is one of the cruising life's great debates and personal dilemmas.

SECOND CHOICES

• Catch the melted water from the cooler and use it to wash something (preferably an outside something, just in case the water is not as crystal clear as the ice was).

• Use morning dew to clear yesterday's salt off the deck.

• If you're cruising in a place where it would be safe, convenient, and sensible to jump over the side, alternate saltwater baths with fresh.

While Joy dish soap was the standard

bath soap for years, now special products are made for the purpose. (One from Sun Shower, one from Davis Instruments.)

SEAWATER PUMP

• For cruising offshore, use a seawater pump. The alternative—scooping buckets of water—is not only inconvenient but also potentially dangerous. (Even with a watermaker on board, you might need the seawater pump as a backup.)

ONE LESS THROUGH-HULL

Boatowners who don't like unnecessary through-hull fittings put sink drains into that category. Water from a galley sink drain can often be diverted to connect into a cockpit drain hose. A head sink could drain into the head itself to be pumped out.

PLUMBING HELPS

• An independent and very informal study showed the two chief reasons live-aboard boats sank were toilet failure and pressure water installed with a hose bringing shore water into the boat. Boat plumbing is not made for that kind of pressure.

• Some heavy-duty pumps are equipped with a built-in check valve to protect against damage from city water pressure.

• Install a separate regulator (with a pressure gauge) to protect the boat's system from damage that might be caused by excessive dockside water pressure.

• Keep Teflon tape on board to seal all water connections.

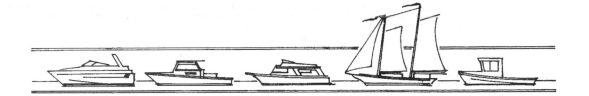

Water Taxi

The dinghy is the family car. As the usually *only* car, it must serve all purposes: sports car for fishing and dive trips; station wagon for shopping; water taxi for visiting, picnicking, dating, and running the dog to shore.

The perfect dinghy would row readily and tow effortlessly. It would come aboard simply and stow unnoticeably. If it planed under power and sported a salty-looking sail rig, so much the better. Might as well expect it to clean and wax itself too.

Since Superdink remains elusive, juggle the variables until you're most comfortable with your compromise.

VERSATILE INFLATABLES

An inflatable dinghy may be the only sensible option for a small boat; it will add the least weight and store in the smallest space. (Davits are not necessary.)

• Inflatables are stable, and their multiple chambers provide a built-in safety factor of flotation.

• With the right size inflatable-and-outboard combination, you can water ski. (A 12-foot, 25-hp combo is a good minimum.)

• An inflatable dinghy that also has a separately inflated keel will be stiffer and easier to control.

• Disadvantages: they don't respond well to rowing or to landings on gravel, rock, or coral.

ADD-A-HULL

A rigid inflatable is not the contradiction its name suggests, but rather a combination. A rigid hull attaches to inflated tubes. It has the weight advantage and stability of an ordinary inflatable, but it's faster and has better maneuverability. It won't stow in as small a space as the regular roll-up inflatable.

• In the true spirit of getting what you pay for, expect to pay a higher price, because you'll be buying a good compromise.

HARD DINGHIES

A hard dinghy, whether fiberglass, aluminum, or wood, is more sturdy and can probably hold more than an inflatable of a comparable size. Most row adequately, and some row extremely well, providing a good source of exercise as well as transportation.

SAILING SKIFF

A sailing dinghy may not be the most stable platform, but its versatility makes up for that minor disadvantage. (Unless you ask the person who is struggling to exit the water after rolling over Tippydink.) Usually, a sailing dinghy gives you a choice of exercise, fun, or solitude. And it can get you to the supermarket too.

DIFFERENT DINKS

Where space is seriously limited, consider two other options: a collapsible, "folding" dinghy, or one that breaks apart on purpose to store in nested half sections. They're both a bit on the odd-looking side, but they have happy owners.

BUDDY BOARDING

If you've been buddy-diving from a tippy hard dinghy and you want to get back on

board, have your buddy hold the bow down and level (from the water) as you scramble over the transom. Then it's your turn to do a balancing act from the inside as your buddy follows you.

STEP HELPS

If you have trouble climbing into an inflatable from the water, buy (or make) a lightweight ladder that's cushioned in the right places to protect the dinghy fabric from ladder burn.

BOAT-TOP CARRIERS

• On a sailboat, a hard dinghy can stow upside down over the forward hatch or standing on edge and tied inside the shrouds (not advisable in rough weather.)

• Powerboats lash dinghies on deck in made-for-the-purpose chocks. Any boat of the appropriate size can hang the dinghy from davits.

• Inflatables can deflate halfway or completely, to roll or fold into whatever space is available. Tie them in place.

SNAP DAVITS

Powerboats can carry an inflatable or a hard dinghy on the transom or swim platform using Snap Davit mounting brackets. Installation is simple: attach hinged davit fittings to platform or transom, and their snap-in brackets to the dinghy.

PAINTERS

Polypropylene is often recommended for towing line; because it floats, it cannot get caught in the big boat's prop when the line gets slack. However, it doesn't hold knots as well as other line, and it must be watched carefully and replaced often, as UV destroys it.

• An alternative for floatability is to put some cork or foam floats on a nylon towing line. Buy the floats at a store that sells commercial fishing supplies.

RAM DEFLECTOR

The bow of a dinghy in tow can act like a miniature battering ram when the big boat stops quickly, or with a following sea. Bow cushions come in many shapes. A baggy-wrinkle fender is very salty, reminiscent of tugboat bows. A right-angle of dock fender material is neat. An old sneaker is ugly, but it works.

TOWING BRIDLE

Rig a towing bridle for an inflatable using four attachment points: one led from each end of the transom, and one from the towing D-ring on each side at the bow. Bring all four together in front of the dinghy to a ring or a knot, then attach a painter to the ring or knot. Adjust line lengths so the actual pull is on the transom lines, with the bow lines adding directional control.

• Put a snaphook on the end of the painter; for temporary tie-ups, snap to lifeline, stanchion, or stay. Cleat the line for overnight stays.

TOWING OPTIONS

• Tow an inflatable dinghy with the bow hauled up out of the water and resting on the transom. (Watch for chafe.)

• Tow a hard dinghy with the bow eye (reinforce it, if need be, with a backing plate or extra fiberglass). You want the towline low, so the bow lifts and the dinghy doesn't swamp.

• To lessen the drag from a towed dinghy, try using a towline long enough to allow the dinghy to ride the front part of the second wave.

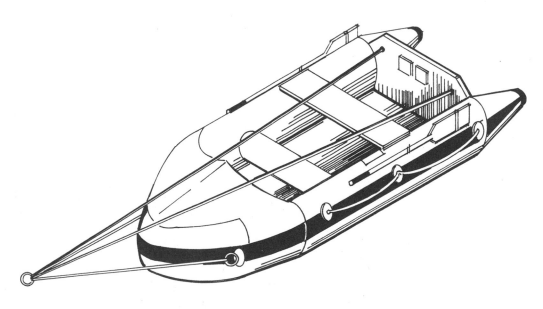

• When towing the inflatable, watch for chafed spots from the towing line. When you see one starting, change the angle of the offending line; if that's not possible, put a patch of sacrificial fabric over the area.

• As you try different towing methods, keep track of boat speed so you'll know if your efforts are making a difference.

PAPER KEEPERS

The dinghy's registration should be with you in the dinghy.

• Put the paper into a small zip-top bag and fold tightly. Tape the packet onto the inner surface of the outboard cover. Be sure the bag is taped flat so it clears the outboard's motor parts. The registration package can be left in place for months. (Check the tape from time to time.) When the marine police stop by with their checklist of requirements, you can produce the paper.

• Have the registration paper laminated. Put it into a boat-acrylic envelope with grommets at the top; tie it onto one of the dinghy "handle" lines.

• Roll the registration paper and put it inside a screwtop plastic bottle (such as a small peanut butter jar). Seal the cover with duct tape, then tie the jar to the motor's bracket handles. (A thin line fits the indentation just under the screwtop.) It's not exactly easy to get to, but since you are obediently abiding by the rules, the police will probably never ask to see the paper. (Watch for condensation, if the bottle gets too much sun.)

• Before stowing the registration, make photocopies to file in case of mildewed or stolen paper, or a purloined dinghy.

LETTERS AND NUMBERS

Paint registration numbers on an inflatable dinghy with artist's acrylic paint. Thin it with water to a workable consistency; use a stencil, if you wish. If the paint fades after a few months, recoating is easy; the edges of the original numbers catch the new paint.

DINGHY DECAL

The dinghy decal should be placed at the bow of the boat, but many people have problems keeping it on an inflatable. Put the decal on the boat while it's fully inflated. Clean the fabric well to remove dirt, salt, and wax. Use a bit of sandpaper to rough up the surface where the decal will be. Use the divided backing paper to adhere first one half, then the other, pushing out air bubbles as you press the decal in place. It should stay the year, unless it gets rubbed off at a crowded dinghy dock.

DINGHY STORAGE

• Make a small canvas cover to fit over the bow section of the dinghy to keep water off cushions, jackets, groceries. A watertight bag underneath is added dry insurance.

• Buy a ready-made nylon bag shaped to tie into the V-section.

• Keep a cooler (with a hinged lid) in the dinghy; use it as a seat, as dry storage, or as a cooler. Tie the cooler handles to the dinghy's side lifting handles.

• Keep a waterproof, tight-closing shower bag/beach bag/diaper bag in the dinghy to carry camera, mail, a few tools, and perhaps a handheld fathometer.

TRAVELING BAG

When going ashore in the dink, most women carry a favorite tote bag to keep purse, book, sunglasses, and correspondence neatly confined and carryable. As often as not, there is a small puddle of water sloshing back and forth on the dinghy floor. To keep the water away from the bag contents, sew some large wood beads on the bottom of the bag. With the bag raised off the floor by the width of the beads, the fabric will stay dry.

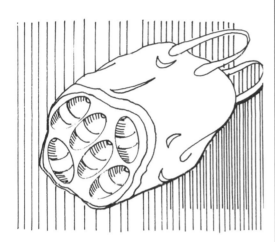

OAR HOLDERS

The oars for inflatable dinghies are not used often; they stay on the dinghy floor waiting for an emergency, and everyone hopes they will never be necessary, because they are not very efficient. Still, an inefficient oar is better than nothing at all, and they're expensive to replace.

To prevent fallout—a common occurrence for dinghy oars—tie the oars onto or into the dinghy by whatever method is most convenient. If "convenient" means

leaving them on the floorboards, attach a lanyard to a seat or some fitting so if an oar goes swimming, it will stay with the boat.

HOLDING OARS

If you must actually use your inflatable's oars sometime, hold and move them like paddles; you'll go farther faster. (With two people paddling, you can make good time.)

DEPTHSOUNDER

Use the dinghy anchor as a lead line. Mark the line with an indication of acceptable depth for the big boat, then use the line to check out possible anchoring spots. The marking could be done with a small knot; the anchor itself serves as the lead. (Where there is sufficient tide, you might want a few more marks on the line.)

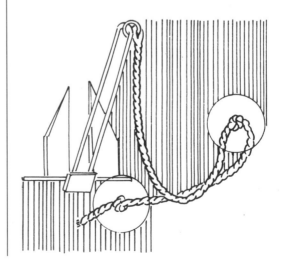

DINGHY ANCHOR

Keep the dinghy or small-boat anchor in a canvas bag, with its rode. By holding mud or rust captive, it keeps the boat cleaner. It should also prevent the tangle of kinks and knots that occur when any line is given free range. (A mushroom anchor is safest in an inflatable; no sharp edges to scratch fabric.)

DINGHY LIGHTS

Dinghies are not exempted from navigation light requirements, as marine patrol officers are only too happy to point out. Use clamp-on or suction-cup attachments to carry appropriate lights powered by C- or D-cell batteries.

PFDS

Keep the proper number of personal flotation devices in the dinghy at all times. Write the boat name or your name or the dog's name on each device with indelible ink. Most people use the oldest PFDs anyway, which may not do much for the spirit of safety requirements, but is less of a temptation to borrowers.

VHF

The handheld VHF radio should accompany you in the dinghy whenever you leave the big boat. If its own carrying case is not watertight, use a cushioned, zip-sealed sports pouch (or at least a zip-top bag).

FOOTLESS PUMP

If you don't need or want the unique exercise benefit of a footpump dinghy inflater, use a hand pump, or take the easiest route with a 12-volt model.

BE PREPARED

Even a dinghy needs a few emergency supplies. Otherwise, when the outboard quits and the dinghy starts drifting off to sea some dark and stormy night, the outboard itself will become an expensive anchor.

• Keep a few distress things in a watertight pouch or bag in the dinghy: some beach shoes, an old nylon windbreaker or throwaway foul-weather jacket, a distress flag, a flashlight, a whistle.

• Put some reflective tape on dinghy and outboard. When the dinghy drifts away some night after somebody does a bad tie-up job, a scanning spotlight will pick up the runaway quickly. Hopefully.

EASY BAILER

Make an easy-to-use bailer from the 1-gallon container than once held laundry detergent. Buy a brand with a molded-in handle and an ordinary screw-on top (not the cap-within-a-cap type.) Cut off the bottom of the bottle at a bit of an angle (make the handle side the short side) so when you hold it to bail, it will show a scoop shape.

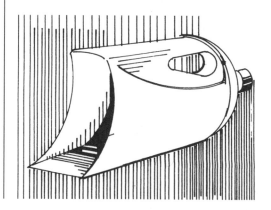

RUBRAILS

If you have a hard dinghy, and especially if it's aluminum, line the top rim with a split plastic hose, rubberized rail, or canvas dock-cushioning material. You'll avoid having to patch dings in the gelcoat or scrub metal marks from the hullside. Friends will be more friendly too.

GLASS BOTTOM

If you have a hard dinghy and cruise in an area of clear water and colorful sea life, put a Lexan window in the bottom. Cut an opening in the dinghy, and seal the Lexan replacement with great quantities of silicone caulking. A good help in finding shells, fish, or entertainment.

BARNACLE REMOVERS

Dinghy bottoms get foul too. The putty-knife scraper that works on the big boat will destroy an inflatable; instead, try to remove barnacles by scraping with a plastic applicator or a small block of soft wood. (The wood will shred rather than gouge the dinghy fabric.) Too much scraping will thin the rubberized coating.

• Another good scraper for inflatables is a piece of PVC pipe. Hold it upright to scrape flat surfaces. Hold it almost horizontally, and you can scrape out the groove next to the black tubing.

• Prevention is the best way to deal with barnacles. It is now possible to purchase antifouling coating for dinghies, a much-needed product that will be much appreciated by anyone who has ever tried to de-barnacle or de-grass an inflatable's bottom. According to the manufacturer, MDR, the dinghy can be taken out of the water, deflated, and rolled up, then relaunched without affecting the paint's antifouling properties.

SPECIAL PAINTS

• If your dinghy is made of Hypalon, reinforce scraped or thinned spots in the fabric with Flexipaint, a liquid Hypalon coating.

• A special sealant made just for inflatables can fill pinholes in the fabric from the inside, extending the life of the dinghy. Look for Inflatable Boat Sealant Kit, from:

Inland Marine USA
1017-C S.E. 12th Ave.
Cape Coral, FL 33990
813-458-0302

CLEANERS

Use cleaners made specifically for inflatable fabrics; they not only clean, they also add a protective coating to help repel the next batch of dirt and grime.

• One retailer, whose sole business is inflatable boats, recommends Starbrite Inflatable Boat and Fender Cleaner/ Protector for most boats, and Marykate for white inflatables. Another recommends Marykate for all. For warranty purposes, check with the dinghy's manufacturer.

• At anchor, haul the dinghy up a few inches off the water, just enough to keep growth off the bottom. (This discourages thievery, too.)

REPAIRS

• Keep fabric patches and contact cement for the inflatable, and check the cement occasionally to be sure it hasn't dried up. How-to directions include preliminary cleaning and a light spot-sanding. If you ignore either step, your patch may curl up and disappear in too short a time.

• Round the corners of a patch; draw a pencil line around the outside so you can keep the contact cement confined to the exact area where it's needed.

DINGHY HOIST

If you don't have davits, carry a block and tackle to hoist the dinghy or the outboard.

• Sailors can use the boom vang. Hook one end of the vang to a halyard, the other to the dinghy; then use the vang's block and tackle to hoist (rather than the halyard itself). It is possible to hoist the dinghy with the halyard on a mast winch, but that requires someone standing at the mast. With the vang, two people can stand on deck to control the dinghy as it lifts.

• The same block and tackle can hoist the outboard for stowing on board. Rig a bridle for the outboard; hoist it on a bracket mounted to the stern rail. The bracket can be a permanent installation; or make it removable, to stow in a locker till it's needed.

OUTBOARD STOWING BRACKET

Make a teak bracket to mount the outboard on the stern rail. Cut two squares of 1-inch (or thicker) teak, wide enough to accept the clamps of the outboard. On the inner surfaces of both wood pieces, rout a half-circle groove so the wood can fit over each side of the stainless tubing of the stern rail and still touch.

Screw or through-bolt the wood pieces together. Countersink and plug the screw holes for a more finished look.

If you have a vertical stanchion positioned under a straight section of toprail, you can use a "T" groove for a more secure fit.

SNUGGING LINE

When you are at anchor and the wind is against the current, the dinghy may start bouncing against the hull instead of quietly trailing behind. Try pulling the dinghy bow up to the boat transom so it rides tight against the big boat.

STEERING EXTENSION

For easier steering, extend the outboard handle with a length of PVC pipe. You'll be able to steer from a position farther forward in the boat. Use whatever diameter PVC fits most snugly over the handle.

DINGHY I.D.

• Carve—or at least paint—some identifying word or number on the underside of a floorboard.

• Paint the outboard, overall, so it's too distinctly recognizable for a thief to want, or with some small symbol that might later serve as positive identification.

• Painting the dinghy with an all-over spatter motif is a good theft deterrent, if you can stand to look at it.

THE NAME GAME

Give the dinghy its own name rather than marking it with the big boat's name. A "tender-to" at the dinghy dock could suggest to a would-be thief that the big boat might be empty. A very brazen would-be thief could steal the tender-to, go to the big boat, burglarize it, and use the tender to carry off the plunder.

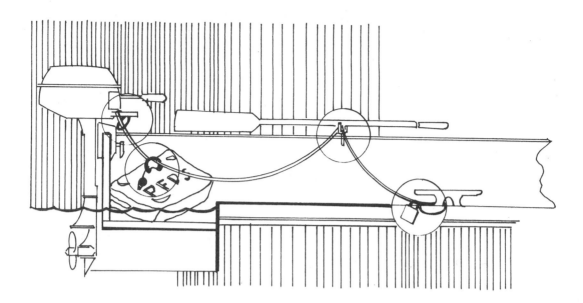

LOCKUPS

There will be times and places where you'll feel more comfortable locking the dinghy to the dinghy dock.

• Get an adequate length of stainless steel cable with an eyesplice at both ends. (Buy the cable at a hardware store and have the loop ends swaged.) Run the cable through as many dinghy attachments as you can: outboard, gas can, oar locks, cushions. Drill a hole in the oars if need be so you can include them too. Lock the cable through a cleat or around a plank on the dock with a combination lock.

• Use vinyl-coated cable to secure outboard to dinghy and dinghy to dock. Even though a determined thief can take the time and make the effort to cut the cable, he will more likely look for an easier target. The cable should also discourage afternoon joy-riding by local adolescents, and if nothing else, will show the insurance company you were trying.

Or Think Positively

Mark the dinghy obviously and permanently with the name of the big boat. If the dinghy escapes some night, you might get it back if the finder knows who to look for.

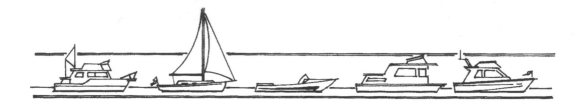

Found Time

Boating—especially its cruising aspect—opens many doors, with the right combination of time, opportunity, and exposure to different people, places, and things.

Hobbies, crafts, and basic fun travel well, but cruising can change the focus of the familiar and give reason to the new. You probably wouldn't paint sand dollars if you lived in Oregon. You couldn't do much underwater photography in New Mexico. You might not read certain books if you didn't go to a lot of book exchanges. And while kite-flying itself doesn't change with geography, ambience does.

The best part is that you can get rid of all those vague "someday when I have time" thoughts. Someday is now. And you have the time.

SHUTTERBUGS

Photographers have not only time, but constantly changing opportunities on many levels. First is the basic record of fun for the family album. Next are the show-and-tell photos to send to friends. You can concentrate on photography as creative art or commercial venture; either way, if you're good, it becomes a potential source of income.

UNDERWATER PHOTOS

For serious underwater photography, Nikon set the standard with their Nikonos series of waterproof 35-mm cameras. With certain lenses, the Nikonos can be used on land too, though the lenses are limited to wide-angle and close-up shooting, which are the camera's specialties.

The snapshot photographer who doesn't want to make that kind of investment can still choose a waterproof camera: Sea & Sea and Minolta also offer 35-mm models, and Kodak's one-time-use camera is understandably popular.

Throwaways

Kodak's Panoramic disposable camera is well suited to boating scenes, capturing whole harbors and sailboat-race starting lines.

Snapshots

Contrary to what some camera salespeople may say, you don't need an underwater camera just because you spend time on a boat. With reasonable care, ordinary cameras live just fine on board.

When the camera's around your neck and you're on deck, in the dinghy, or sightseeing on shore, protect it from spray or drizzle by covering it with a plain clear plastic bag. Cut a couple of small holes for the strap to come through; put the bag on with the opening pointing down. When you want to take a picture, lift the bag quickly and shoot.

Don't leave the bag on for any length of time; you don't want to create condensation.

Photostow

Reserve the driest drawer on the boat for camera gear.

• When transporting camera and lenses, especially in the dinghy, use an inflatable zip-top sport bag with an additional Velcro flap closure.

• When traveling, keep the camera in its bag, safely wedged somewhere inside the boat; you can grab it quickly when you want to use it, but it won't be exposed to sunlight all day.

• Buy small, individual packets of silica gel (a moisture-absorbing material) to put inside camera bags or film storage boxes. One larger package can be dried in an oven for reuse. Buy these from stores that sell camera equipment; most photofinishers do not carry them. (Silica gel is also sold at craft stores; it's used in flower-drying.)

• Keep film in the coolest place on the boat. Freezer or refrigerator is best, but let film warm up before attempting to load it into the camera or the film may break; cold makes it brittle. A surplus ammo box or a plastic storage box can be placed low in the boat for any cooling effect the water may provide.

Lens Protectors

• Whether or not you choose to experiment with other filters, buy at least one: a skylight or haze filter will cut down some glare and reduce some blue, but mostly it will protect your lens.

• Add some contrast to your boat photos with a polarizing filter: sky will be darkened, haze minimized.

• Lenses will need a lot of attention to keep away the misty film that settles onto all glass surfaces. Keep a small chamois, or any soft, lint-free cloth, for wiping lenses.

Or keep a supply of standard lens-cleaning tissues in a dry spot.

Budget Protector

If you're traveling overseas, film and processing will be very expensive—two to three times as much as U.S. prices. Bring your exposed film home for processing.

Action Camera

Video cameras let you send the best kind of letters home, and dupes of those letters later become a great record of a cruise for the travelers themselves.

While camcorders are user-friendly, some concentration is still necessary to do a good job of filming. Otherwise, videos will be just as boring as home movies sometimes were.

Usually, one person takes on the role of cinematographer. Instead of random shooting, plan a tape with a story line of what you want to recall from this trip, or what you want to show Mom, or what you'd like to send to the school. If you make a written list of the highlights you want to share, you're more likely to remember to shoot those things. Then the spontaneous happenings just add variety to your established theme.

Picture Protectors

For long-term cruising, keep all negatives (and all the photos that didn't make the scrapbook) in moisture-proof boxes; otherwise they'll be permanently bonded in a short time by the sticky surface of the paper or negative. Dry storage is necessary for slides, too, or they'll develop spider webs of contagious

mildew that will spread to other slides and eventually ruin the entire box.

SKETCHBOOK JOURNALS

• If you have the inclination (and hopefully some natural talent), take along, and use, sketchbooks. They don't take much space, are easily transportable on shore leave, and, when filled, provide a personal and unique visual log.

• You may choose basic black in pencil form or with felt-tip or ink drawing pens. Colored pencils are a nice option; pastels are generally messy, but some artists prefer their blendability.

ARTIST'S SUPPLIES

• For real painting, watercolors are an obvious choice on the basis of size of material, as well as their fast working and drying time. You can purchase or make a kit that holds all necessary supplies in a box you can carry like an attaché case.

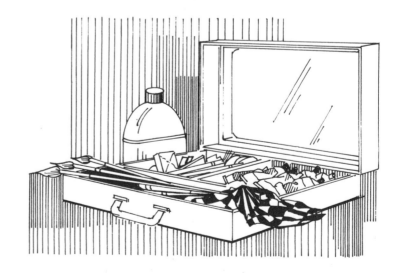

- Take a small folding chair or a camp stool to shore with your art supplies, just for the comfort of it.

- Oil paints are a problem on a boat because they take so long to dry. If you have a pet on board, the problem is compounded by animal curiosity and hair. But anything is possible. Plan appropriate spaces to devote to drying areas. For this obvious reason, one artist paints only small canvases while on board and lines them up in a custom-made drying rack.

- Acrylics are a popular substitute for oils. They mix and clean with water; they dry fast, they're practically indestructible, and, if you're a beginning painter, they're much more forgiving than oils.

- Whether you use oil or acrylic, canvas panels (canvas glued to cardboard backing) store in much less space than stretched canvases, and you're much less likely to poke a hole in one.

SCISSOR ART

A revived traditional craft, "scherenschnitte," suits boat living. This scissor-cutting art produces charming pictures or patterns cut from paper and displayed against a contrasting background to frame for bulkhead hanging or gift giving.

DECORATIVE ART

Many artists like to use found objects as their figurative canvas. Miniature paintings can be done on shells; sand dollars are a popular choice because of their flat surface. Flat rocks and bleached driftwood boards also provide painting backgrounds.

FABRIC ART

- Fabric painting is another way to personalize travel experiences. Use patterns drawn from the nature you see along the waterways: birds, fish, reef life, flowers. Decorate pillowcases, tote bags, or clothing (wrap skirts, T-shirts, sweats).

- To paint clothing, buy or make a cardboard backing form. Slip the garment on the stiffener for easier control.

- Craft stores sell a lot of fancy pencil-paints, but plain artists' acrylics, in liquid or tube, produce artwork that will last through as many washings as the fabric itself.

GLASS ART

One remarkable onboard artist manages to produce stained glass items while working on the dinette table of a 34-foot sailboat. Storing the glass panels and the tools and generator required to power them is a greater challenge than most might care to face, but it *is* possible. (If you see *Glass Lady* along the waterway, ask to see the newest creations.)

METALCRAFT

Less messy than glass, designs made with a metal punch find useful purpose or serve as decoration. Make a lantern shield, an insert for a locker door, a decorative hang-up. Make Christmas ornaments all year, solving the question of Christmas shopping.

Use copper or tin; craft stores sell it in pieces measuring from 5 inches by 7 inches up to 12 inches by 18 inches. You might be able to get scraps of thin-gauge aluminum from a company that uses it. "Tools" are the metal punch and a spray of clear acrylic coating that discourages greening and salt-air corrosion.

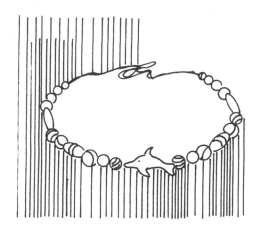

WEARABLE ART

Materials for metal-wire or wood-bead jewelry take very little storage space. A fishing tackle box or artist's paint box keeps small items separated and organized.

For some jewelry projects you'll need only epoxy adhesives; others require a soldering gun. One determined artisan carries a small electric kiln on board so he can manufacture his own miniature ceramics. He sculpts tiny likenesses of birds or fish, fires them in the kiln, and uses them to add a focal point for a color-matched necklace or bracelet of beads.

WOODWORK

Scrimshaw, the most traditional mariners' art, is no longer socially acceptable unless it's done on fake ivory. Whittling and woodcarving are almost as traditional, and the output is always admired. With a few carving knives and a small set of chisels, you can create useful or decorative items for the boat, or to sell. One man specializes in fish, another in birds. A how-to book can get you started, but mostly it's a learn-by-doing process.

NEEDLEWORK

Colored thread and yarn and twine are the basis of many kinds of needlework.

File each project in its own holder, so everything's at hand whenever there's time. Plastic milk crates stack well. Wicker baskets (some come with fabric covers) are attractive as well as practical. Canvas tote bags keep projects readily transportable from ship to beach, ship to neighbor's ship, ship to laundromat.

Cross Stitch
Cross-stitch projects are especially good on a small boat: small patterns, small thread, all confined in a small workspace.

Plastic Canvas
Plastic squares are the basis for a lot of useful and good-looking gifts. Choose patterns that connect to boating, travel, and nature. Do a picture frame or a framable picture. Christmas ornaments or a gingerbread house. Bulkhead hangings, rugs, place mats, coasters, tissue box holders. . .

Knitting
Cruising gives you time to do all the someday projects that have spent years

filed on a closet shelf or in the back of your mind. Of course, the ski sweater may have lost its immediacy, just as the afghan might be overkill on a boat sofa. But some knitted clothing or crocheted blankets or pillow covers may still be practical. You'd make a hit with boating friends with crocheted angels and stars, scaled down to fit the size of a boat Christmas tree.

Quilting

Quilting efforts don't have to be applied to queen-size bedspreads. In reduced form, quilting can produce a unique pillow sham, a decorative bunk mat, or a wearable vest.

KNOTWORK

Knotwork is the original boat craft, still the same melding of function and form.

• A good knot book is a necessity. The classics by Hervey Garrett Smith (including *The Marlinspike Sailor,* International Marine, 1993) give clear instructions for the standard Turk's head (probably the most popular decorative knot) or monkey's fist (more useful to today's boater as the grasp on a key ring instead of the weight at the end of a heaving line).

• Mariners practiced recycling long before the idea went mainstream. When a line chafes, or breaks, it may lose its job as anchor or dock line, but it still has purpose. Use it to make a knotted step mat, a fender, a bow bumper, or a rubrail for the dink. Thinner line might wrap around oar handles, steering wheel, handrail, and anywhere else a secure hold is needed.

• If you're too new to boating to have a bunch of old line, buy ends of rolls, usually available at a discount from standard per-foot charge.

Macramé

Macramé carries knotting to decorative heights.

• Make functional boat things like curtains, floor mats, or netting for lifelines, or knot some frivolous people-things like a purse, tote bag, or belt.

• Macramé jewelry continues to be popular with boaters. Small shells or bits of beach glass inspire necklaces and bracelets (including ankle bracelets) that fit right into the surroundings and the lifestyle. Materials are confined to an assortment of colored twine and possibly a few jewelry findings, though traditional necklace and bracelet connections are done with appropriate knots.

• Macramé—and other decorative crafts—have created a kind of Junior Achievement business opportunity for some ambitious cruising children.

THERAPY

One side advantage to any kind of handwork: when the weather's awful, you have something to concentrate on other than the lightning show and the thunder sound and wave action that might otherwise disrupt your cool.

WORKLIGHT

A small clip-on light with a flexible neck gives focused illumination for any small project. Plus, it allows you to read at night without disturbing others.

SEWING MACHINE

For some people, a sewing machine is more necessity than hobby tool. Useful for all onboard fabric fixing, it can also provide a means for earning some extra money. A floating cottage industry of canvas or sail stitching or repair is not unusual on a cruising boat.

SEWING KIT

A bar of bath soap with a fabric cover is a good boat pincushion. It keeps pins safe and accessible, and it helps them slide into fabric. A magnetic needle holder is an obvious help. Folding scissors can tuck into the smallest compartment of a sewing box.

SOUND INVESTMENTS

Few boat folks choose to sacrifice the sounds of civilization. One solution to inevitable differing tastes in music is to provide everyone on board with his or her own "floatman." Personal choices can be tuned in without intruding on anyone else's space or hearing.

• Install a 12-volt automobile cassette player, with speakers in as many places as you want. Separate controls for each

speaker will send the sounds only where they are desired.

VIEWPOINTS

Videotapes can be rented in the most unexpected places, so television sets with videocassette players are standard on all sizes of cruising boats. Many carry at least a small tape library for tape trades in the anchorage.

• Expensive antennas can correct the reception problems caused by a boat swinging at anchor. A reasonable alternative is an old-fashioned rabbit-ear antenna sold at Radio Shack for use in camper vans. Hooked to some outside structure, it works fine most of the time. There may be some fuzzing as the boat swings, but it's a workable choice.

BOARD GAMES

• Onboard games may be better than television for whiling away evening hours. But choose carefully: a game like Scruples can cause minor irritations to escalate into major confrontation, and the fun stops there.

• Play Scrabble against yourself. Whether you're singlehanding or just can't find a willing opponent, you can still get the benefit of mental exercise. And you always win.

• Turn games into a learning challenge by making up your own questions or puzzles to be played in the manner of Pictionary or the trivial pursuit of a given subject related to boating or the cruising lifestyle.

CARD GAMES

Bring along some playing cards. Keep the family busy together, leave the children to their own games, or veg out with a few games of solitaire.

READING GAMES

• Even in the age of video, book exchanges survive: sometimes boat to boat, sometimes through marinas, sometimes at used-book stores in waterfront towns.

• Fly a "Books Aboard" burgee. Developed by the Florida Center for the Book, in cooperation with the Center for the Book in the Library of Congress, the burgee shows the green-and-white library logo and tells others you have books to trade or talk about. For information, contact:

Florida Center for the Book
100 S. Andrews Avenue
Fort Lauderdale, FL 33301
305-357-7401

To order a burgee, send a $20 donation; make check payable to Broward Public Library Foundation. Proceeds are used to promote reading and combat illiteracy.

• Keep as many reference books as will fit on your bookshelves on the topics that relate to boat travel: fish, coral and reef life, shells, birds, stars.

STAR GAMES

Get a star finder for the latitudes you'll be cruising, plus appropriate references. Even if you don't need the calculations of celestial navigation, get a sextant and learn the basics, just for the self-satisfaction.

BIRD COUNTS

Birds are everywhere, and before the end of a cruise, everyone on board will be a birder to some degree. Keep binoculars handy (best if each person has his or her own). Keep identification references, and have each person keep a list of sightings.

HIGH FLIERS

• Find room on board for a couple of kites. The whole family can spend a happy afternoon flying—or watching—kites, whether they're the standard classic drifters or the more active stunt models.

• Taking that enjoyment a giant step further, a man whose lifelong hobby is radio-controlled model planes found the way, and the space, to bring some along. It helps that the models can be taken apart: wings hang from overhead brackets, while bodies wedge into a locker. The planes, along with a glider and an experimental saucer, provide hours of fun for flier and spectators alike.

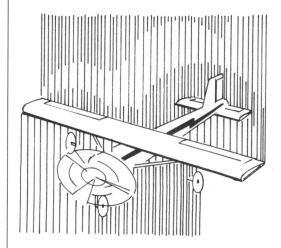

SCALE FUN

• In the Chesapeake, skipjack fleets still exist in model scale, sailing against rival towns in a regular annual regatta series.

• For the powerboaters, minidestroyers can be seen patrolling marina slips, while tiny runabouts look for racing competition. Hours of fun go into the building and the playing.

SHELL COLLECTING

• If you're planning to collect shells, be optimistic about finding large ones. Keep a supply of aluminum containers or plastic boxes in the dinghy; you'll need them for fragile specimens. Zip-top bags are always good for smaller, tough shells.

• To clean shells, you might soak them in a bleach solution, but too long a soaking damages the shell before it gets rid of the coating. Rather, scrub shells with a wire brush till deposits are gone.

• If a shell has a dead creature inside, try rinsing with a solution of about ¼ cup chlorine bleach to 1 gallon water. If that doesn't empty it completely, you'll welcome the chance to take it off the boat. Try to leave the shell on shore for a few days, where ants can clean it out for you. If that still doesn't work, pack it with sand and leave it for a few days (pick a shady place to leave the shell so it doesn't lose color). Then empty and repack, and repeat until the inside is clean.

Shell Displays

• Some people use spray varnish or nail polish as a protective coating for their treasures, but if the shell has good color when it's found, an application of mineral oil will bring up the color naturally, without distortion.

• With a straw basket to contain them, shells can be displayed as tabletop centerpiece or cockpit decorations. Narrow boat shelves are naturals for a lineup of shells.

Shell Protectors

Strips of plastic canvas make mildew-resistant drawer dividers where shells will store safely. With the canvas, spaces are customized for each shell; the drawer is ready for instant display whenever another collector comes aboard.

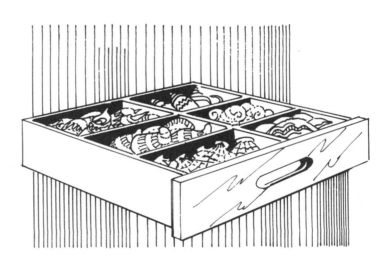

Shell Finder

If you're in a clearwater place, a look bucket will help you find shells or just sightsee the underwater world from the comfort of your dinghy. A glass-bottomed cedar bucket is the most sturdy, but you can make an acceptable substitute with a plastic bucket, a circle of Plexiglas, and some caulking. One manufacturer offers one with inflatable sides; it can be collapsed for flat storage.

Shell Distributor

You can keep just so many shells, especially on a boat.

• After your first extended cruise, give the folks back home gifts from nature in their Christmas stockings: large shells are good bookends; medium-size shells are planters for air plants; small ones hang on shell chimes.

• Chimes are easy to put together. Many shells already have tiny holes from natural erosion, but if they don't, use a tiny drill bit. Tie rows of shells a few inches apart onto monofilament line. Then hang four or five strands from a piece of driftwood found on the shell beach.

• Small, flat shells of the same type and color can border the dirt surface of planters.

• Tiny shells might fit the scale of the nieces' dollhouse, to line a garden path or sidewalk entry.

• The eroded center coils of whelks and augers make graceful Christmas tree ornaments.

• Fossilized shells are natural paperweights.

• And some people glue a bunch of small shells onto a mirror frame.

SNORKEL WORLD

If you are cruising to a land of crystal waters, buy snorkeling equipment and learn to use it. A simple mask and snorkel will introduce you to complex new worlds; few people fail to experience a thrill on seeing their first coral reef.

• Store snorkel and scuba gear (masks, snorkels, fins, knives) in a covered plastic box with holes cut into the bottom for water to drain.

• Or, keep each crewmember's gear in a separate mesh bag, identified by color. Easy to find, easy to grab, easy (and possible) to dry.

• Clean your diving mask with toothpaste; it helps prevent fogging.

WATER FASHIONS

A wet suit is desirable for snorkeling and necessary for scuba diving. Even when air and water temperature are warm to hot, your in-water time will be limited without the protection of a wet suit. For most casual diving, the short-sleeved, short-legged style is adequate. For more serious diving, find out in advance what protection is appropriate for the areas you plan to explore.

SCUBA DIVES

Always dive with a buddy, but remember: Having a buddy doesn't mean you—or your partner—can be lax or foolish or ignorant. Choose your buddy carefully and prepare yourself as if you were diving alone.

Be honest with yourself regarding your capability. Logic warns that overweight individuals and smokers may have trouble with proper breathing, stamina, and generally decreased efficiency. Abusers of alcohol or other drugs not only put themselves at risk, they endanger their diving partners as well.

DIVE TANKS

• It's important to keep dive tanks secure so they can't roll around with ordinary boat motion. Make a platform for the tanks. Build a low-sided box to accommodate however many tanks you carry. Cut semicircles into the two end boards so tanks will lie in the cutouts, and strap them in.

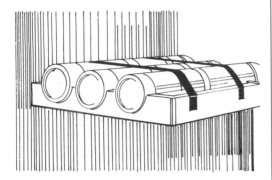

• Most tanks can be stored horizontally for the few weeks of a usual dive trip, when you're using them regularly, but for long-term storage, keep them vertical. Any sediment will settle to the bottom, where it will be seen more readily in a required visual inspection. Aluminum tanks should be stored upright all the time.

• Try not to store tanks in direct sun; excess heat creates excess pressure. A tarp suspended above the storage area will create shade and allow air circulation, a better arrangement than a tarp tied directly on top of the tanks.

• Use a freshwater washdown to clean off gear after each use. The bug-sprayer shower adds some water pressure help if the boat is not equipped with a real outside shower.

SAFE STOWING

Confine a diving spear with a piece of PVC tubing strapped on deck or tied between two lifeline stanchions. A 6- to 8-

inch piece of hose or surgical tubing might also be used to cover the business end of the spear; a retired tennis ball can find new purpose as a cover for the spear barb.

FISH TIPS

Basic fishing gear is recommended in Chapter 3. Here are some reminders.

• Check regulations in each state or country regarding licenses, seasons, species, and sizes. Watch for areas closed because of pollution. Be aware of the possible danger of ciguatera and other seafood-related illnesses. (See Chapter 21, pages 218 and 219.)

• New fishermen especially need to be reminded: Don't get hands or thumbs on the line; it can burn you. Don't get line around fingers or hands; you could lose a finger.

• Bring along a fish scale and a small tapemeasure; you might like to know what you're catching, and you might need to know, where weight or length limits apply.

• Have good fish reference books on board, covering all areas you may be cruising.

• Best fishing is found when approaching or leaving harbor or shore.

• Best fishing is at the drop-off of shore/bank to deep water.

• Best fishing is when the barometer is rising.

• Best time to fish is from just before sunset till midnight.

• Best time to fish is just before dawn.

• Best fishing is on an incoming tide.

• Best fishing is on an outgoing tide.

• Best fishing is when the moon is blue.

FISH RELEASE

Release undersize or unwanted fish as unharmed as possible. Using a glove or a cloth, grasp fish gently near the tail. Try not to damage the area around the gills. If the hook is easy to get to, remove it as gently as you can. If it is deep in the mouth, cut the leader. (If the hook is not stainless steel, it will dissolve in a few days.) Put the fish back into the water; if he's sluggish, "swim" him back and forth a bit to force water through his gills.

POLE STOW

Fishing rods will last longer with less exposure to weather.

- Stow them on racks overhead in the wheelhouse, above saloon bunks, over V-bunks or quarter berths—in short, anywhere you won't bonk your head on the reels.

- If storage is a problem, buy a rod that breaks apart.

- Clean all gear with a freshwater rinse after each use; occasionally, clean with a metal cleaner and protectant to prevent corrosion.

SAILBOARDING

Sailboards are a great source of exercise, and not much can match them for pure exuberance on a breezy day. And they ride along on cruising boats fairly easily. On sailboats, tie them to shrouds; on powerboats you have more choices, on deck or cabintop spaces.

Protect your board from nicks and scratches by stowing it in a canvas bag. Let the sail dry out on deck, then bag it and store it inside.

WATER SKIS

Skis are good toys if teenagers are aboard. Skiing keeps them occupied, gives them a chance to socialize with neighboring teens, and, with luck, tires them out.

- Ski gear can be kept to a minimum, but the dinghy and its engine must be up to the job. A 12-foot inflatable sportboat with a 25-hp outboard is probably the minimum, but it's certainly within the range of carryability for average-size cruising boats.

JET POWER

Mini jetboats—also known as personal watercraft—are the newest water toys to decorate the decks of large powerboats. Traditionalists who find excessive noise distracting wish jet owners would be very personal with these watercraft and play only in their own back water, but personal watercraft enthusiasts are not willingly confined. These sporty craft are a fact of boating life.

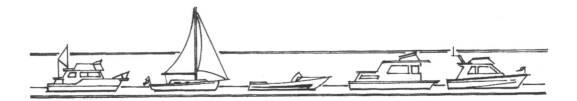

18 Warning Flags

Nobody wants to think about preventive safety, because that forces you to consider all the bad things you're hoping to prevent, and *that* could put a damper on a day on the water (no pun intended). Denial, while convenient, is unrealistic, foolish, risky—wrong any way you look at it.

Instead of thinking safety, think seamanship. It has a much better ring, and if a simple change in perception can prompt positive action, it's a change for the best. Besides, it *is* good seamanship to be conscious of and concerned about the safety and security of boat and crew.

FLOAT PLAN

Some people think this is one more government form that should be avoided, but it is only an abbreviated way to say: whenever you go out on a boat, tell a responsible person when you're leaving, where you're going, and approximately when you expect to be back. Think of a worst-case scenario; it may convince you to take the time to file a plan.

DESIGNATED DRIVERS

Boating friends who drink need a designated driver.

• Alcohol speeds the mind-dulling effects of overexposure to sun, sea, glare, wind, motion. It affects your judgment, your coordination, and your reaction time.

• Operating a boat while intoxicated is not only ill advised, it's illegal. Different states have different penalties; don't learn the hard way.

• Telling statistics: About half of boating fatalities involve alcohol. Fifty percent of drunk men who drown are found with their fly unzipped. And every one of them no doubt assured himself he was "fine."

SAFE BASICS

You don't want to spoil anyone's anticipation of boating fun, but you should make guests aware of the location of safety equipment. Basics include PFDs, fire extinguishers, radio. As you travel, you might gradually add information about anchoring, signaling devices, or whatever seems pertinent to your boating situation.

Make sure everyone on board knows where the first-aid kit and book are stored; no rule says Mom (or whoever did the stowing) will always be available to play nurse.

WRITING ON THE BULKHEAD

• Post basic rules of the road in a place convenient to the helm. This is especially important for weekenders, because of the high volume of traffic. Read the rules until their directives are second nature. (Laminated, waterproof cards are a sensible presentation for quick grasp of facts.) Then drive defensively anyway, because the next boater may not have the cards on the boat or the rules in his head.

• Post brief, clear calling directions close to the radio. Make sure no one has questions about how to call for help, since you may be unable to answer them in an emergency.

• Post in conspicuous areas crew-overboard procedures and CPR instructions. These are important if there are children on board, and they're good for guests too; you may assume they're already familiar with these aspects of boating when in fact they are not.

• Boat kids learn about responsibility early. If your children are old enough to be left on board without an adult, then they are also old enough to be aware of problem procedures. Teach them to use fire extinguishers and radio, and also what to do if a sibling or a pet goes overboard.

OUNCES OF PREVENTION

• When deteriorating weather conditions threaten to bounce pots off the stove, practice personal safety prevention. Wear long, lined mitts and a heavy apron. Unless your galley has a tiny, wedge-in U-shape, give yourself the leaning support of a heavy canvas strap.

• Add strips of nonskid tape to ladder steps—especially helpful when shoes and steps are wet.

• Add a second row of lifelines, find an appropriate pattern for netting, or buy nets ready to tie on. Whether for children, pets, or nervous crew, if it creates confidence and diminishes anxiety, it's a good addition to the boat, nautical machismo notwithstanding.

• Privacy is fine, and everyone needs some alone time. On board, however, everyone should keep track of everyone else in a quiet, nonintrusive way.

PFDS

Eighty percent of drowning victims were not wearing PFDs. Apparently, some people don't heed the reminder that PFDs can't work if they're not worn.

• Find a vest that's comfortable enough so you will wear it; learn which type is most reliable for the job you may someday demand of it. Buy one that's adequate for the kind of boating you do.

• On a calm day, have the whole crew put on PFDs and go for a swim, so everyone gets familiar with the feel of his or her "device." This is especially recommended for children, but could certainly benefit anyone. Then do the same thing on a wavy day, in controlled circumstances: one by one, and attached to a tether with a dinghy standing by.

• Check the fit on each child's PFD. Pick up the child by holding the shoulders of the PFD. If it fits right, the child's chin and ears will not slip through the head opening.

• Because of the convenience, many boaters opt for wearing a Seacurity, an inflatable horseshoe buoy that packs into a small case to wear on a belt. The Coast Guard has not approved inflatable products yet, so you can't include them in your total number of approved required PFDs. But people who wear Seacurity like and trust it, and since liking a PFD is the key

to wearing one consistently, it's worth considering.

FOUL-WEATHER COLOR

• No matter how attractive you find blue or white foul-weather gear, think about how visible it would be against the color of wavy water. Not that you are supposed to wear it in the water, but if you're going to fall in, chances are good that you'll do it on a day when weather forces you to wear it. In the interest of giving yourself every possible advantage in such a situation, wear *colorful* foul-weather gear.

• Put strips of reflective tape on foul-weather jackets, PFDs, and safety harnesses, so a search light will be more likely to see you.

SAFETY HARNESSES

• Ignore the people who say safety harnesses are a pain. A harness could be a good pain sometime if it keeps you out of the water. Set up your attachment line and practice with it so you're comfortable using it before the time when you *must* use it.

• Mark names on safety harnesses in big letters so you can pick yours out even while you're still half asleep. (If only two people are on board, you wouldn't worry about a choice.)

• Never leave the cockpit without wearing a harness, or without telling another person what you're doing.

• Sew a heavy-duty luggage handle onto a harness. You may need to add extra canvas strapping to attach the handle, which provides a substantial grip for hauling a person back on board. (An

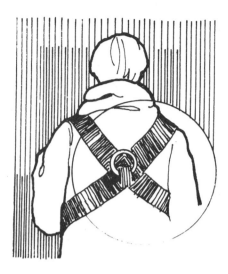

O-ring might also work; a halyard could snap into the ring quickly.)

OVERBOARD

• Practice crew-overboard procedures. Explain to children that "pickup the cushion" is not just a game, so they'll pay attention. Just as there have been rescues credited to the television show "911," familiarity with emergency procedures might save a life in a real boating situation.

• A crew-overboard pole should be easily throwable to mark the approximate place of an overboard accident; it's especially helpful in the wavy conditions that might cause a fall-in. On sailboats, mount the pole at the transom next to the backstay. Attach a short length of PVC pipe onto the stay at top-of-pole height. Roll the flag around the pole top and slide it into the PVC. The weighted base of the pole can sit in chocks; a slight lift and a downslide sends the pole into the water.

• Make your own crew-overboard pole. Attach a lead weight to the bottom of a fiberglass rod; add a Styrofoam float just above the weight, and put an orange or red flag on top.

• Check either homemade or store-bought versions periodically; a crew-overboard marker that lies flat in the water is useless.

• A lot of boats carry a MOM, or Man Overboard Module. MOM[8] is an overboard rescue system. Packed neatly into its case, the compact unit mounts on the stern rail, for easy access and fast deployment. In an overboard emergency, a quick pull on the release handle sends a self-inflating horseshoe lifebuoy, a marking pole, and a sea anchor into the water. (Buoy and pole will be fully inflated in seconds.)

MOM[9] adds a floating platform to the system. Besides enabling the overboard person to get out of the water, the platform can be hoisted to bring the person back on board.

• For overboard rescue, Lifesling's good ideas start with the printed directions on the outside of the pack. The system was developed for shorthanded rescues; one small person can rescue a heavier person by (1) getting a flotation collar to the person; (2) pulling the person back to the boat; (3) hauling them on board. Actual lifting tackle is not included with the Lifesling. Some sailors can use their boom vang, though the manufacturer recommends a separate lifting tackle to be sure you have enough line to lift the person off the water.

Powerboaters can use Lifesling too. If the boat has the appropriate superstructure, the block and tackle can be used to hoist the victim out. In some cases, the overboard person may be able to climb onto a swim ladder or platform. Each boat is different; each crew should try out their own plan of action. Even if you can't haul the person on board, you'll be able to hold him or her close until help comes.

BOTTOM FINDERS

Before there were fathometers, lead lines helped to keep keels off river bottoms, lake beds, and sea floors.

• Attach a lead weight to the end of a line marked for depth. From a position at the bow, while the boat is traveling very slowly, throw the lead into the water ahead of the boat. As you move up to where the lead hit bottom, hold the line as nearly vertical as you can, and read the marking on the line.

• A lead line may be low-tech, but it has two advantages. The piece of lead is shaped with a gouge in the bottom, so it can bring up a sample of the holding ground. More important, since you are at the bow of the boat when you read the depth, you may have enough time to back down before you touch bottom. (Depthsounders usually read from about midboat length; by the time it warns you, it's too late to react.)

Another Alternative

Use an easy-to-cast rod and reel with a weight at the end of the line where a hook would normally be. (The weight must be heavy enough to pull a bobber under.) Attach a bobber at a significant depth mark, perhaps 6 feet. As you approach a questionable area, cast the weight ahead of the boat. If the bobber pulls under, proceed. If the bobber sits on the surface, back down fast. With this lead line, you can read water well ahead of the boat's actual position.

DIRECTION FINDERS

• Be sure your compass is as accurate as it can be. You can't steer a perfect course in the best of times; if you start out aiming on a course that's already off a few degrees, it can make a considerable change in the direction you actually travel. Hire a compass adjuster to minimize the deviation of your compass, or buy a how-to book and try it yourself.

• While such compensation will help, don't dismiss a deviation table, the record of deviation figures for various headings that applies only to your boat.

• A second compass is good insurance; the hand-bearing compass is suit-

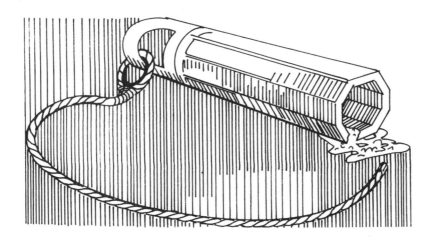

able for temporary or emergency use, though it is not meant to be a primary compass.

MAGNIFIERS

Good binoculars are important, but you don't need the absolute best. While super-optics may be on your wish list, a reasonably priced Bushnell binocular is more than adequate for ordinary piloting requirements.

• A rubberized coating protects the binoculars and helps prevent the deck from getting dinged.

• For marine use, 7×50 binoculars are always recommended. The 7 indicates magnification power; with any higher power, the binoculars would be hard to hold steady from the unstable platform of a boat. The 50 is the diameter, in millimeters, of the front lens; this relatively large lens has good light-gathering capability.

• For help with coastal navigation, try binoculars with built-in range finder and compass heading.

• Permanent-focus binoculars may not be as optically correct as adjustables, but when many people are using the same pair, they could save a lot of aggravation.

LIGHTS

Carry a spotlight (easily connected and preferably portable) and/or a good flashlight to help spot unlighted markers at night, or to scan a riverbank or shoreline. In clearwater areas, you can read the bottom well enough to enter an anchorage at night (presuming conditions are quiet enough to allow you to *see* the bottom).

PROBLEM PREVENTION

• A boat running through an anchorage may pick up another boat's anchor line on its prop. Sometimes it's possible to free such a wrap without cutting the line. First, take the strain off. Pull up the anchor rode a few feet in front of the stranded boat. Attach a smaller line to the anchor rode with a rolling hitch, and take the smaller line back to the anchored boat, snugging it enough to force the original rode to go slack. Let out more scope from the anchored boat, if necessary, so you can pull the wrap off the prop. When it's free, retie the anchor rode in its original position. (With an I/O boat, the prop can be tilted up to work on the tangle; with other boats, you might need to go into the water.)

• On night watch or anchor watch, a set of earphones can help keep you—and only you—awake with your favorite music, or a book-tape of *Moby Dick*, if that seems more appropriate.

• When going through an area with a lot of crab-pot floats, pass on the downwind or downcurrent side of the float. The traps usually have long lines that could easily be pulled in by the prop if the boat passed on the windward side.

• If you do pick up a line, the prop wrap will probably kill the engine. Try to find the end of the offending line; pick it up and hold it taut while you try to restart the engine in reverse. If you're lucky, a quick spin will throw off the line.

• If you're running in an area with a cross-current, stay on the "upcurrent" side. If you go aground, you won't get pushed on farther, and if you're lucky you might get pushed off.

• Always watch ahead and behind so you can compensate for a sideways set before it becomes a problem.

HOOK INSURANCE

• When anchoring, always back down on the anchor. This does more than check its set; it gives you the necessary feeling of security to keep you comfortable at anchor. Nothing ruins a good night's sleep more completely than worrying about a dragging anchor.

• Other anchorers will thank you too. The toss-and-hope school of anchoring does not inspire confidence in already-anchored observers.

• If the water is clear, use a look bucket to see that the anchor is well set. Or dive on it for an even closer look.

• Always take rough bearings of your position in an anchorage so you can relate it to something when you are awakened at

3 A.M. by howling wind and torrential rain. (Even if a wind or current shift has changed your direction, you should be able to judge position relative to shore stations or other boats in the anchorage.)

• An informal survey of loran owners revealed that nobody used the anchor alarm, because nobody bothered to learn how to use it. In those few cases where you might actually be able to drift out of a harbor entrance and out to sea, it seems a far better idea to have an alarm wake you before you start nicking other boats in your exit path.

• If a predicted weather system would create a bad situation for your anchored boat, move while you are still able. "Wait and see" is too risky a strategy.

FIRE FACTS

• To burn, fire needs fuel, heat, and oxygen. Get rid of one, get rid of the fire.

• Baking soda will snuff a small galley fire. If a flare-up is confined, covering it with a metal pot lid may cut off enough oxygen to stop the fire.

• A 3-foot-square fire extinguishing "blanket" is sold to smother fires. Look for them in marine supply stores or catalogs. Keep one near the stove, one near the cabin heater.

EXTINGUISHERS

• The U.S. Coast Guard requires a specific number and type of fire extinguishers, depending on boat size. These are minimums only; it's important to keep an extinguisher any place you might use it. You will always need one quickly, so the more accessible they are, the better.

• Alcohol is considered the safest cooking fuel, because an alcohol fire usually can be put out with water. However, there are exceptions (the alcohol fire could start a grease fire, and water could spread that one), so always keep a fire extinguisher near the stove.

• Put a small, hand-operated fire extinguisher in the engine room. You may be able to put out a small fire before the automatic system is triggered.

EXTINGUISHING AGENTS

Fire extinguishers are labeled with a letter code and a picture showing its purpose. One way to help you remember what the letters mean:

Type	What's Burning	Extinguishing Agent
A	PAPER	WATER
B	FLAMMABLE LIQUIDS	A BUNCH OF EXTINGUISHERS
C	ELECTRICAL	CO2 OR DRY CHEMICAL

B's memory help is admittedly reaching, but B extinguishers are the most widely used, so it is less critical; all extinguishers can be used on B fires. Besides, even a bad attempt at association can fix the subject in memory.

• Dry-chemical agents leave a powder residue. CO_2 is a gas, so it creates no cleanup problem. Foam (rarely used) is hardest to clean up.

• For years, Halon gas systems were used to protect engine rooms, and portable units provided another extinguisher option. Environmental considerations led to the banning of Halon, but a replacement agent—FE-241—is available for the fixed systems. (By increasing the size of cylinders in engine-room installations, Fireboy was able to modify existing systems so they could use the new chemical.)

DON'TS TO REMEMBER

• Don't use water on a flammable liquid fire (B); it spreads the fire. (Think about oil floating on water.)

• Don't use water on an electrical fire (C); it conducts electricity. (Think about safety warnings regarding bathtubs and radios.)

• Don't use foam extinguishers on electrical fires; the foam contains water.

• Don't worry about cleaning up the residue from a dry-chemical fire extinguisher; it sweeps up fairly easily. (Surprisingly, people do complain about the follow-up cleanup, when it would seem more appropriate to be grateful there is something to clean.)

DO'S TO REMEMBER

• To use a fire extinguisher most effectively, direct it to the base of the fire, with a back-and-forth sweeping motion. The discharge time of small fire extinguishers is less than a minute.

• Practice using a fire extinguisher, even though you'll have to take it for a recharge. Each crewmember should do it once, or at least watch.

• At one time, local fire stations would check and recharge extinguishers. They no longer do so, but if you can't find listings in the local phone directory, they will tell you where to take your extinguishers.

• CO_2 (carbon dioxide) extinguishers should be checked annually, by weight. If the cylinder is rusting, get a new extinguisher.

• Check the gauge on dry-chemical extinguishers and recharge as necessary.

DETECTORS

• Smoke detectors work in boats too. The bigger the boat, the more separate staterooms, and the more detectors you need.

• Install detectors to warn of any dangerous fume accumulation: gasoline, exhaust, hydrogen (from batteries), or propane/butane. Detectors sound an audible alarm and show a warning light.

• See Chapter 1, pages 3 and 4, for a reminder on proper installation and careful use of propane.

PLUGS

Once you've bought the package of emergency wood plugs, don't leave them stowed "somewhere." Through-hull fittings can disappear with a lightning strike, and elec-

trolysis can cause the gradual or sudden deterioration of the most substantial-looking metal. Keep a plug next to each through-hull, tied to it if that's the only way to be sure it stays put.

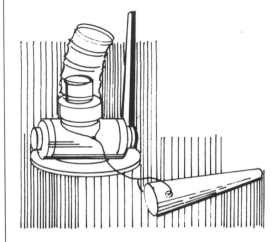

LIGHTNING

Accepted wisdom says connect and ground all large metal; if lightning strikes, it will follow the easiest path along the connected route to exit via the grounding plate. It sounds good. Don't touch metal parts in a thunderstorm. Don't stand on deck in a thunderstorm. (See Chapter 11.)

• If you like to keep track of approaching thunderstorms, time the interval between the lightning flash and the thunder rumble. Divide the time by five, and that figure tells you how many miles separate you from the thunderstorm.

WATER PUMPS

If the boat is taking on water faster than bilge pumps can get rid of it, and assuming the inboard engine is still working: Close the seacock and remove the engine's raw-water intake hose. Attach one end of a separate section of hose to the intake fitting and put the other end into the bilge. Normal running of the engine will pull water out of the bilge and send it out with the exhaust. (Cover the bilge end of the hose with screen to keep bilge yuck out of the water running through the engine.)

If this is a remedy that could be used on your boat, be sure you're carrying a separate piece of hose.

- If you're taking on water, help the bilge pump do its job by putting it in a colander to prevent the pump from getting clogged with bilge debris.

- If you're taking on water through a hole in the hull, use hatch boards, shelving, locker lids, canvas, rags, anything that can be held on with duct tape, caulking, or underwater epoxy. (Yes, it really does set up on wet surfaces.)

BILGE ALARMS

- A float switch can trigger an audible and visible alarm when bilge water gets too high. It can also turn on the bilge pump when you're not there to push the button. And some pumps have a built-in switch, so turn-on is automatic. Pick one.

- Don't rely on electric bilge pumps alone; have a manual pump on board too, fixed or portable, with a larger pumping capacity than you think you'll ever need.

PFD ADD-ONS

- Attach a whistle to each PFD: a small investment for a big attention-getter.

- Personal strobe lights should be permanent attachments on PFDs too; the farther offshore you travel, the better and brighter light you should carry. (Check batteries regularly.)

VISUAL DISTRESS SIGNALS

- The official distress flag displays a black square over a black circle on an orange background. A plain orange towel would probably send the same message.

- If you don't have either, fly the yacht ensign upside down and hope whoever sees it recognizes that as an unofficial distress signal.

- If you see someone, wave anything red (windbreaker, shirt) back and forth as a signal you need help, or use the most basic of distress signals: raise and lower your arms in a steady repetition.

- A small mirror is a good signal-sender. Buy a couple of stainless steel mirrors at a camping or outdoor supply store. Keep one handy, and put one in the emergency kit.

Flares

Keep one set of flares in your emergency kit and another in a more accessible place on board. Review launching instructions with everyone on board. Check for current dates on flares.

- Keep outdated flares for spares. If you accumulate too many, or some start to look locker-worn, turn them in to a fire or police department, or a Coast Guard auxiliary.

AUDIBLE DISTRESS SIGNALS

- Movies may take credit for implanting the SOS signal in many a mind. If you recognize no other code, remember dot-dot-dot, dash-dash-dash, dot-dot-dot. Sound it any way you can send it.

- Making noise continuously sends a distress signal too. Use a foghorn, air horn, bell, or whistle.

VHF CALLS

• Practice the procedure for emergency calls on the VHF. Use "Mayday" only for a serious threat to life or property.

• Learn the phonetic alphabet, or post it near the radio. It saves a lot of frustrating repetition when spelling the boat name or your own.

ABANDON-BOAT PLAN

Establish an abandon-boat plan. Make a checklist of what goes with you, listed by priority. An inland runabout's list will be considerably different from that of an offshore fishing craft or a circumnavigating sailboat. While a small boat within sight of shore can attract attention with the basics of flashlight, whistle, or mirror, an offshore boat will need sophisticated gear like an EPIRB, a desalinator, and a liferaft.

• Once you've made the list, put it where you can find it easily, and hope you never need to read it again.

LEARN TO BOAT

Boating courses are taught by the U.S. Coast Guard Auxiliary, the American Red Cross, and the U.S. Power Squadrons. To receive a printout of courses available in your area, call BOAT U.S., 800-336-2628. The U.S. Coast Guard also maintains a Boater Safety Hotline; call 800-368-5647.

ANTIBOARDING DEVICES

Plan what you will do if someone should attempt to board your boat at night, either at anchor or at a dock.

• Keep a spotlight handy inside the boat, and also a camera with a working flash attachment. If someone comes to the boat with what seems a poor reason, stay inside (so you're still locked in), but open a port or a hatch so you can shine the light in the intruder's face and/or take flash photos. Either will have a temporary blinding effect, throwing the person off balance. Hopefully, the light show will have the desired chase-away effect.

• As an antiboarding device, thumb tacks on deck (as per Joshua Slocum) are still a half-practical idea (even though the other half conjures a cartoon scene in which a sleepy captain forgets to sweep the deck). Anything that would make noise if bumped would accomplish the same attention-getting result. (Tin cans or jingle bells on the lifelines. Strategically placed trip lines.)

FOOLERS

• When you're leaving the boat for a day on shore, hang out some laundry and leave a light on inside. *Don't* leave anything on deck that could be used to pry open the hatches (a winch handle makes too good a pry bar).

• Use a second dinghy (a sailing dink or a recently retired inflatable) as a reverse decoy. Trailing off the boat transom when everyone goes to shore, it might serve as a deterrent to evil-intentioned thieves, who will surmise that an attached dinghy means someone is on board.

LOCK UP

Install the hardware to enable you to lock the boat from the inside. Barrel bolts are good and strong.

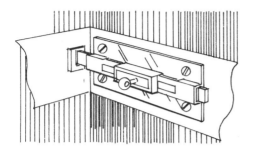

GUNS OR NOT

• Regarding personal safety: If guns are your choice, be sure you know the regulations of each state or country you visit. Follow them strictly, or you may lose freedom, boat, or both.

If you do carry firearms, be sure everyone on board knows how to handle them properly.

• If asked by the authorities how much ammunition you are carrying, don't estimate. Give an exact count, or a later count may put you in the impossible situation of accounting for something that never existed.

• If you're not a gun person, think about Mace. If you make a mistake, you won't cause any lasting harm, but it will temporarily incapacitate someone whose intent may be to harm you. Call local law enforcement agencies to check on regulations.

• You can also carry an innocent-looking pen that is actually a pepper spray. Nontoxic and nonlethal, it will prompt violent coughing and temporary blindness, effectively disabling a would-be aggressor.

RECORDS

Keep a record of identifying numbers on theft-prone items (electronics, cameras).

Better yet, engrave one familiar name or number on all of them. Even though the chances of recovering your property are slim, the insurance company will know you tried.

INSURANCE

• Request a rider, or a separate price quote on the boat's insurance policy, for a lower deductible to cover the dinghy and outboard.

• Even if your insurance company doesn't request it, you should have the boat surveyed at regular intervals. Not only will timely surveys catch potential problems, they will also establish a record of regular safety checks—a favorable consideration if you should decide to change insurers.

SAFETY IN NUMBERS

If you're planning to cruise to an area where security might be questionable, try to cruise with other boats.

TRAVEL ADVISORIES

Information on health or security conditions that may affect U.S. citizens is available from regional passport agencies in the U.S., and from:

Citizen's Emergency Center
Room 4811
Department of State
Washington, DC 20520
202-647-5225

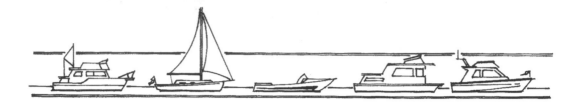

Mess-About Time

If you followed a program of regular boat care, you would diligently catch and fix all potential problems while they were still at the potential stage. A dab of putty on a deck ding, a squeeze of caulking on a leaky seam, a fresh coat of paint or varnish over a scrape, and all's well for another few months.

The reality is, you probably don't follow any program. You look at something long enough to stop seeing it: familiarity breeds a kind of invisibility, helped along by a lack of motivation.

If you're doing things the hard way, maintenance chores are a pain. If you can learn some easier ways, the time spent maintaining just might take on a hint of reward.

STRIPPERS

• When it's time for all-new varnish, ordinary paint remover will take off the old; industrial strength or marine strength will do it faster. Use bronze wool with the stripper to clean out the last residue of old varnish.

• Never use steel wool for anything. Tiny broken bits will hide in every corner and crevice and diamond shape in the deck pattern, to surprise you soon with a terrible case of rust pox. Stick with bronze wool, or try 3M's synthetic steel wool, guaranteed not to make synthetic rust spots.

• If you're trying to remove paint in order to varnish the wood, you may have to resort to scrubbing with a stainless steel brush to get to the paint imbedded in the grain. Try not to scrub any deeper than necessary; sand down most of the grooves and let the new varnish fill the rest.

• Keep a rubber-cement bottle (the kind that has a brush built into the jar lid) to use when applying paint remover in corners or small surfaces. Don't *store* the stripper in the jar; it may melt the glue or the bristles of the brush.

• To remove paint from fiberglass, buy a stripper formulated for that purpose. Other brands may soften the gelcoat and raise an orange-peel texture.

• Peel-Away, a relative newcomer to stripping, claims to be environmentally safe. It does not damage the boat's gelcoat or your skin, and will even remove antifouling paint.

ALTERNATE STRIPPERS

• If you're removing paint from a wood surface that you plan to fiberglass, don't use a chemical stripper; it may affect the bond of resin to wood. Try a heat gun, or grind off the old paint.

• A heat gun makes fast work of stripping paint or varnish from wood. Practice using it on scrap wood. You must hold it close enough so the paint blisters, but not so close that it chars the wood (*most* important if you're stripping a surface to refinish it bright). Don't use a heat gun on fiberglass; you might damage the laminate.

FILLING DINGS

• If imperfections are very shallow, polyester putty is great: it dries fast and sands easily. But if the ding is deep, polyester may eventually shrink just enough so you can see the outline of the repair.

• Wood-colored plastic fillers are not exactly permanent either, but the color is usually much better than a resin/sawdust mix.

• Epoxy putties take longer to dry and are a lot harder to sand, but they won't shrink, so you won't be fixing the same spot again later.

• In spite of a long drying time, Marine-Tex is a favorite of many yard inhabitants. It stays white, it stays put, and it lasts. Once set, it is likened to cement or steel. (Use Marine-Tex with a piece of copper screening to repair a leak in an exhaust pipe. What starts as a temporary repair stays fixed.)

• Some people complain that two-part putty never dries. This is probably the result of an improper ratio of hardener to putty. Mixing equal parts is easy enough, but a 5:1 mix apparently causes problems. Most people mix the two parts the same way: They start with a plop of putty, then guess how much hardener would be 20 percent of the plop. If they would start with a dollop of hardener, then add five similar-size mounds of putty, the mixture would be close enough to right.

• If you have a heat lamp, you can hurry the cure of any putty.

RESIN THICKENERS

Make your own strong putty by adding thickeners to epoxy resin.

• WEST System epoxies are much used; the company has a full range of fiberglassing materials, including different types of thickeners for different types of repairs.

• Mix a fine powder into the resin when applying it to a vertical surface so the resin stays in place and doesn't drip away.

• Use a microballoon mixture for filling and fairing deeper grooves and uneven surfaces; microballoon putty is fairly easy to sand.

• Cotton fibers mix into a thicker putty to fill seams and round inside corners.

• A thickened epoxy will fill cracks in teak, but varnish over the repaired wood; ultraviolet weakens epoxy.

• If you're rebedding hardware and screw holes have been stripped, use epoxy putty to fill the old holes, then redrill.

• When using epoxy putty to repair cracks and holes, tape around even the smallest spots; it will be easier to sand each raised spot later. Remember to remove the tape *before* the putty sets hard (take it off within a half hour).

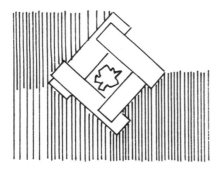

• Keep a running list of holes to be patched. When you've filled one, you'll have places to use the extra goo you mixed up. Or use tiny strips of long-lasting blue tape to mark the spots; it will stay on for weeks, or until you get enough repair spots to make a putty mix worthwhile. Or until you get tired of looking at tiny strips of blue tape.

GLAZING

Glazing is a means of filling minor scratches and dents on a painted surface with a thinner, usually one-part putty. Glazing should give you a nice, smooth surface for the new coat of paint, but if your glazing filler is not compatible with the paint, you'll waste the filler, your time and effort, and maybe the new paint. Be sure the putty covers the existing paint without any lifting, and that it takes the new paint without softening.

POLYESTER OR EPOXY

Polyester resin is less expensive than epoxy by a big percentage. It dries fast, so you can work faster. Epoxy is stronger yet more flexible, and it sticks better to more surfaces.

• When choosing resin for a repair, remember that it's okay to use epoxy over polyester, but not the other way around.

• You can't fiberglass over a painted surface; get to bare wood or glass. (Some suggest removing gelcoat from the area you're patching.) The surface must be clean and dry; rough-sand for best adhesion.

• Be sure to mix resin and hardener thoroughly to avoid spotty curing. (If it happens, you'll probably have to start the project all over, wasting both time and materials.)

• If you're using polyester resin for a fixing project, be sure to buy *finishing* resin, not laminating resin.

FORGET THE MEASURING CUP

When mixing resins (or two-part primers and paints), use a can or paper container with straight—not tapered—sides. At the bottom of a square-edged paint stir-stick, mark off a series of equal spaces. Hold the stick upright against the bottom of the container, and add appropriate amounts of whatever you're mixing. For example, if it's a 3:1 mix, pour paint until the liquid reaches the top of the third space, then add enough catalyst so the mix reaches the top of the fourth space.

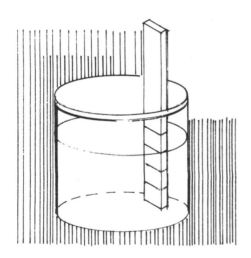

MIXING HINTS

• Never mix resin in a glass bottle; as resin begins to harden, a combination of temperature change and a slight expansion in volume could break the glass. Use paper mixing pots or metal cans.

• If possible, avoid working with fiberglass resins in direct sunlight. A 75°F day would be ideal.

• With polyester resin, on a hot day, use less hardener; when it's cold, use a bit more.

• Epoxy usually cures fairly slowly, but in a Florida summer, be careful; it will kick off before you're through applying it. Find out whether the manufacturer has a different catalyst to slow cure time. (In cold climates, you can speed curing with a heat lamp or a hair dryer.)

• To add pigment to resin, mix the coloring agent into the resin before adding the hardener. (If you add some color to the last coat of finish resin, you'll use fewer coats of primer or paint.)

GELLING

When working with resin, the mixture in the pot will harden faster than what you're applying in thin "sheet" form. If you begin to feel heat from the resin container, don't dismiss it as your imagination. It's probably time to quit using that batch, because it will soon be a blue or gray or pale yellow rock.

• Don't try to use the polyester resin once it starts to gel in the container. That last frantic 30 seconds of application will dry into a lumpy mess requiring way too much sanding time just to start over. The same caution applies to epoxy resin, and the sanding will require more effort.

SMOOTHING

• One of the secrets of smooth fiberglassing is to flow the resin *on*; don't try to brush it out. Like many such secrets, it sounds much easier than it is.

• When applying epoxy resin to a vertical surface, mix some fine powder thickener into the resin to discourage epoxy's tendency to sag and drip down.

• Distribute resin over fiberglass cloth quickly and evenly with a clean, smooth plastic spreader.

CUTTING CORNERS

Don't try to bend fiberglass cloth around—or into—a square corner; you must round the surface, or the cloth won't stick. It will lift away from the sharp edge when resin is applied. Round an exterior edge by sanding it down; fill an inside corner with putty.

COVERING A SEAM

To cover a crack or seam, use fiberglass seam tape. After the initial layer of resin fixes the cloth in place, add enough coats of resin over and around the tape so when you sand it smooth, you don't sand into the cloth. (Make a putty mixture of resin and thickener to fair the seam edge into the background surface before applying final finish coats.)

The same procedure applies to a surface patch. Always round the corners of your patching material for easier fairing.

PATCHING A HOLE

To patch the hole in the hull after removing a through-hull fitting: From the inside, bevel the edges of the hole. Clean and sand inside and outside surfaces around the area. Tape a piece of plastic over the outside surface, and secure a piece of flat wood over that to provide a stiff backing. Use a wood plug for part of the patch, or build up the entire thickness with multiple layers of fabric or matte, or with alternate layers of fabric and matte. Use epoxy resin; such a patch

is too important to worry about adhesion. Build up layers in sections, allowing them to dry to a tacky state in between. When the hole is plugged, sand both sides smooth and cover with one or two layers of fabric, overlapping the repair by at least an inch all around.

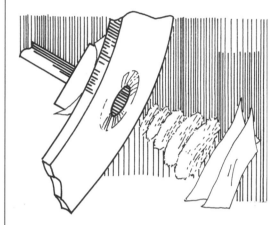

DECK DELAMINATION

If decks develop a delamination problem, you can play doctor. Drill a bunch of ¼-inch holes about 1 or 2 inches apart wherever you feel the delamination. Thicken some epoxy resin slightly and inject the mixture under the top skin of the deck.

Weigh the surface down so the top skin and core (or next layer) reattach. Then fill the holes and refinish the deck.

BLISTER REPAIR

• The most common treatment for a blistered bottom is to sandblast or grind off all paint and open all visible blisters. The boat is then left for as many weeks as possible, so any water inside the laminate will find its way out. Presumably, once the blisters are opened, there is no gelcoat to *trap* additional water, so it's acceptable to leave the boat outside in the sometime rain.

Once the hull is dry, fix the holes with epoxy putty; once the patches are sanded, coat the entire hull with three coats of epoxy as a primer and barrier coat.

• A more drastic blister treatment is to peel off all the gelcoat, then repair and recoat with epoxy, as above. Peeling is not a do-it-yourself-easily project.

SIMPLE SEPARATION

If you want to fiberglass the top of a wood cabin, but leave the sides bright, the place where the two finishes meet can be a source of trouble. An early solution was to cover the seam with a strip of heavily caulked molding. Ultimately, water got behind the molding, then behind the varnish, ending a nice, bright finish with a bunch of raised varnish blisters.

Epoxy putty can help. After fiberglassing the top, cut the cloth about ¼ inch above the eventual dividing line between painted top and varnished side. Then build up a thick layer of epoxy putty to cover the cut edge of the cloth, and to form a raised lip at the place where paint will end and varnish begin. (With the seam covered, water can't seep into the fiberglass cloth; with the putty raised away from the surface, water can't get behind the varnish.)

OVERCOAT

As tough as epoxy is, it cannot take exposure to ultraviolet light. Cover epoxy repairs or paint on a clear finish that has UV inhibitors. Even epoxy-saturated wooden boats are overcoated with varnish.

WORKING WITH WOOD

• To minimize a bad dent in wood that is to be finished bright: If the surface is already coated, remove the varnish. Wet the area; the wood will swell, raising the grain. When it dries, it can be sanded smooth, and if it's not completely level, at least it will be closer.

• For small holes or patches, mix carpenter's glue or epoxy resin with some fine sanding dust from the same wood. It will dry darker than the wood, but it will be a permanent patch.

• Before using epoxy to glue wood pieces, seal the wood with shellac or thinned varnish to prevent the epoxy from deep-staining blotches in the wood.

• When refinishing wood, don't leave it bare any longer than necessary. Seal it so it can't absorb moisture, because damp wood won't take a finish.

COPYING A CURVE

To transfer a curved shape from a pattern to new wood: Place the pattern next to the wood. Using a child's compass, place the point against the old curve and the pencil tip on the new. As you move the compass point along the edge of the pattern, the pencil will draw an accurate curve onto the new wood.

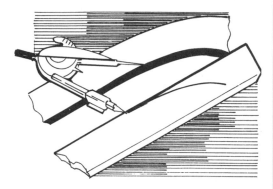

PLUGS

If you're putting wood plugs into countersunk holes on a surface that will be finished bright, dip the plug in varnish before tapping it in place. *Note:* antique boat restorers could lose points if they fail to line up the grain of the plug with that of the wood surface.

For a painted surface, you could dip the plugs into glue or epoxy.

GOOD WOOD

Teak is a desirable boat wood for its rot-proof quality, but cypress and locust are rot-resistant and can add handsome color and grain.

TOOLS

• If you have a big repair or construction project to do, buy professional-grade tools. Good tools cost more, but if you try doing a job with toy tools you'll just pay more in yard bills because you'll be there so much longer.

• If you need to take down a nonskid pattern or get rid of gelcoat, use a belt sander or a random orbital sander (no swirls).

• If you choose the belt sander, get one with the attachment that keeps it level, or you'll create more work for yourself with a deck full of dips and waves.

DRY SANDPAPER

Keep sandpaper in zip-top bags to be sure it stays usable. It's easy to leave a pack (or worse, a whole box) of sandpaper sitting out where it's handy. It's just as easy to forget it's there when the rains come.

SANDING HELPS

• Fold a piece of sandpaper around a plastic spreader or a wide plastic putty knife to sand in corners and to smooth out repaired lumps without creating new dents.

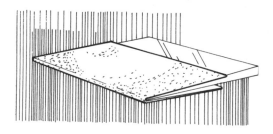

• Buy industrial-strength sandpapers for your orbital sander. It makes a huge difference in time and effort and is well worth the added expense. If you can't find them at the boat store, go to a store that sells automotive paint supplies.

• Save the used belts you remove from the belt sander, or buy new ones, to cut apart and use for hand sanding in hard-to-reach places. The heavy-duty cloth/paper won't shred when you fold it to fit into small corners, and it will do the actual sanding much faster than ordinary paper. Wear gloves, or it will sand your fingertips too.

• Make your own sanding block to fit those particular areas on your boat that must be hand-sanded. Cut the bottom flat shape to a suitable size. Glue a smaller block of wood on the top to use as a handhold. Round the top edges so it won't hurt your hand.

SCUFFER

When you want to paint a deck that has a molded-in nonskid pattern, it's impossible to sand away all gloss without taking down the pattern. Scuff the surface enough so it will take paint by scrubbing with a scrubbie pad, with or without the added abrasive of a powdered cleanser.

SANDAWAY

Remove as much sanding dust as possible before you paint or varnish. Brush it off with a whisk broom. Use a tack cloth (it grabs stray dust with its slightly sticky surface). Wipe off the surface with alcohol or paint or varnish solvent. *Use a lot of clean rags.*

TACKY TIPS

• It cannot be repeated often enough: don't trust bargain—or even standard—masking tapes for painting jobs unless you *know* the tape will be removed in a couple of hours. If you find yourself faced with baked-on masking tape that someone else used, you can ease removal somewhat by soaking with mineral spirits, acetone, or other solvents that may be handy. (Gasoline works well, but for all the obvious reasons it's not a first-choice recommendation.) Whatever cleaner you choose, test it first in an inconspicuous place to be sure the solvent will not damage the surface you are cleaning.

• Available in assorted widths, 3M's smooth blue plastic tape will peel off easily, even if it has been stuck in position for weeks (though, hopefully, it will never be necessary to test its longevity). The ⅛-inch roll makes an easy job of taping around curves; to mask a wider band, extend the initial masking with the same company's Long Mask, a blue crepelike-textured tape. It's less expensive than the smooth tape, but is also long-lasting. Buy these tapes from automotive paint stores if you don't find them at marina or yard.

SPATTER GUARDS

• Plastic paint tarps catch drips but can't absorb them, so the paint sits there until it dries, or until you walk in it and carry a paint-plop pattern beyond the borders of the project area. Heavy fabrics are best, but who has room to store them? Instead, save old sheets to use as drop cloths. You can put them over the plastic tarps, or use the elastic corners of fitted sheets to hold the tarp around all surfaces you want to protect.

• When painting or varnishing drip-prone vertical surfaces, keep coating and cleaner in a small widemouthed bucket, to move along as you move along. Mineral spirits and rag or paper towel are immediately handy to mop up drips before they have a chance to set or to multiply with your footprints.

It's especially important to pick up varnish quickly. You won't see it until it dries into a deck of yellow measles.

SMUDGE GUARD

Keep the plastic lids from cottage cheese, margarine tubs, potato chip cans—any lid with a small raised edge. When you have just painted/caulked/varnished/puttied small touchup spots, and you don't want to sit on, lean into, or brush against them, put a lid over each patch and tape it down.

These covers are especially necessary if you have a pet on board. Trying to remove epoxy putty or silicone caulking from a fuzzy foot is not fun, for you or your fuzzy-footed friend.

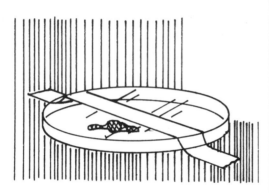

HULL PAINT

The two-part miracle paints are super glossy, and super tough, and they show super brushmarks if you do it wrong. Standard enamels and single-part urethanes are much easier to work with (just watch the video), and also much less costly. (You may have to repaint a year or two sooner than with the two-part paint.)

• Some people have good results painting the hull with a brush, even with two-part paint. Keep the wet edge of the paint moving. Work with a partner. One per-son applies the paint with a roller; the other follows, smoothing the paint with a good badger-hair brush. Use up-and-down strokes for less chance of long, horizontal sags. Use brushing thinner, but sparingly; if you use too much, you'll lose the high gloss and solid coverage you're after.

• If you choose to have the hull sprayed by a professional, see if you can do the preparation: that's the most time-consuming part of the job. Be aware, however, that the paint will not fill or cover any leftover scratches or lumps; in the right light, it will exaggerate them. If you expect a perfect paint finish, do a per-fect prep job.

• Commercial fishermen in Maine use latex housepaint on wood and fiberglass hulls. It breathes, it's easy to sand and recoat, and it lasts as well as oil-based yacht paint.

INTERIOR PAINT

• Don't try to hide mildew by covering it with paint, which will just flake off as the mildew continues to grow. Wash surfaces thoroughly with a chlorine bleach solution (½ cup to 1 gallon water) and let it dry completely before attempting to apply paint. (Add a mildew inhibitor to the new paint; call Boatek at 800-336-9320, and ask about M-1 additive.)

• A much-recommended enamel undercoat: Z-Spar 105, overcoated with Z-Spar's gloss white or your favorite color.

CLEANUP HELPER

If it's not practical to remove hardware from a painting area, and taping such things makes you nervous, try coating the metal with petroleum jelly. When you do get paint on the metal, it will wipe off easily. (Be careful not to drop the petroleum jelly on the places you want to paint or you'll have reverse measles.)

BOTTOM BRANDS

Read and heed manufacturer's instructions regarding bottom paints. If the new one is not compatible with the old, you pay for everything twice: paint cost, yard time, and your effort. It's too costly and too messy a job to risk all those repeats.

PAINT CONTAINERS

• To control the amount of paint on your brush, stretch a wide rubber band around the can vertically and wipe the brush against it, so paint drips right back into the can—not onto the can's rim or down its sides.

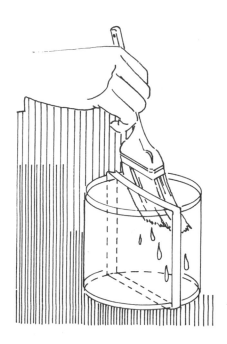

• Pour paint, and especially varnish, into a separate container, rather than using it out of the can itself. Tuna or pet-food cans are a good size for varnish. Plastic 1- or 2-liter soda bottles can be cut down to paint-can size.

Check any plastic with the paint you'll be using: cottage cheese containers, for example, melt when filled with certain paints.

PAINT TRAYS

• Paper liners are sold for use with paint trays, but you can use aluminum foil too. A plastic bag might work with some paints, but check compatibility; melted plastic is probably not an acceptable paint additive.

• A square or rectangular disposable foil or aluminum cake pan makes an acceptable substitute paint tray. Prop one end up to duplicate the angle of flow; then all you're missing are the grooves to smooth out excess paint. Since you're probably using the tray for bottom paint, a perfectly smooth roller application is not critical.

TOUCH-UPS

It's always best to catch and fix the scrapes and pinholes quickly. Once water has a chance to sneak under paint or varnish, you'll have to fix a much bigger area of air bubbles and lifting paint.

• Keep a small amount of varnish or paint handy in a spice jar or a small jelly jar, and use it to touch up nicks and scratches as they occur. Soft, square-ended artists' brushes—one for each coating—work well and clean and store easily.

• For really small spots, recycle and use a nail-polish jar with its own built-in brush. Or spot-paint with a bit of rolled-up paper toweling or a cotton swab, and don't bother with any kind of brush.

PAINTING OUT OF CORNERS

Make a neater job of painting in corners. Cut a throwaway foam or bristle brush to either a chisel edge or a modified A-shape. Even disposable brushes can be cleaned and kept for a time (except, of course, for those that melt in the more exotic paints).

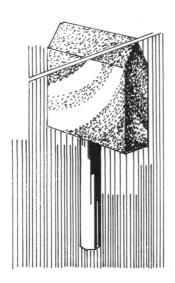

BRUSH CLEANERS

• If you're doing a project requiring multiple coats of paint or varnish, recycle the cleaning solvent. You'll save a little money on paint thinner and simultaneously minimize the amount of solvent going into waste disposal.

Have ready two or three small "washing" cans and one larger, sealable jar. Wash brushes in a succession of thinners until clean, then pour all the liquid into the jar. By the next day, solids will

settle to the bottom; the clear solvent on top can be poured carefully back into the cans for reuse.

• If you know you'll be painting again soon, it's not even necessary to clean the brush. Remove most of the paint by brushing it out on paper. Pour on enough solvent to saturate, then wrap the brush tightly in aluminum foil or plastic wrap. (A paper-towel liner inside the wrap helps keep the damp solvent against the brush.) The next day, brush out most of the thinner and start painting.

• To keep brushes soft and flexible, after you clean them, give them a final rinse in water containing a splash of fabric softener.

• While the boat is stationary and you're working on an ongoing painting project, you might want to keep brushes suspended in thinner so they can't dry out. Save a tall can for the thinner. Drill holes near the tops of the brush handles. Pass a piece of heavy wire through the holes and place it on top of the can so brushes hang in the thinner.

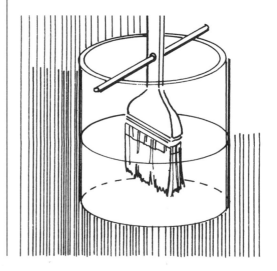

BRIGHTNESS

To maintain varnish, it's almost necessary to establish a time schedule and stick to it. By the time you see a problem, it may be too late. You can ignore paint "just a little longer," but varnish is unforgiving. You wait, you start over.

• If you have the time to wait for good drying between coats, use Epifanes. The company's literature explains that it starts out with more solids than other varnish, and it holds up longer in southern sun. People who use it notice the solids (one can goes further), and they appreciate the longevity.

• Those who like to put on many coats fast recommend Interlux Jet Speed Varnish, overcoated with Schooner.

• It's true of paint, but especially so with varnish: many thin coats are better than one thick one. The finished coating will be more likely to level out, and it should last longer.

• Varnish wood dowels simply: Drill a hole in one end so dowels can be hung in a row. Varnish the entire all-around surface of all dowels at the same time.

• When you're ready to apply the final one or two coats of varnish, don't sand. You want to keep as much of the varnish buildup as possible, and by this time—if you've done it right—the surface will be nearly level. Use a scrubbie pad just to get rid of gloss, so the last coat(s) will adhere.

TEAK CARE

It often happens that the newest teak care product will be the most popular for a time. This time, it is Sikkens Cetol Marine. It's not a varnish, but it looks like varnish, and it requires fewer coats. It can be spot-touched-up if spots deteriorate, unlike varnish, which demands a do-over once spots get too bad. (Use it on other kinds of wood too.)

SAVE THE LEFTOVERS

• When you've used more than half a can of paint or varnish and will not be using the remainder soon, the liquid may not keep well. If possible, get a clean, smaller can, available from paint stores and some hardware stores, to transfer the coating.

• Put a circle of aluminum foil or waxed paper on top of the liquid inside the can, to keep air away from most of the surface. This helps prevent surface drying; more of the coating will remain usable, in its correct proportion of solids and solvent.

• If paint skins over or gets lumpy in the can, strain it before trying to paint with it. Add thinner as needed.

• Mark a line on the outside of the can showing the approximate level of paint left inside. When you want to do a painting project later, you'll know, without opening the can, if you need to buy more paint.

• Stow paint products in the coolest locker you can find, or you'll have solidified paint no matter how carefully you treat the cans.

PAINT RECORD

Keep a record of the paints you've used. Note not only brands and colors, but also what solvents, thinners, and cleaners you used with each paint, and how much paint covered how much area. You won't remember. Recordkeeping is most important with bottom paint, to avoid a costly mistake.

CAULK TALK

When caulking, what you buy may be more important than how you apply it. Many excellent caulking products will do their excellent job only if used for their intended application. That seems obvious, but it's easy to make a mistake, so read labels carefully before making a choice.

• A common recommendation where super strength is required to seal two parts together is 3M-5200, but another brand, such as BoatLIFE Life Calk, might work better for seam caulking. Silicone is specified with installations of plastics.

• Some caulking can be sanded, some not; some painted, some not.

• When using a caulking gun, pull the handle to start caulking flowing, then, holding the gun at about a 45-degree angle, push the bead ahead of the gun as you move along (don't try to pull the gun backward, which would leave a bead of caulking trailing behind). A combination of steady tension on the handle and steady forward motion (and practice) should give you an even bead.

• Despite the tempting price tag (on a per-ounce basis), there is no savings in buying a large cartridge of caulking if you have only a small job to do. While you can keep an opened cartridge for a short time, it will eventually solidify or get lumpy, making it unusable.

TEMPORARY KEEPER

To keep a caulking cartridge after it's open, take a long, thick nail and put it into the nozzle so it reaches all the way to the caulking, not just into the nozzle. Wrap a small plastic bag around the nozzle and tape the bag shut. Tape the bag to the nozzle. Put the whole cartridge into a larger bag and seal it. Depending on the temperature, and the type of caulking, it may stay usable for a few weeks to a couple of months.

CAULK SMOOTHER

To smooth out a just-caulked seam, dip your finger in mineral spirits or another solvent, and move it along the caulk line. (If a consistent indentation would be appropriate, use a popsicle stick.)

• Both mineral spirits and alcohol have been recommended for smoothing and cleaning 3M-5200. Read labels on other brands; whatever cleans it can probably be used to smooth it.

GOOD GLUE

For jobs where you'd normally use a contact cement, try Liquid Nails. It's much easier to use, and the finished job is often

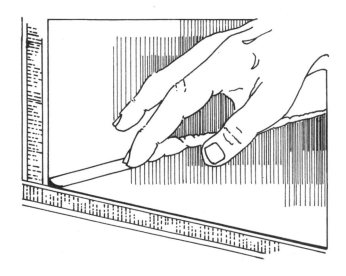

more secure. Some examples: glue a vinyl liner to the overhead, carpeting to the hull side, or Velcro strips to hatch frames. You don't have to buy a cartridge; Liquid Nails is sold in a smaller tube size as well.

NEW CHROME

If you've removed hardware to facilitate fiberglassing or painting, now's the time to have items rechromed so everything old will be new again.

NEW VINYL

• Mend cuts and tears on vinyl fabrics with a tube of vinyl repair, available at most big hardware stores. V.L.P. sticks the cut edges of vinyl back together. It may not be totally invisible, but if it stops the small tears from becoming big rips, it can extend the life of the seat cushions, and that should be the main objective.

• For a more finished repair, take it to a professional; they can melt in new fabric sections with heat.

SCREEN PATCHES

• Patch a small hole in a screen with a dab of varnish or epoxy or clear silicone caulking.

• Transparent tape on both sides of a larger tear holds for a while. Then you put on new tape for the next while.

• To really patch a screen, sew a new piece over the hole, and seal the edges with varnish.

SMALL PATCHES

When a screw hole strips, use wood matches or maybe toothpicks to fill out the hole. Dip the match into epoxy or carpenter's glue, or even varnish, to make the repair more permanent.

The same type of repair works to reattach a locker knob, a teapot lid, a ladder bracket, whatever.

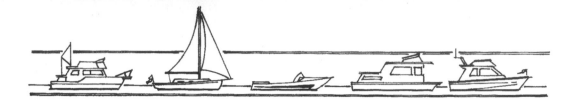

 # Hard Time

No doubt some true mess-about boatowners actually enjoy yard time, but for ordinary people it is the least desirable (though arguably the most necessary) of all boating time. A boat with a dirty or barnacled bottom doesn't go very far very fast. A boat with a dirty or scuffed top is an embarrassment for the owner. A boat with any structural problem is a danger for everyone on board.

One yard owner takes great delight in wandering around the work area cheerily singing an inimitable rendition of his own composition, "The Boatyard Blues," in an apparent, if warped, attempt to lighten the collective mood. Between choruses, he noted that the best way to get out of a yard fast is to follow the route of best preparation.

BE PREPARED

• Know the yard's policies and rules. Ask all your questions *before* you're hauled, so neither you nor the yard manager will have to deal with any surprises at an inopportune later time. Besides costs, ask what's allowed and what's not.

• Make a list of jobs to do, in priority order. Make a companion list of tools and materials you'll need, allowing a percent of extra material for the inevitable unexpecteds. Yard jobs tend to grow and grow and grow.

• Be sure your extension cords and water hoses are long enough to reach power and water outlets, so you'll be able to work when you're ready.

HAULOUT

• Show the lift operator a blueprint or boat spec sheet so he'll know where to position the lift straps. If you don't have a spec sheet, take a photo of the boat profile the first time you're hauled, and keep it for future reference.

• Before you go into the lift, use some easy-off tape to mark the lifting places on the boat.

• Carry some extra-wide waxed paper to put between the hull side and lift straps so gelcoat or paint won't get scratched in the haulout or drop-in process. The yard people will smile tolerantly on the outside as they laugh loudly on the inside, but you'll feel better, especially if you've painted the hull recently.

BLOCKING

• Ask to have the boat propped on big-enough crossbeams (8 × 8s are nice) so you can have access to the very bottom of the keel, to find and fix all the gouges you put in during groundbreaking excursions.

• Encourage yard personnel to block the boat as close to level as possible. If you plan to be in and out in a few days, it's not very important, but if you spend weeks in a yard, it gets tiresome walking uphill and downhill or on a permanent tilt. What initially

seems a slight angle becomes all too noticeable in time.

DRYDOCK LIVEABOARD

• No matter how sturdy your ladder, *tie it* to the boat. Leaning is never steady enough. Pad the contact places with foam or rags to prevent scratching. (Heavy-weight cotton socks have the right shape and cushioning factor for covering ladder ends.)

• If you've planned a lengthy yard stay, organize individual jobs so they're

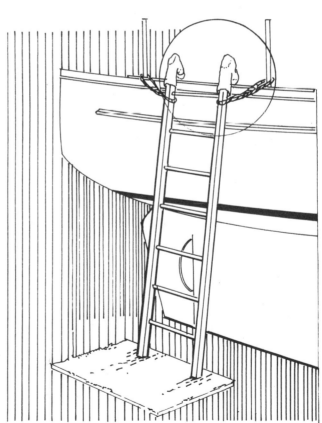

not all in progress at the same time. To ease the pain of boatyard living, try to keep some area of the boat as undisturbed as possible.

• If you're living on board, you'll no doubt be using the galley. Yard owners may not appreciate the gray water draining onto the ground on a regular basis. Put a section of hose into the through-hull fitting outside, and direct the water into a bucket; then empty the bucket in the yard's bathroom. Similarly, a portable toilet on board saves night-time ladder trips.

KEEP YARD DIRT IN THE YARD

Buy rug samples or remnants at a flea market. Put one mat at the bottom of the outside ladder, one at the top, one at the entry, and one at the bottom of the companionway. Some people insist on removing their shoes at ground level, but this gets tiresome if you wear tie shoes and are in the yard a long time. The mats are easy to shake out, will wash well enough in a good rain, and by the time they're ready to fall apart, you're out of there.

DRYDOCK COOKABOARD

While you're trying to do boat work, cooking every day takes too much time. Try fixing a bunch of food at once for later heat-and-serve meals. (This works only if you have cold-keeping capability.) Better yet, frequent the local supermarket's deli, if budget will allow.

TO-DO LISTS

Your yard list will likely include a number of outdoor projects. Make a second list of indoor jobs. On bad-weather days, you'll be less frustrated if you're still working on

something to do with boat care. Plus, it may be the only way those secondary jobs will ever get done.

WORK SCHEDULE

• If you intend to make a lot of changes on your boat, try to schedule only one major project each season; too much yard time has a definite dampening effect, not only on boating fun, but also on motivation to carry out the complete plan.

• Before you're hauled, decide if anything needs to be done outside the yard (electronics repair, custom metal work, or anything else sent for or sent out). Take care of those items first so you won't find yourself sitting around waiting for something that could have been finished earlier.

• You can shorten the time spent in the yard's work area by scheduling only as much work as must be done in the yard, and doing the finishwork later. The bad part of this arrangement is once you leave the yard, work thoughts tend to leave your head.

LAST COATS

If you'll be doing a lot of varnishing in the yard, leave the last finish coat to be done away from the yard. You'll never find a dust-free time there; you'll just be frustrated by a lint-covered surface.

BACKYARD ADVICE

When you're in a do-it-yourself yard, you'll get lots of advice whether you ask for it or not. Some will be very good, some not. Since your advisers won't be volunteering to redo the work if you guess wrong about who's right, don't guess. If you have any questions about materials or methods, ask the manufacturers and do what they suggest. (Always ask who you're talking to; it saves lengthy explanations to a new person if you must call back, and you have a name to blame if the job doesn't go well.)

STEP SAVER

• Put a long line on a canvas bag or plastic bucket, and use it for hauling stuff up to the boat deck or for dropping stuff down to ground level. If you're single-yarding, this won't help much, but with two people it avoids a lot of up-and-down trips chasing forgotten materials.

• Keep a lot of small carry bags or buckets, and fill each one with the materials needed for a different work project. When it's time to work on a particular job, just grab the bag and you're ready. (Attach a checklist to each, if necessary.) Have a paint bag, a varnish bag, a glazing bag. Don't forget the shower bag for daily self-cleaning.

PAINT BOOTH

A hauled-out boat provides a perfect "bracket" for painting odd-shaped items. For example, to paint the anchor, let it hang down a few feet from its usual place at the bow. (If you're spray painting, cover the forward area of the hull to protect from overspray.) Since aesthetics are not so critical with anchor coating, you can use a brush. Either way, you paint all sides at one time.

YARD HELPS

• If you'll be spending a long time in the yard, keep your good white drinking-water hose stowed in its locker. Buy a cheap garden hose that will become a throwaway; water hoses get scraped, cut, resin- and paint-spattered, and run over. As you're leaving the yard, cut the cleanest sections from the hose to use for chafing gear on anchor or dock lines.

• The electric cords you bring to the yard should be heavyweight and heavy

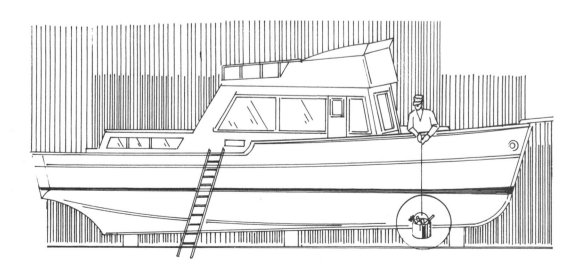

duty to handle the power demands of all your tools.

• Before plugging a power-tool cord into the extension cord, tie the two into a loose knot so you won't be chasing the extension cord down the ladder. The knot connection is obviously more important if you're using power tools while the boat is in the water. A falling cord may only trip the circuit breaker, but you'll be delayed by drying time.

PEOPLE PROTECTORS

• When fiberglassing or painting inside the boat, open all ports and get a good-size fan to direct bad air out as it's bringing new air in.

• When working with any chemicals (such as those in strippers, resins, or paint), wear the kind of gloves that are suitable for use with paint remover. Ordinary throwaway rubber gloves may melt from contact with solvent. Fabric or leather-palmed gloves are useful for sanding, but buy many spares, as fingertips can wear out quickly—especially if you're using coarse paper.

• Wear the type of respirator suitable for the work you're doing (packages describe intended use). A soft, paper dust mask may be acceptable for ordinary sanding, but not for sanding or using antifouling paint. To protect against the mist from spray painting, you need a respirator with replacement filter cartridges. Be sure the respirator fits properly, or there's little point in wearing it.

• Don't ignore cautions regarding the use of certain paints. If you have any breathing difficulty or heart irregularity, no matter how minor, you probably shouldn't work with the chemicals used in today's high-tech paint products.

• Remember the old stories about spontaneous combustion, and don't confine oil or paint rags in a small space, unless you're conducting a controlled scientific demonstration for your school-age child.

EYEGLASS SAVER

• If you wear eyeglasses, keep an old pair for work glasses. Despite the best of intentions, paint will decorate glasses by the spatter method, by fingers pushing glasses back on the nose, and by hands taking glasses off to mop the face. Also, paint and solvents will melt plastic lenses and frames.

• Wear safety goggles over your glasses for fiberglass work or bottom painting, and to keep out sanding dust or saw slivers.

• If you don't wear eyeglasses normally, wear safety goggles for the same reasons.

SAVE YOUR HANDS

Disposable rubber gloves help some, though they're not very strong. Heavy paint stripper–resistant gloves are good, but many people insist they can't work with gloves. At least use a protective hand cream, or coat hands with liquid detergent before getting into paint and caulking; they will clean up easier, without the use of harmful solvents.

SAVE YOUR CLOTHES

• Coveralls are always a good idea, but especially so when bottom-sanding. Wear a shirt and shorts or swimsuit underneath, so you can take the coveralls off and leave them under the boat; you definitely don't want bottom-paint dust on deck or inside the boat. (Be sure to leave shoes on the first mat at ladder top.)

• Boatyard clothes are often one step away from the rag bag anyway, but for

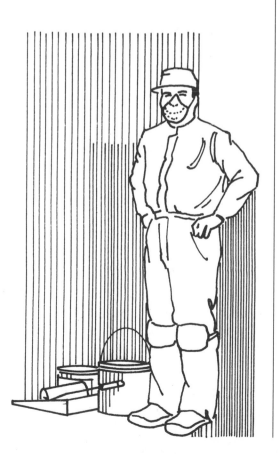

really messy jobs like bottom painting or fiberglassing, buy appropriate clothing (anything that fits) at a thrift store/flea market, and throw them away when you're through.

SAVE YOUR KNEES

Buy or make foam knee pads and wear them, no matter how silly you look. (Nonskid decks make particularly ugly knee blisters.) The alternative is to drag around a cushiony foam kneeling pad wherever you go.

SAVE YOUR HAIR

Wear a cap or a bandana to keep most of the sanding dust and paint spatters out of your hair and off your scalp. It is a lesson in frustration to try to shampoo out blue bottom-paint sanding dust; it starts out gooey and goes through a putty stage before it grudgingly departs.

SELF-SURVEY

Think about having a survey done as long as the boat's already out of the water. Yard owners should be able to recommend a competent surveyor.

• If you've spent enough time in a yard to absorb a lot of information about boat ills, you may want to do the survey yourself; if you can't be objective, however, you're wasting your time.

Make a master list from an old survey report and copy it for your annual self-survey.

METAL CHECK

• Examine all through-hull fittings, shaft, prop(s) strut(s), rudderpost.

Replace zincs whether they look bad or not; it's a small expense, and better to start out all new.

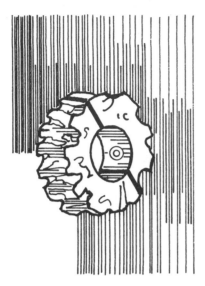

• To check for damage from electrolysis on through-hulls or shaft, clean the metal and scrape the surface with a small, sharp knife or file. If the metal shows a dull or matte pink cast rather than shiny bronze, examine it further. If flakes of pink scrape off with your knife, you have a problem, and perhaps two problems. First, replace the damaged metal piece. (You may want to switch to a composite material for through-hull.) Second, see if you can find a cause. (The problem may not have originated with your boat, but with another docked or moored close by.)

PROP CHECK

If you use your boat a lot, you may consider having the prop(s) reconditioned every couple of years. Take it to a prop shop; they'll check the pitch, smooth out the dings, and give you a smooth, clean prop. It's a small amount of money to pay

for a big improvement; it could eliminate vibration and improve performance and fuel economy.

HOSES AND WIRING

Part of your informal survey should include an inspection of all the hoses and fittings in the fuel system, and also a thorough check of wiring; look for any cuts or nicks, exposed wire, loose connections.

DRY ROT

If you can poke a fingernail into wood with very little resistance, it is no longer good wood. Once it is rotten, it will shred into soft, brittle slivers with very little pressure between your fingers.

Small areas can be treated with a penetrating resinous hardener made to cure dry rot. Larger patches should be replaced with new wood. Try to trace the path of the rot so you can prevent its recurrence.

DAMP CORE

You'll hear a damp core in a fiberglass-sandwiched deck as a literal squish, or perhaps you'll feel it in a spongy deck that gives slightly beneath your feet and diminishes your confidence in your once-solid platform. Repair usually means replacing the core material.

Cut the top skin and peel it off. Remove the water-soaked core and replace it with a closed-cell, non-water-absorbing material set in place against a piece of resin-soaked fiberglass mat. Fill the gaps and reglass the top skin.

BLISTERS

Blisters are too easy to recognize because you don't want to see them. They look exactly like their name. On some boats, they are relatively few and far between. Other hulls are a giant case of gelcoat hives.

If you find blisters, ask the yard manager about having the hull sandblasted—this part of the repair is not a do-it-yourself job. See "Blister Repair," Chapter 19, page 189, for general instructions about the rest.

GROUND CHECK

Don't forget to check the very bottom for grounding gouges or scratches. These can sometimes be deep enough to expose the laminate, and nobody wants exposed laminate; it's an invitation to water to come inside. Fix all spots with epoxy putty.

MISPLACED WATERLINE

If earlier hull-painting has misplaced the boat's waterline, you may be able to correct it by moving the line up in places. A "true" waterline (where the boat sits in the water) may still be visible, even after a high-pressure-hose cleanup, showing where dips or upturns occur. Your painted waterline will be above this floating waterline, but it gives you a starting place.

Stand behind the boat, eye level at waterline: the line should be on the same horizontal plane. With another person handling the masking tape, you should be able to correct the up-and-down curves.

Once the bottom edge is taped, the rest should be easier. The line is usually wider at the bow, so a graceful upswing there is expected. As the line comes to the stern, the painted line will be wider, because it is on a flatter portion of the hull; from profile view, it will look the same width as a section farther forward.

• When the waterline is right, scribe it in place so you won't ever lose it again. This should be done on a paint-free surface so you can cover the scribe with a coating of resin to prevent water seepage under the gelcoat. Be careful not to *fill* the indentation.

NONSKID DECK

Check the traction of a new coat of nonskid by wetting the surface with a hose. If your shoes still slip, the deck's not ready to leave the yard.

STEERING CENTER

While the boat is out of the water, turn the rudder until it's lined up straight or centered. Then put a Turk's head or some other permanent marking at the top center of the wheel. Later, when you're back in the water, you'll know at a glance when the rudder is centered.

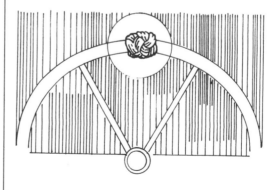

SAIL GEAR CHECK

Sailors should check winches; spray turnbuckles, cars, and track with an anticorrosive agent; and clean and do maintenance on roller-furling units.

Check for wear on the rigging; shrouds may show broken or loose wire, or may be discolored. Look for cracks in swages or broken seals on the caulking on end fittings. Check stitching on the sails.

MAJOR PURCHASES

When you're building a new boat or modifying an old one, don't make major purchases on warranted items (like engines) until you're close to installing them. You want the warranty to be valid for as long as possible after installation, but unfortunately the time span starts when you buy it.

MAJOR ALTERNATIVE

One sailor solved the problems of boatyard living in a unique way: "We carry our own sling; anyone with a hook can lift us out. We also carry a portable toilet for temporary 'yard' use."

STORING THE BOAT

To a lot of boaters, "storage" conjures the winter scene of boat tarps covered with snow in a lonely lineup at the often closed-for-the-season yard. But increasing numbers of boaters are taking their boats out of that kind of storage, cruising a few months in southern waters during the snow months, then storing the boat for the summer season in the south and returning to their northern jobs. Some storing suggestions apply to any location; some are geography-specific.

Takeouts

If your to-do list has any time-consuming maintenance projects that can be done from home (rather that wasting next year's

cruising time), take off the items that need the work. Don't forget any special materials you may have on board.

Remove all outside electronics and pack them in a dry locker inside. Better yet, take them all home, if you can, for the safest possible storage.

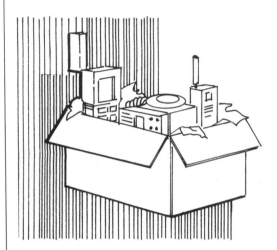

Decommissioning

Engine manuals give instructions for winterizing or decommissioning the engine. The big generalities include: change the oil, drain water or add antifreeze (if north), do something with the batteries (preferably take them home), and spray everything with an anticorrosive.

Battery Care

• Remove batteries from boats stored in cold country. A frozen battery will not revive. Store them in the garage or basement; charge them as necessary.

• In the southland, some people leave batteries in place with a small solar panel providing a daily trickle charge.

Fuel Tanks

There is still disagreement about whether fuel tanks should be left filled or empty. "Full" prevents condensation, but long-stored fuel may deteriorate. If you choose "full" anyway, add a stabilizer.

Outside Strip

• Take down all antennas, all canvas, all lines, anything that could be damaged by constant wind.

• Take in all seat cushions, remove fenders and lifebuoys, stack it all inside to keep it dry and out of ultraviolet light.

• Sailors should remove all sails, give them a good freshwater washing, dry well, and bag and stow them below. If they need restitching, let the sailmaker store them awhile.

Inside Stuff

• Take clothing and towels out of lockers, especially those prone to hull condensation, and pack them in fabric laundry bags or pillowcases.

• Take books off the shelves and put them in paper or fabric bags.

• Put desiccant packets inside clothing and book bags. (Buy reusable silica gel in bulk quantity at craft shops; it's used for flower-drying art. Then make your own packets.)

• Prop seat and bunk cushions on end and move them away from any known leaky ports. Prop open underseat lockers.

• Don't pack things in plastic bags. Long-term condensation with its wet and dry cycles is as bad as a constant water drip.

• Put a scented dryer sheet or a bar of bath soap into the bags with clothing, bedding, and towels.

• Put baking soda in the cooler or refrigerator. Most people prop the lids or doors open.

Food Leftovers

• For northern winter storage, leftover canned goods can't stay. Even if the frozen cans don't actually explode, they'll probably pop their seams enough to leak, and that is a mess you won't want to face.

• In southern storage, leave canned goods on board (except for the potentially dangerous sauerkraut). Many dry foods can stay also, provided they're in plastic storage canisters. Don't leave food in foil packets or cardboard boxes, even if they are also encased in zip-top bags; given enough time, creatures will chew through it all. And don't leave flour, pancake mix, or cornmeal that may be harboring weevil eggs.

Tarp Coverups

• No matter where the boat is stored, the tarp may need to be cushioned in places where it touches sharp corners. For each corner cushion, put some foam rubber in a small plastic bag. Cover the bag with a fabric sleeve made from an old pant leg sewn at both ends. Tie the pad in place by whatever means works; it will save the tarp from a chafed hole.

• In northern yards, tarps often fit over a specially constructed framework that shapes the fabric to allow ventilation and prevent pockets from forming and filling with the heavy, cold white stuff.

• In southern yards, tarps are used to try to keep out sun and rain. For a secure tie-down, one clever recycler found an innovative use for 2-liter plastic soda bottles.

Filled with water, the bottles act as

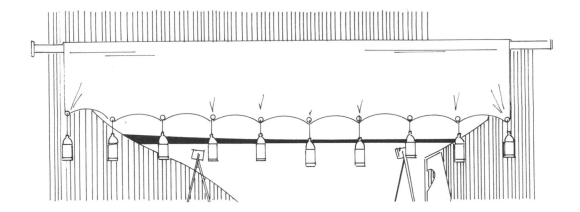

weights to hold the tarp in place. Tie them onto the tarp every few feet; even if they bump the hull, they can't hurt it. The bottle weights replace shock-cord tie-downs, which work fine for a time, but after too much sun exposure they give too much, and a loose tarp suffers from overflapping.

Rainaway

Often, the tarps covering a stored boat will rip from wind or disintegrate from sun; rain pours in along with dirt and leaves, and scuppers get clogged. The cockpit may fill, and water will find its way inside the boat as it "sinks" on land.

• If the boat is to be stored during a rainy season and you won't be able to check it periodically, take a cue from commercial fishermen and consider putting in a drain plug (even though it means drilling a hole in the hull).

The plug should be accessible and installed low enough in the hull so water would drain out before it could fill up the bilge to engine height; if it could be positioned on a slanted section of hull, debris would be less likely to clog the hole.

• If the cockpit has recessed scuppers, there's another alternative: Use a 4- or 5-inch length of PVC pipe of a diameter that will stand upright in the scupper recess. Drill a number of small holes near the bottom end of the PVC so water can flow through, but leaves cannot get to the drain to clog it.

Mildew Control

Humidity may create a problem during summer storage. Some boats store with no mildew problem; some drip green; some get black boat pox. The first storage year is always somewhat of an experiment, and its outcome depends on a combination of factors, including air flow and the boat's own insulation.

• To absorb excess humidity, leave charcoal briquettes or cat litter in foil or plastic containers in lockers, under bunks, and in other such spaces.

• Hang bags of mildewcide crystals.

• When you leave a bunch of mildew-deterrent packets made of paraformaldehyde, you'll coincidentally deter would-be thieves too. In a closed boat, the anti-mildew chemical burns the eyes and nose; a person could not stay in the boat without airing it out first, and it's doubtful a thief would choose to be that obvious.

Airflow

• Solar vents are the perfect solution for moving air through a stored boat. If you can arrange it, put in one vent as an intake and one as exhaust, and create your own steady airflow through the boat. Remember to place them in an area that won't be covered by the tarp.

• Mushroom vents can be placed anywhere. While not as good as the solar vents with fans, they're an improvement over leaving the boat closed up tight.

Keep the Wildlife Out

• Birds may nest in a sailboat's masthead, and mud daubers can sneak into the tiniest of places on any boat. Discourage their homing instincts by stuffing all access holes except those that must remain open to carry away accumulated rainwater.

• Cover the cowl vents with foot sections cut from pantyhose. Air still gets in, but even tiny no-see-ums can't get through the fine mesh. (Useful any time, any place where gnat-size bugs are a problem.)

Bug Control

When you leave, put out bug traps and poisons. When you come back, bug-bomb the boat if you see evidence of insect habitation.

In-Water Storage

Instead of putting the boat "on the hard" during the summer, you may choose to keep it in the water at a marina dock, on a private dock, or on a mooring.

• If you choose any of these options, try to find a responsible person to open up the boat occasionally to air it out; to start and run the engine for a while periodically; and to check after a heavy rain to pump out, fix the tarp, or unclog scuppers.

• The biggest problem of summer in-water storage is hurricane season. If the boat is in a possible storm path, you might be required to move it. Ask for recommendations for a trustworthy person to do this; it is not a favor to ask of a friend. Finding the right person may be difficult, so be prepared for an unscheduled boat visit.

• If you're at a dock, there's always a risk that some homeless critters—such as mice, rats, possums, raccoons, and stray cats—may establish squatter's rights. Do what you can to keep them out of the boat interior, but resist the temptation to leave rat poison out on deck. Marina mascots and boatowners' pets often go wandering.

• If the boat's on a mooring, your trustworthy boatwatcher might put out a storm anchor for extra holding in case of a threat from a summer storm.

CHECKLIST

Make up a checklist for your boat—what to do when you leave it, and what to do when you come back. It's surprising how much you can forget about boat living in six months' time, and such tasks as unplugging mud-dauber holes, plugging drain holes, and opening water intakes are too important to trust to memory.

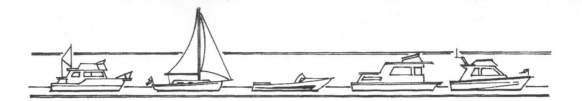

Good Crewkeeping

Everyone wants to stay healthy and fit. If you want to spend time on a boat, it's almost a prerequisite.

In our health-conscious society, people are taking more interest in and responsibility for their own health care. Such awareness is essential for people who cruise for extended times away from medical help, but everyone benefits from a knowledge of health care or fitness alternatives.

It's finally okay to be a health nut.

EXERCISE TIME

Boating shouldn't be sedentary, but it's possible to get too comfortable when you're anchored in some quiet spot and have nothing more pressing to do than contemplate the sunsets. With the fitness awareness of recent years, people feel guilty if they don't get physical about something other than ordinary boat handling.

• Establish a routine for activity. Daily is best, but three times a week is the minimum.

Hike

The sightseeing you want to do coincides with the exercise you need to do. Hiking shoes are essential; then set a pace for your shore wandering that goes beyond stroll speed. You can always backtrack to the highlight places for a browse.

Jog

• Dawn beach jogging is popular; it becomes a challenge to be the first to put footprints on the tide line. Be prepared with the right shoes.

• Take along a pair of lightweight nylon/rubber wet shoes to protect feet when walking on rocky shores. They'll give some protection from accidental encounters with sea urchins or stingrays.

Bike

If your boat can carry bikes, it should. Beyond the convenience of being able to travel farther for needed supplies and sightseeing, biking is one of the better all-around exercises.

Row

While a rowing shell would provide the most complete exercise, a rowing dinghy is a decent substitute. Rowing doesn't work too well with inflatables (the idea being to actually go somewhere at the same time you are exercising), but if you can carry or tow a hard dinghy, it's a pleasant way to maintain muscles and stamina.

Paddle

Paddling an inflatable like a canoe not only gets you where you want to go, it pro- vides a very focused upper-body exercise. And blisters, if you're too enthusiastic.

Tai Chi

You don't have to embrace a total phi- losophy of mind, body, and spirit to reap the benefits of the exercise aspect of Tai Chi. Perfectly suited to boat living on both the space and the activity levels, the grace- ful stretching exercises keep the body toned and flexible, and any regular exer- cise generally improves mental attitude, whether or not that's part of your plan.

With the help of video, you can have an in-boat teacher. Known for his Kung Fu expertise, actor David Carradine also produced a Tai Chi video. With its visual direction, people of all ages and any physi- cal capability can do as much or as little as they choose.

Aerobics

• The more energetic and ambitious exercisers can bounce along with any of the aerobic or workout videos currently fighting for top tape billing.

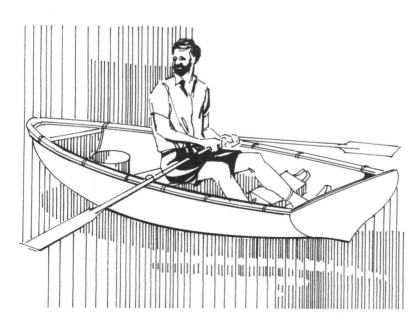

• How-to instructions can be found in old-fash- ioned book form, too, for those who would rather not be bombarded with a background of someone else's favorite music.

• Among the cruising commu- nity, groups often congregate on available beaches to follow a leader in a daily workout. The foredeck is a suitable platform too, providing nobody is trying to meditate in the forward stateroom.

Dance

A few people revive the almost forgotten routines of childhood dance classes. While tap dancing (on a portable floor panel) is usually limited to children who still attend classes, ballet routines are a wonderful way to work out muscles and fantasies.

Stretch

For a space-saving, muscle-conditioning, all-in-one exerciser, get a ShapeMate. This stretching strap is promoted as a "gym-in-a-bag," duplicating any muscle conditioning exercise done in a gym. Not mentioned in the advertising copy but noted by an advocate: it is helpful in combating the stiffness and pain of arthritis.

Lift

Small dumbbell weights are easily carried and easily used on board. You'll find instructions when you purchase the weights, or buy a separate book or video for the kind of program that's suitable.

Jump

Get a jump rope and return to childhood with a mix of singsong rhythm and coordinated jumps on the foredeck or shore.

Water-workouts

Swimming, diving, boardsailing, and water skiing are the obvious ongoing sources of fun that coincidentally provide great exercise. (See Chapter 17.)

Horseshoes

They stow in a small space, and a beach is a good place for horseshoe pitching: one giant sand pit.

Shore Sport: Where There's a Will

Boat travel needn't preclude golf or tennis either. Cruising routes have been planned around the accessibility of courts and courses. And whenever enough boaters congregate near a handy beach, a volleyball net is sure to follow.

SUN FACTS

• The closer you are to 0 degrees latitude, the more intense radiation is year-round.

• The two hours before and after noon (sun time, not daylight saving) are the most harmful hours to be exposed to sun.

• Clouds don't absorb UV radiation; they just diffuse it, reducing intensity only by half.

• Reflected sun can burn you too, as it bounces off water, fiberglass, or sand.

Tan Facts

"Tan" means wrinkles, the leather look, early aging, and very possibly skin cancer. Sun worshippers choose not to believe, or do not care.

• Some medications—diuretics, birth control pills, tranquilizers, some antibiotics, and some antihypertension drugs— may increase UV sensitivity, which increases your need for sunscreens and sunglasses. Check with your doctor or pharmacist about any medication you take regularly.

• Skin cancer is the most common type of cancer in the United States. Current estimates are that 40 to 50 percent of Americans who live to age 65 will have skin cancer. The good news: it's curable in over 95 percent of cases.

Sunscreen Facts

• If you want to control sun exposure, there are two kinds of protection you can apply. A physical barrier, like opaque zinc oxide, blocks out the sun effectively but is very messy to use. Sunscreens screen out ultraviolet rays.

• The sun protection factor (SPF) rating on sunscreen lotions indicates the time you could stay in the sun before burning. Example: if you would ordinarily burn in 5 minutes of exposure, with an SPF 10 it would take you 50 minutes (5 times 10) to burn. Look for a rating between 15 and 30. Beyond 30, there is no real added protection.

Sun Hints

• Put on sunscreen 15 to 30 minutes before going into the sun.

• The waterproof screens *do* work.

• Ankles and the bottom of feet are especially tender when they burn; protect them.

• Stay out of the sun between 10 A.M. and 2 P.M.

• Anyone prone to sun poisoning (which raises a hive-like rash) should be doubly careful.

Sunburn

When you get a sunburn, soothe it with tea, vinegar, baking soda paste, or any over-the-counter burn medication. Gel from the leaf of an aloe vera plant is most comforting, if gooey.

SUNGLASSES

Putting dark lenses in front of your eyes is not good enough anymore; they must be the right *kind* of dark lenses.

• Always buy lenses with UV protection; they block 95 percent of radiation to protect the eye from sun damage. (Exposing eyes to ultraviolet light contributes to cataracts and retinal damage.)

• Polarizing lenses cut surface glare, allowing you to see into the water. They're good for "reading" water (judging depth by color) when eyeball navigation is your only navigation aid.

• Photochromic lenses darken and lighten with the surrounding light, but some don't clear completely inside. Also, if you are in a shaded area (flybridge, wheelhouse, cockpit under a bimini) the glasses will lighten, but if you are looking out at sun and glare on the water, you *need* the darkening. Better to have real sunglasses, so you can control the times you want dark lenses.

Lens Colors

Gray or smoke lenses allow the most true-to-color view and are considered best for boating. Brown or green lenses are the next best, but they do distort colors some. Blue, yellow, and other odd colors create too much color distortion.

To Clip or Not?

Prescription sunglasses are better than clip-on lenses hooked onto your regular eyeglasses. The clip-ons cause distracting reflection and distortion; plus, they may scratch your lenses.

Rust-Away

Solve the problem of rusting metal frames by buying titanium. You can also buy superflexible nylon frames; even the hinge is nylon, eliminating that potential rust spot.

Misplaced Glasses

• Keep spare sunglasses and magnifying glasses on board if you have a habit of losing them.

• Put holders at places you normally remove glasses (in the galley, at a desk, next to the radio), and maybe you'll be able to find them with a retrace-steps routine.

• Eyeglass straps are necessary on prescription glasses, and they're handy for ordinary sunglasses too. The straps are a small inconvenience; good glasses are too expensive to have to replace due to negligence.

• If you drop a lot of glasses overboard, try putting foam floats on the side pieces. They are initially very distracting, but at least you'll have a chance for retrieval.

Glass Repair

When you lose the tiny screw that holds the side piece on your eyeglasses, and the handy fix-it kit doesn't have one the right size, use a thin wire. It you don't have thin wire, peel the paper off a twist tie, and use the wire as a twist tie.

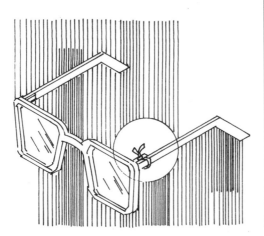

MAL DE MER

• It's no secret that seasick prevention medication must be taken *before* you get into the situation that might make you sick, but people like to test themselves or the theory from time to time. By the time they fail the test, it is too late to take the medication and they are sorry to have posed the question.

• Ginger is a seasick preventive. (It's reputed to help morning sickness, too.) You can brew your own ginger tea by simmering a few thin slices of ginger root in a pint of water for about 20 minutes. Then you must sip it, an ounce at a time, all the boating day. You can also go to the local health store and buy ginger tea bags or ginger capsules.

• People who tend to get seasick like to use the skin patch and the wristband. The pills work, but they do make people drowsy.

• Give yourself a better chance to stay sea-well. Don't eat heavy or greasy foods the night before a boat trip. Stay away from alcohol and caffeine.

Mind Over Mal

• If you start feeling unsteady, stay outside in the air. Focus on a landmark, or on the horizon if you can't see shore. Stay out of the path of exhaust fumes. Munch on saltines or pretzels.

• Try steering the boat; concentrating on a job may help you through the worst of the woozies.

• Some people head straight for a bunk, but most feel better sitting upright.

• If you get sick, don't be embarrassed. It happens to almost everyone at some time, contrary to what some braggarts may claim.

HYPOTHERMIA

Nobody's favorite subject, but one that requires familiarity for the just-in-case possibility.

If you fall into cold water, you want to think about minimizing loss of body heat. Keep your clothes *on*; cover your head if you can. Try to get out of the water (on a swim platform, for example), but swim only if it's necessary to reach a floating object; don't try to swim far. (Too much activity will release the already warmed water between your body and your clothes.) Keep still.

If you're alone in the water, hold your knees up to your chest in the "heat escape lessening position" (H.E.L.P.). If others are also in the water, huddle together.

On the boat, be prepared with detailed instructions for treating hypothermia. Symptoms include shivering; confusion; loss of coordination; cold, blue skin; weak pulse; irregular heartbeat; and enlarged pupils. Once the victim is out of the water, remove clothing, but keep physical activity to a minimum. Start rewarming by wrapping in a blanket. Apply hot water bottles, if you have them, to head, neck, chest, and groin. Put the victim into a sleeping bag with another person to transfer body warmth and speed rewarming.

Don't apply heat to arms and legs. Don't massage or give a hot bath. Don't try to give food or drink if a person is unconscious. Don't give alcohol.

The information above is condensed from a brochure funded by the U.S. Coast Guard and available from Boat/U.S. Boating Safety Foundation. To receive "Hypothermia and Cold Water Survival," write:

Boat/U.S. Foundation
880 S. Pickett Street
Alexandria, VA 22304

STINGERS

• If you step on or otherwise surprise a sleeping stingray, you may get stung, but it's more a reflex action than an aggressive maneuver. If you see the barb, remove it carefully. Wash with salt water; apply diluted ammonia or urine, then soak in hot water. If you show any symptoms of an allergic reaction, such as dizziness or difficulty breathing, get medical help.

Flats fishermen always slide their feet when wading, to prevent getting stung.

• If you swim into a jellyfish—either the translucent white variety or the turquoise Portuguese man-of-war—you'll unwillingly keep some of its tentacles, which will be stinging by the time you can exit the water. Neutralize the poison

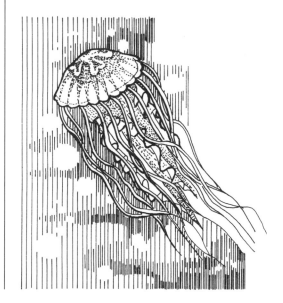

with alcohol; apply a paste of baking soda and water, then scrape off the clinging tentacles with a dull knife. (Other neutralizers include vinegar, diluted ammonia, urine; if you don't have access to baking soda, use beach sand.) Take aspirin for the pain or an antihistamine for the itch.

The Portuguese man-of-war sting can cause an allergic reaction (respiratory or cardiac problems) in some people. If symptoms seem severe call a doctor, or refer to your onboard medical kit for further treatment recommendations.

• Spiny black sea urchins sting unwary and unprotected feet. Treat a sting with the same alkaline substances you'd use for the jellyfish: vinegar, ammonia, urine, alcohol. Aloe gel may have a soothing effect on any sting.

• Meat tenderizer is available seasoned or unseasoned. Buy the no-flavor version, and keep it on board for sting relief.

HEALTH HELPS

• Everyone's favorite cleaning agent has some people benefits too. Baking soda is a mouthwash, a toothpaste alternative, a stomach soother. Put a baking soda paste on minor burns and stings; clean your hands of fish smells with baking soda (and/or lemon juice.)

• To take baking soda as an antacid to relieve heartburn or sour stomach, mix ½ teaspoon baking soda into ½ glass water.

• Ginger ale is still a good stomach settler. Some recommend drinking it flat; some like the bubbles.

• Nobody's old favorite—castor oil—has a surprise benefit: It's good for a number of skin problems. Applied regularly (once or twice a day), it will remove some kinds of warts or moles and scaly

spots on skin. Nonbelievers should try it anyway; it can't hurt, and you might be surprised too.

• To discourage swimmer's ear, rinse ears with a half-and-half mix of alcohol and vinegar.

Aloe

If you believe the believers, aloe vera is the miracle plant used to treat acne, anemia, arthritis, bedwetting, gum disease, nasal congestion, radiation burns, and tuberculosis—among other things.

• You can buy aloe juice in mainstream establishments. It is said to improve digestion and get rid of ulcers, constipation, and colitis.

• Aloe is most well known for soothing the pain and hastening the cure of sunburn and other minor cuts and burns.

• Keep an aloe plant growing on board. It is a true survivalist plant; even black thumbs can't destroy it. To use, break off

a leaf and squeeze the gel onto the cut or burn site. Expect it to be sticky.

ALTERNATIVE HEALTH CARE

A focus on prevention and natural curatives appeals to cruising boaters, who don't always have instant access to doctors or hospital care. But alternative remedies should not be used casually. Learn as much as you can about whatever method you may choose to use; be aware of limitations, and realize that even "natural" products can have side effects.

Homeopathy

Webster's defines homeopathy as "a system of medical practice that treats a disease by the administration of minute doses of a remedy that would, in healthy persons, produce symptoms of the disease treated," an idea not unlike the principle behind vaccines.

• A reference book can suggest what you might want to keep on board for your crew's specific problems: asthma, high blood pressure, bladder infections, seasickness, whatever. For information, write:

National Center for Homeopathy
801 N. Fairfax Street, Suite 306
Alexandria, VA 22314

• To obtain remedies, look in health food stores, or write:

Standard Homeopathic Co.
210 N. 131 Street, Box 61067
Los Angeles, CA 90061

Naturopathy

A combination of homeopathic remedies, herbal medicine, nutrition, and other natural approaches fall under the umbrella of naturopathy. The natural remedies, and often a change in diet and lifestyle, aim to boost the body's immune system and encourage self-cure.

For information, send SASE to:

American Association of Naturopathic Physicians
2366 Eastlake Avenue, Suite 322
Seattle, WA 98102
206-323-7610

Accupressure

For some people, accupressure reportedly achieves the same results as acupuncture, sans needles. It may be worth learning, for possible help with headaches, arthritis, and other conditions that cause chronic pain.

DIAGNOSES

Keep a family health reference on board. It can help you separate those problems that can be allowed to run their course from those that need medical attention fast. *The American Medical Association Family Medical Guide,* available in bookstores, includes a useful section of self-diagnosis charts.

MEDICAL/FIRST-AID KIT

The size and type of medical kit you carry will depend on your usual boating locale and activity. If you're always within sight of shore on a busy inland lake, you'll get by with a small first-aid kit for cuts and blisters. At the opposite extreme of full-time offshore cruising, you must carry as much as you can for all the emergencies you can think of.

MEDICATION AND SUPPLEMENTS

• Get prescriptions from your doctor for basics, like antibiotics and pain pills. Know how to use all the medicines you're carrying.

- A book describing medications can provide a ready reference when you can't conveniently call the doctor or the druggist. If you're taking prescription drugs on an ongoing basis, ask the doctor or the pharmacist before you leave on a cruise if there is anything you should avoid, such as other prescription medications, over-the-counter drugs, or foods.

- A cruising boat may not always provide the right foods every day. A daily vitamin supplement for the crew could supply whatever the boat diet is missing.

Safekeeping

- Keep prescription drugs in their original bottles, labeled and dated. Put the small bottles inside other bottles to ensure dry storage.

- If you're traveling in a foreign country, don't take pills out of their original containers to mix them with others in a pocket pillbox or bottle.

- Keep a separate, tight-sealing container—preferably plastic—for all your medical supplies, so all will stay dry and accessible. If you carry medication that needs to be refrigerated, keep a moisture-tight jar or box in the same place in the ice chest.

Safer Not Keeping

Get rid of out-of-date medications. It's easy to forget how long pills have been in the locker, especially when you don't use them. Schedule a clear-out session twice a year.

Don't Forget

Some medical aids that are often forgotten:

- Ophthalmic ointment and eye patches.

- A dental putty that fills cavities temporarily. (Hard to find, but a blessing to have when a filling falls out.)

- Benadryl for minor allergic reactions, and a kit for unexpected serious allergic reactions. (If you've never been stung by a fire ant or a jellyfish, you don't know if you have an allergy. Be prepared.)

- See if your first-aid book shows what you might need for poisoning, and add it to your list. Pets or visiting children should probably be your main concern. Mistaken identity is the usual source, especially if you're recycling plastic bottles and the new label falls off in the damp boat environment. If you put soap in a soda bottle, don't trust tape-on labels; use indelible marker and write in large letters. Draw a skull and crossbones for emphasis.

- If a poisoning occurs, and you're close to help, call the local Poison Control Center or the nearest hospital emergency room.

WARNINGS

No Harvesting

Be aware of problems associated with some seafood.

- Warnings are posted, usually by a state agency, wherever shellfish are considered unsafe to eat. Illness can be a mild case of vomiting or diarrhea, or a serious paralytic reaction.

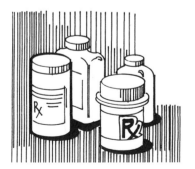

• Areas may be closed because of naturally occurring toxins, bacterial contamination, or industrial and agricultural runoff. Watch for signs tacked up on posts. Closed areas sometimes apply to shrimp and finfish as well. If in doubt about the boundaries of the restricted area, ask (or watch) the locals.

Ciguatera

Ciguatera is a type of fish poisoning caused by eating reef fish, usually the larger barracuda, grouper, snapper, or jack. Not everyone who eats the same fish will necessarily get sick; of those who do, not everyone will experience the same symptoms. Most common are digestive upsets: vomiting, cramps, diarrhea. Partial or temporary paralysis may occur and heart rhythm may be affected. Other symptoms may persist, or recur, for months: tingling in mouth or lips; aching or numbness in limbs; and the one symptom most peculiar to ciguatera, a reversal of hot and cold sensation. An ice cube burns; hot water chills. If you show any of these symptoms after eating fish (usually within 2 to 10 hours, but they could appear as early as 30 minutes and as late as 48 hours), seek medical help. Though treatment is mostly a matter of waiting for the toxin to leave your system, a doctor can monitor and perhaps ease some of the secondary problems.

Researchers continue to look for testing methods, but presently there is no way for fishermen or cooks to test an individual fish. You cannot kill the toxin by freezing, marinating, or cooking.

BACK ATTACKS

On a boat, there are too many opportunities to aggravate a back problem; it's practically impossible to avoid situations that might trigger a bad back attack. If you've ever been treated for a problem, follow your doctor's recommendations to help ward off future attacks.

Here are two possibilities suggested by Dr. Michael O'Shea of the Sports Training Institute. These exercises keep back muscles flexible and healthy, and they can be done easily on a forward deck or a large enough saloon.

Full Spinal Stretch

Start with back flat on deck, knees bent up to chest, hands on thighs as if holding legs up. Slowly curl your head up toward your knees. Hold in position; you'll feel the stretch along the length of your spine. Slowly uncurl back to starting position, then repeat.

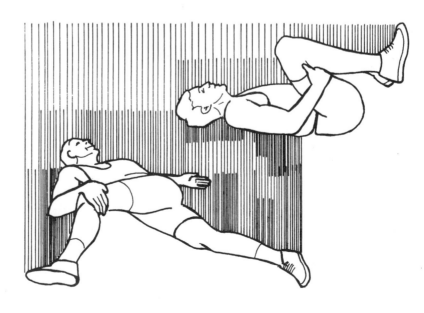

Low-Back Stretch

Begin with back flat on deck, legs extended. With right hand, pull your left leg up and over the right leg. Keep shoulders on deck. Turn head to left, then grasp your left leg under the knee and pull left thigh up and sideways toward waist, still keeping leg close to deck, to stretch lower back and buttocks. Hold, then return to starting and stretch other side.

SHORESIDE WORRY

In some areas, shore excursions or dog walks could lead through Lyme territory. A serious problem for owners as well as pets, Lyme disease is carried by the tiny deer tick. While it is difficult to see the tick itself, a bite will show within 24 hours as a readily identified, raised, circular red mark.

Early antibiotic treatment is essential; go to the nearest doctor or hospital outpatient facility for appropriate medication.

Lyme has been found all across the U.S., though it is most prevalent in the Northeast.

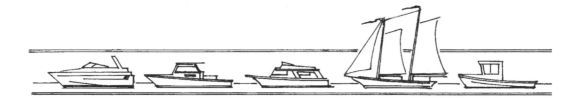

My Boat/ Your Boat

It's fun to have company. Sharing boating time with friends and family gives them a chance to experience boat life, and it gives you a chance to see through their "fresh" eyes. It's the best possible opportunity to make the term "quality time" mean something, whether it's time with kids, grandkids, or best friends.

It's easy to invite experienced boaters, but it's more interesting for you and your guests if they're new to the lifestyle. Recall your early ideas about boating so you can better prepare your guests. Think of ways to make the most of the time they're on board. Then enjoy.

BE FLEXIBLE

• The one personality trait boat guests need most is adaptability, for their sake and yours. Narrow minded, narrowly focused, or uptight types don't do well on a boat.

• Keep your guests' first visit short. Some people cannot adjust to boat life even when they want to, and with one unhappy camper, everyone on board will suffer.

• "Don't take lubbers to sea."

SCHEDULES

"Let them find you: Don't create deadlines." An understandable attitude from the boater's perspective, but the land person has a limited time and a specific time frame for a vacation; trying to locate a sometime traveling boat would not be a favored way to spend that time.

Don't create *unrealistic* deadlines. Allow plenty of leeway when arranging to meet people.

INCLUDE THE KIDS

If friends have children and you don't, invite the whole family anyway. You can usually find other children for your visitors to play with. It's a great learning experience for children, and it's fun for you to be able to watch them.

• Keep a few small-child things on board—coloring books, crayons and paints, tiny stuffed toys—for rainy-day play.

ITINERARY

A few weeks before their scheduled arrival, send your guests a list of titles, or the actual books, so they can read about the place they're coming to see. Ask them to think about what they might want to do with their time. You can tell them if it's possible, on a time and distance basis, but at least you'll have a starting point. Nobody likes to hear a standard "I don't care" or "It's up to you" in answer to the question "What do you want to do?"

GUESTS BEARING GIFTS

When guests ask "What can I bring?" they want a real answer too. Give them one. If they're the kind of friends who would not come without bearing gifts, make some suggestions of what you'd like to receive. This is not tacky; it makes better sense than leaving them to guess about something they know nothing about. (Resist the temptation to request a new radar.)

SHARE ALIKE

Some sharing of expenses is a nice arrangement. One couple established a set fee for daily provisioning, even when they buy supplies in advance. This is a common practice with friends and family, but in some places it might be interpreted as "paying guests," so don't advertise. You don't want to be mistaken for a charter boat if your license reads pleasure or recreational.

DRESS RIGHT

Send your friends a list of the kind of clothes they'll need, or they may show up with completely inappropriate resort wear, with fabrics that won't travel well on a dinghy. They may not bring sweaters if the boat is at a tropical island, because they don't know about cool nights at anchor. They may not realize that wearing a skirt would be a nice gesture of respect for local custom.

Tell them to bring mostly casual clothes, but one yacht club outfit if you and they enjoy eating out at places that require such attire.

PACK RIGHT

• Allow one bag—soft luggage or duffel—per person. No exceptions.

• Explain ahead of time they may have to live out of the bag, empty drawers and "closets" being nonexistent.

• Tell them to leave hair dryers and makeup mirrors at home.

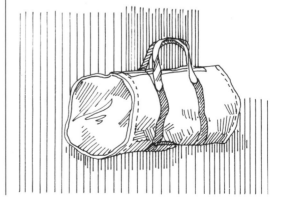

NO SOLES

In the forewarning letter, include a reminder about shoes. While you assume most people know about deck shoes or ordinary sneakers, they may associate "hard-soled shoes" with dress shoes, and not think about sandals, which often have leather soles.

MONEY CHANGING

If they're joining you in a foreign country, suggest to your guests that they change money before leaving the United States. Bank rates might be more favorable than those in the local establishments in a foreign country. (This won't be necessary where currency is on a par with U.S. dollars and both are used commonly, as is the case in the Bahamas.)

PAPERWORK

• Don't forget to tell guests if they need a passport, birth certificate, shots, customs forms for camera gear, or other documents.

• If they're coming on board in a foreign country, explain that they should list themselves as crew to avoid the misinterpretation that they are paying passengers.

CAMERA GEAR

Remind nonboaters that a boat atmosphere is not the best for camera equipment, and it's to their benefit to have a good, shock-resistant, waterproof bag. They may decide to bring only disposables. Whatever their choice, they should bring as much film as they think they'll need. Even when available, film may not be stored under optimum conditions, and in hot climates that can ruin it.

HEALTH CONCERNS

• If you have a pet on board, let your friends know the animal is with you; people with allergies may not be able to stay on board. Try to keep the pet's routine as ordinary as possible, especially if your visitors are strangers to the pet.

• If they're not boaters, warn your guests about the possibility of seasickness. Suggest they not eat a heavy meal the evening before their arrival. Have saltines and pretzels and whatever other favorite preventive you may have on board. (One family went through boxes of ginger snaps in preparation for a cruise. And one quartet of siblings were so worried about being seasick they nearly made themselves sick by overeating the saltines and pretzels. Somewhere there is a happy medium.)

• If your guests want or need to eat something special, tell them to bring it. That way no one has to spend time searching for something that may not be available locally.

• Tell everyone to bring any medications they might need, both prescription and over-the-counter items. If they need refrigeration for their medication, find out if ice is suitable, if that is your onboard cold-keeping system.

• Remind them about sun protection.

BAD HABITS

• If your friends smoke but the boat is generally a no-smoking area, explain that the smoking area is outside the cabin. (Tell them *before* they buy their airline tickets so they have the option of declining your invitation if they perceive the ban to be a problem.) When they arrive, explain further about downwind.

• It's doubtful friends would need to be told about Zero Tolerance (the absolutely no drug regulation), but if someone wants to bring a new acquaintance back to the boat, remind everybody that this could be a lose-the-boat offense. Zero means zero.

SHORE SHOWER

On the let-them-know-ahead-of-time list, explain about marina showers so they'll have a transportable shower kit, which will coincidentally keep bath items neatly confined on board. Stress minimum in the bottle and jar department, and tell them about flip-flops for shower floors.

COMMUNICATION

Not having telephone access is a new experience for today's communication generation. Mention it so the folks back home are not left waiting and worrying.

ARRIVAL

• Your guests may not be as young or agile as your usual crew. Arrange for appropriate boarding helps: a good ladder if anchored; sturdy steps if dockside.

• Put together a guest kit for your friends' arrival: a bottle of sunscreen, so they'll have no excuses (yours will have a higher SPF number than whatever they brought, but they'll think of reasons not to use it anyway); a visor, to shade head, eyes, and nose; eyeglass straps, because they won't have spare glasses.

SHOW AND TELL

If you've shopped for food before your friends arrived, give them a quick menu plan. Show them where the grab-at-will snacks are. Explain what should be saved for planned meals (this will give them some time to think about which dinner they may volunteer to prepare). If you're lucky, you'll have one friend who insists on taking over galley duty full time. Some folks really enjoy it, and you can have a vacation too.

INDOCTRINATION

Without seeming like an alarmist, you should take some time for an indoctrination session. Use of the head is tops on many a list. Carefully explain careful use of water. Take a few minutes with fire extinguishers and flotation jackets, then maybe a practice call on the VHF. The rest can be explained bit by bit. Don't forget to assure them they're going to have a splendid time.

SAFETY CHECK

Make up a permanent list of things everyone on board should know. Show guests the list when they arrive, and leave it handy for referral. Use the following as a starting point, and add as many items as you want.

- The location of PFDs

- Instructions for VHF radio use

- The boat's call sign

- How to use the stove

- How to use the head

- The locations of fire extinguishers, bilge pump switch and/or handle, flares, and first-aid kit; and instructions for their proper use

BEST FOOT BACK

The nonboaters among your guests may think they're helping when they put forward a foot to fend the boat off a dock. Caution them ahead of time that it is difficult to maneuver around a boat if they're on crutches.

SENSITIVITY SEMINAR

Attention captains: be sensitive to guests' concerns about weather. It is not your job to frighten them so they'll never come back. You may see a small weather front as a chance to get an extra push in the right direction; they may see any rain clouds as a danger to stay out of. You may enjoy the roller coaster ride of wavy water; they may discover a cause of seasickness.

LIVING ABOARD

Nonboaters often are embarrassed about using the head. Today's houses have guest bathrooms with each guest bedroom; privacy is the name of the architect's plan. Larger boats can duplicate that with separate cabins, but average boats have a one-for-all situation.

Try to laugh away any unease. If that doesn't work, you might be able to allow everybody some alone time during the day to provide a temporary feeling of privacy.

LOG KEEPERS

Give everybody a personal log when they arrive (small notebooks will do) and encourage them to keep a record of daily happenings and impressions. Compare notes the day before they leave; it is sometimes funny and always fascinating to see how different the logs can be.

TOWEL I.D.

To avoid a laundry bag filled with half-clean towels, assign towels to each person.

- If you have assorted colors, it's easy to keep track of who's blue and who's green.

- If you have many towels the same color, mark them with some identifying symbol on the tag, or on a corner of the towel itself, using indelible marking pen.

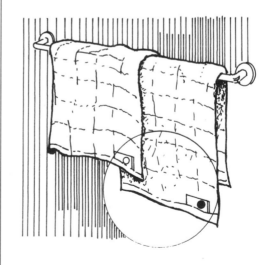

BEDDING I.D.

- If all guests are using the same color sheets to make up bunks each night, label them too, so everyone continues to use the ones they started with. (This is *very* important to some possessive teens.)

• Lightweight sleeping bags are easier to handle and identify than sheets and blankets. Buy or make sheet-weight liners for the bags to keep laundry to a minimum.

(See "Spare Room," Chapter 6, page 66, for a way to store guest bedding.)

SPARE PILLOWS

• If you don't have enough pillows, consider inflatables. You could try making your own with a heavy-duty zip-top bag full of air.

• Even simpler: stuff a pillowcase with bath towels, sweatshirts, or boat sweater (those old favorites that keep you comfy on a night watch). No one will notice wrinkles.

BOAT CAMPING

Visiting children like to sleep out, whether in a tent on the beach or under a tarp in cockpit or at forepeak. Air mattresses have come a long way since backyard Scout rallies. A self-inflating mattress is designed with separate-but-connected air chambers to conform to any body's shape.

LOANERS

• Keep a few lightweight white cotton shirts and some drawstring-waist pajama-type pants on board. When the guests who never burn turn lobster color, you can loan them the sun-bouncing outfits to wear until they heal. No "I-told-you-so" will be necessary. If you have very smart guests, they may borrow the outfit *before* turning red.

• Be prepared to loan sweatshirts and sweatpants, too, when evenings turn cooler than anticipated.

• You probably keep a small supply of hats and visors on board already; add a few pairs of inexpensive sunglasses, including clip-ons. They may not be the best protection, but they'll be better than nothing to temporarily replace forgotten or fallen-in glasses.

• Among the keep-for-guest attire, a child's hat is necessary for sun protection, even for an afternoon cruise. A fabric bonnet takes almost no room to store, and a forgetful mom will be most grateful.

WAKE-UP CALL

Establish a breakfast time beyond which everyone is on his own. If there are late sleepers in the group, give them the bunks farthest from activity centers, but don't try to organize time around their schedule. Politeness has distinct limits on a boat.

HELPERS

• One family welcomes kids and grandkids for week-long visits with one standing rule: "Do the dishes while you're here."

• A good boat rule, with guests or not: whoever cooks does NOT do dishes.

• For the sake of the dishwasher, glasses should be separately identifiable by their own design or color, or by a piece of masking tape with a name written on it.

• Guests often ask "What can I do?" Don't say "nothing." Give them options. Tell them what's available for cooking; you may get a delicious dinner surprise. Demonstrate how you do dishes, then let volunteers do the job. If you have a small boat-fixing project, see if someone else could handle it. Everybody wins.

• Let guests get as involved as they are willing, in boat handling or navigation as well as cooking or boat care.

NEATNIKS

• Some people are natural neatniks; with them, there's no need to explain how important organization is in a small space. For others clutter is a way of life, and no amount of explanation will help. Usually you're aware of these quirks before you invite people; don't expect any miraculous turnabout. Practice not seeing what might upset you, and you'll all have a better time.

• If you'll be spending time at anchor, establish one place on deck for boarding, so unloading of diving gear or shore things will be confined to the same area for easier cleanup.

• Checking shoes or feet after a day on the beach is automatic when you spend time on a boat, but guests don't know about the black beach blobs of oil/tar. If their feet have black polka dots, show them where the kerosene or mineral spirits or paint thinner is stored so dots can be removed before footprints leave dark smudges all over the deck.

• Remind everyone to leave sand on the beach where it belongs. A quick foot dunk before getting into the dinghy will help, and another as you exit should keep sand off the big boat.

SEPARATE SIGHTSEEING

Even families treasure alone time now and then. Depending on the length of the visit, plan some off-the-boat time and perhaps a day of separate activity. You might recommend something on shore that you've already seen and think they'll enjoy. Give them the bikes and wave good-bye.

PRIVACY TIME

Every so often, send the guests forward to sit on the bow for an hour or so. It gives everyone some privacy, plus it gives them a better boating perspective; away from engine noise, they can better appreciate the passing scene.

TOWN TRIPS

If you're anchoring or traveling each day, plan town days for shopping, post office, phone calls, laundry. Divide chores if need be, then meet for lunch or dinner out. This gives your friends a chance to add some favorite snacks or drinks to ship's stores, and it lets everybody satisfy a junk food or ice cream attack.

UNPLANNED TOWN DAY

If the captain must do an engine (or any) repair while friends are visiting, it's best to get everyone off the boat to allow him or her to concentrate on the job and to curse at will.

ALTERNATIVE HOUSING

When the boat's too small for onboard guests, you can still spend vacation time with family or friends. Scout the chosen area well ahead of time so you can find suitable rental options.

SUGGESTION BOX

At the end of a vacation cruise, ask your departing guests to throw ideas into a suggestion box, so next time they (or the next guests) will benefit from their thoughts while the experience is still fresh in mind. Presumably, anyone you invited to the boat is a good friend who will give you good (honest) suggestions.

WHEN YOU'RE THE GUEST

Pitch in for supplies, or bring surprises. Take on cooking chores, or take everyone out. Bring a boat gift, or send a gift certificate from a boater's supply store. Enjoy.

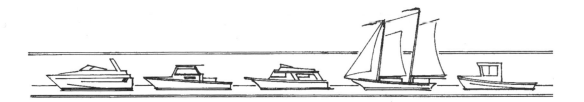

Best Friends

Some pets like boating time. Some tolerate it. And some are made miserable by it.

When you are weekending or vacationing, it's possible, if not easy, to leave your pets with a trusted caretaker. But long-term cruising forces you to make some decisions. How will you manage with a pet on board? How will the pet adapt to being on board? What's fair?

The first two are answered by a two-week vacation. The third question is tough. Pets may not be part of a master boat plan, but if they're part of the family before boating, they'll probably want to stay. A lot of apparently happy animals live on boats.

PET PACK

Pets can't pack their own duffels, so don't forget extra flea collars, comb and brush, skin conditioner, dry shampoo, wet shampoo, nail polish, and an assortment of colored ribbons for the pooches' after-bath time.

STRESS MANAGEMENT

Older animals are less adaptable to change, more prone to anxiety about new places. To help pets adjust to boat life, bring along bed, blanket, toys, anything familiar. Immediately establish "pet's room" inside.

A PLACE IN THE SUN

Set up an outside place for the pets, where they can sit and survey, and where they'll be safe when the water's rough and they rightly choose not to stay inside. "The place" might be a basket, a blanket, or just a platform kept clear for pet occupation.

FEEDING STATION

Regardless of the boat's size, wherever you put your pet's dishes will be the wrong place; passing feet will find them every time.

• Carefully choose a "best" place—convenience is less important than traffic flow. Build a two-dish-size shelf a couple of inches above the sole (so toes can't kick the dishes) and put a low fid around the edge (so pets can't knock dishes off).

• If a built-in feeding station is not practical, buy or make a suitable-size tray with an anti-spill lip. Though portable, it too could be raised off the floor by adding wood crosspieces to the bottom. You can feed the animal inside or out.

PET-ICURE

• Buy specially made nail-clippers for animals. The dog won't be going to regular wash-and-clip appointments, and if any pet's nails get too long, its feet can suffer.

• If you must cut nails with manicure scissors, turn them so they curve away from the foot. When clipping, be careful to avoid the tender inner claw that you may see as a thin pink line. If you can't distinguish the color change, cut only to the place where the claw starts to curl down. Or just clip the sharp end, and do it more often.

HAIR CARE

Regular brushing is most important in the confined space of a boat interior, to help keep the fuzz problem under control.

FAT ATTACKS

You may need to watch your pet's weight. On board, a dog may not get the same amount of exercise as he did in a backyard run. Adjust feeding accordingly, and then try to explain to your favorite loyal companion that hunger is for his own good.

Cats tend to sleep most of the time, no matter where they live, so a weight change is not likely.

CARRY ALTERNATIVES

A pet carrier is a practical item, but for the few times you need one, it takes up too much space.

• To make a substitute carrier (assuming you're not planning to carry a Saint Bernard), empty out two of the plastic storage crates you already have in your locker. Line the bottom of one with newspaper, rags, or a pet blanket. Put the animal inside; invert the second crate over the top and tie the two together. (You may need to add a line across the side with the cutaway openings, especially if you're carrying a cat.) Most animals are relatively content with this arrangement; they can see out every side, and you can reach in with a reassuring pat on the head.

• A second alternative, for cats and possibly small dogs, is to put the animal into a mesh bag. The cat is less fearful than if confined in a dark box, and the owner is less fearful of flailing feet and claws.

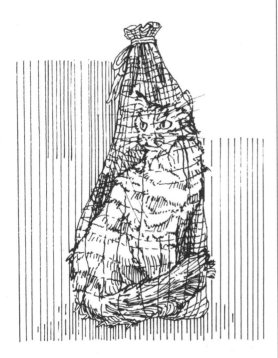

• Kittens can be taught to travel in a canvas duffel bag, at least for a few hours at a time. Enough light and air filters through the fabric to keep them comfortable. Later, the grown cat is familiar with bag travel and crawls in without a fuss.

• You can buy a shoulder-strap bag made specially to tote a pet. Made of nylon and sturdy webbing, Le Pet Bag lets dog or cat ride while keeping a lookout on where it's going or where it's been.

DOUBLE DUTY

One manufacturer has designed a carrier that doubles as a bed. The Pet Taxi is made in two sections, top and bottom. When put together, it looks just like an ordinary pet carrier. When you take it apart, invert the top section and it nests inside the bottom half. Add a pillow, and the pet has a bed.

TRAVELING PAPERS

• A health certificate signed by a veterinarian is usually required to take a pet into another country. However, some countries won't allow them entry at all, regardless of paperwork.

• Regulations exist for interstate transporting of pets, too, but these are not enforced on a check-in basis. Once a year, have all shots updated and get a health certificate, for the pet's protection and yours.

• "Traveling with Your Pet" is a booklet listing regulations for interstate and international travel. (If you are planning a trip to another country, make sure the information is current.) For information write to:

ASPCA Education Department
424 East 92nd Street
New York, NY 10128

HEALTH HELPS

• Ask your veterinarian to recommend a good pet care book. You'll need to practice more pet first aid than you would if a doctor were close by. Be prepared with whatever medications your pet might need, and recognize the signs so you'll know when to give pills, especially if the animal has a recurring health problem.

- If the animal is prone to motion sickness or easily upset by bad weather, talk to the veterinarian about tranquilizers. Experiment with their use before your cruise, to see how the pet reacts. Some pets respond well; others—particularly cats—panic when they realize they can't function normally. It may be that the dosage needs to be adjusted, rather than changing the tranquilizing agent; that's why it's important to test while professional advice is near. You wouldn't want to give a pet medication that made its symptoms worse.

- If a cat has an injury that shouldn't be irritated by licking, make an Elizabethan collar for the cat. Cut a circle of posterboard about 12 inches in diameter. Cut one slit to the center, and cut a center hole a bit larger than the cat's neck. Slip the collar on, and tape the slit closed after overlapping the outer edges a bit. The collar should tilt forward, like a very broad funnel, preventing the cat from turning around and reaching the injury.

POISON PREVENTION

Don't let your pet wander around marinas. Rat poison is a problem you don't want to deal with, but there is a good chance a wandering pet will find some. Not all boatowners are considerate of stray pets.

HEALTH RECORDS

Ask the veterinarian for a printout of your pet's health records. If the pet shows signs of illness while you're traveling, the new doctor will have a professional background report from which to start diagnosis.

FLEA PATROL

Flea control doesn't change much from house to boat, except you can forget about spraying the yard.

- Fleas seem a worse problem in the South: there are more of them, and the animals suffer more. If you have carpeting, keep it vacuumed more than it would seem to need. Wash and disinfect the wood cabin sole. Set off a fogger occasionally.

- On the pet, use dips, sprays, collars, and combs—*not* in combination, but whichever you've had some success with before. All help keep the problem under control, though total elimination is a dream.

- A few mothballs in the vacuum cleaner bag should dispatch those fleas you've collected.

- Boaters have one flea remedy not readily available to house people: if you're cruising in salt water, you have the world's largest flea dip at your transom.

- Other natural flea deterrents, like brewer's yeast and garlic, have been touted for years, and some pet owners are convinced they help. Finicky eaters can find the stuff no matter how well you think you've disguised it within their usual smelly mashed herring in shrimp sauce favorite, but it's worth a try.

- Try rubbing the garlic or the yeast powder on the animal's coat. The odor doesn't linger. They say.

- Fleas don't like cedar, so include some shavings in the pet's bed. (Sew them into a cloth sack or mattress pad.)

- When you buy a flea collar, take it out of the foil wrap package and stretch it to activate its chemicals. Then let it sit out for a week or so before putting it on the animal. Cats are especially sensitive to the smell; if you put the collar on straight out of the box, you may have a yowling, whirling furball to deal with. When claws start skidding around the deck, the loudest yowl may be prefaced by a splash.

PET FLOTATION DEVICES

If your wee beastie is a klutz around the boat, get a PFD and hope you can encourage the animal to wear it happily. (Boots and sport shoes exist, but so far, no deck shoes.)

PET OVERBOARD

Plan for possible pet-overboards.

• At anchor or dockside, hang a section of carpeting off the boat so an animal will have something to grab and climb. A few heavy lines might also help. Floating cushions have been suggested, but it's hard to imagine an animal being able to climb onto a relatively tippy moving surface.

• Keep a long-handled crab net within grabbing distance on deck. Change the netting as often as needed, so it will *hold* the animal if you use it to scoop up an overboard pet. (Cotton netting mildews; polypropylene "melts" in the sun.)

LOST AND FOUND

Losing a pet while traveling may well be an owner's worst nightmare.

• "Finding" information can be imprinted on a tag attached to the pet's collar, or it can be written directly on a fabric collar or a white flea collar. The boat name is probably the most practical information, and possibly the phone number of a back-home person you contact regularly.

• Keep a few photos of your pet on board. If the animal does get lost, a search party will know exactly who to look for.

EASY RIDERS

Small dogs are like stuffed toys, except that instead of decorating the bed, they follow you everywhere. On shore trips, they ride in the handle-bar basket of the bike—in figurehead pose. Another option is riding in a backpack strapped to master's back, guarding the rear.

ANTIBARK

You won't win friends in marina or anchorage if your dog barks from the time

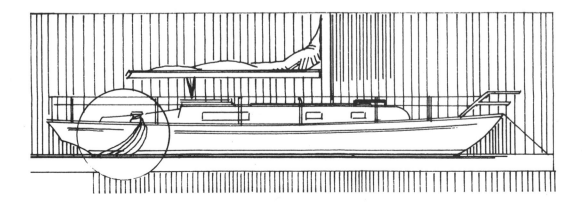

you leave the boat until the time you return. Some dogs do not comprehend "quiet." Try the old leave-the-radio-on trick. Sometimes it works, fooling the dog into thinking someone is home. Or take the dog to a pet behavioral psychologist for an in-depth analysis of pesty loud-mouth barking syndrome.

BATHTIME

• After a good rain, the dinghy will be filled with lots of nice soft rainwater. Don't bail. Bathe the dog instead. This time, it may be welcomed, to get rid of a salt accumulation. (Fortunately, most dogs tolerate saltwater soakings fairly well; only a few sensitive types develop skin problems.)

• You might keep a couple of collapsible bottles just for storing rainwater for the dog's baths.

• Bathe the dog on shore or on the back deck, wherever rinsing (and subsequent shaking) will be least bothersome. One young man managed to train a black lab not to shake after coming out of the water; the owner preferred to towel the dog dry. The lab could shiver (with anticipation and/or perhaps longing), but he would not shake.

• When you can't give Benji or Beethoven a real bath, try a quick coat cleaning with waterless shampoo or grooming powder. Or sprinkle on some baking soda, and brush.

EARLY EXERCISE

If you're cruising when temperatures are in the high 80s, exercise your pets in the cooler hours of the day—early morning is best.

CANINE SWIMMERS

• Put a luggage handle on the dog's harness. When it's exercise time, let the dog swim around the boat for a while; then *you* do the retrieving by hauling your pet up with a boathook or a halyard hooked into the handle.

• Some people train their dogs to jump over the side and take themselves to shore. Others do the opposite, and teach the dogs *not* to jump unless directed to do so. It's too hard to see a black dog in the water at night.

BEACH WALKS

• When you take animals walking on the beach, try to go at low tide; the wet sand won't harbor any fleas.

• If your pup gets into a to-do with another dog on shore, throw some water on the combatants. Or a loud noise will sometimes startle the dogs enough to separate them.

TICK ATTACK

Depending on the territory, after shore romps, check for common dog ticks. To remove, use rubbing alcohol (gin, and presumably other drinking varieties, will do in an emergency) to force the tick to loosen its grip; then, with tweezers, pull the tick straight out. (See Chapter 21 for information on Lyme disease, which is usually carried and spread by the tiny tick associated with deer.)

DOG WALK

If you do a lot of marina hopping, make up a discreet but complete dog-walk kit. Put a deluxe Pooper Scooper (encased in its own plastic carrying bag), a few empty plastic bags, and some paper towels in a handled bucket (a child's beach toy is a good size) or a small canvas tote bag (perhaps plastic-lined.) Find a discreet spot in the boat to hang the bag or wedge the bucket.

WALK ALTERNATIVES

• Some small dogs can be trained to use litter or shredded newspaper, just like cats. One Yorkie is content to use the classified section of the newspaper, which can be left inconspicuously on the head floor and changed as necessary.

• Teach the dog to use a doormat made of plastic grass. Attach a line to one end of the mat, and throw it over the side to clean it. (Assuming you're outside the 3-mile limit.)

• Train a dog to use a flemished line when you can't get to shore. Tie one end of the line to the boat; when the dog is through using it, toss the line over and let it slosh around in the water until it's clean.

(The problem with this suggestion is explaining to the dog that all flemished lines do not serve the same purpose.)

• One clever basset hound trained himself to literally "go" overboard, apparently assuming the ocean was his private litter pond.

NO-NOS

Discipline doesn't go on vacation. If your favorite friend develops a behavior problem, try the easiest deterrent; a spritz from a child's toy water pistol or a spray bottle.

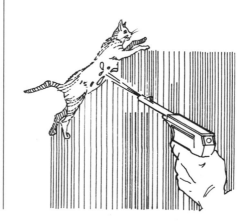

CATS: BEST BOAT PET

• If you can choose a boat pet, choose a cat. They're easy to care for, they're good footwarmers, and sometimes they take responsibility for ridding the boat of uninvited varmints. No guarantees, of course; it depends on their mood.

• Cats like to hide in cozy places where they feel safe. In a house, they go into closets and under furniture. On a boat, they find places you haven't. Make a discoverable spot in cockpit or wheelhouse where the cat can sit watch. They like to be behind a windshield or port, where they get sun without a strong breeze.

• Cats find their own safe places. An empty binocular case or a camera bag is a good cat-size retreat. The chart book's protective cover becomes feline foul-weather gear. (Cats can't read cautions about plastic bags.)

Furball Preventer

• A consistent brushing schedule takes loose hair off the cat, lessening the unpleasant surprises of furballs. No fur in, no fur out.

• Give the cat some vegetable oil or bacon fat or a liquid vitamin supplement to keep its coat shiny and perhaps prevent furballs.

Cat Toys

• A small single sock is the start of a good cat toy. Fill the toe section with catnip or plain foam rubber, just for the bulk. Tie the sock shut and toss it to the cat. (They like something their claws can catch, but not necessarily sink into.)

• Other high-tech toys: rolled up ball of aluminum foil, empty thread spool, twist tie, plastic ring from milk bottle. Despite a reputation for insufferable independence, cats are sometimes very easy to please.

Cat Cautions

• Do *not* give cats string, yarn, thread, rubber bands. The image of lovable kittens romping playfully with a rapidly unwinding ball of yarn is nonsense; cats will try to swallow the yarn. And swallow. And swallow. And swallow.

• Cats like to eat grass; if they can't find any, they'll try plants. Some are poisonous, so if you keep plants on the boat, ask the vet which ones are toxic. (English ivy is one.) One solution is to grow a pot of rye grass just for the cat.

• Don't let the cat go wandering on shore wearing a collar unless it's elasticized. Cats are not completely bright about poking their noses into small places, and could easily get caught by a nonflexing collar.

Cat-Scratch Fervor

Advertising claims aside, cats choose to ignore manufactured scratching posts. They like carpeting well enough—just watch them attack textured wall-to-wall—but most posts are not stable enough; one wobble, and the cat's gone. Often, there's not much room for one in a boat anyway.

• If the aesthetics don't bother you, nail a 2-foot piece of a pine 2 × 4 to a bulkhead. Or put a similar length of 2 × 4 or 4 × 4 flat on deck, so the cat can stand on it while clawing.

• Cardboard offers another possibility. Roll up some corrugated cardboard into the general shape of a plank of wood. Tape the back or underside so it doesn't unroll. The cat will also stand on this while shredding it. Replace as needed.

• Wrap sisal around a stand-on plank.

• One of the better-designed scratching modules is a modified pyramid shape. Rough sisal is wrapped round the triangular post; its exaggerated taper improves stability and scratchability.

LITTER BOX LESSONS

• Even when cats start out to use a litter pan, they don't always hit their mark (meaning the litter inside the pan). Sometimes they abandon the favored squat position and stand straight up, sending a liquid stream well beyond the boundary of acceptability. Both male and female cats can accomplish this trick, much to the chagrin of the cleanup crew. Though a covered litter box may look large and awkward in a small space, it solves this nasty problem. Be sure the cover is molded in such a way that the bottom edge curves over and inside the top rim of the pan; the stray liquid will drain into the pan, not be redirected to the floor outside.

• If you prefer to keep an uncovered pan, make a three-sided "folding screen" of a waterproof material such as a lightweight acrylic. Use plastic tape to connect the three panels. Place the screen inside the box, so drips will also stay inside. And hope the cat remembers to turn around and face front when using the box.

• Be sure an open litter pan is held firmly in place. Use hooks, framework, latches, whatever it takes. Otherwise, in a heavy sea or at a steep heel, the box could tip over when in use, and you definitely don't want a cat to be frightened away from its box.

• You wouldn't want to be out in the kind of weather that could threaten to tip over the covered box.

Consumer Information

• If you always buy a generic or store brand of plain, white, unscented clay litter—which is widely available—you'll never have the problem of a cat not liking and refusing to use a new type of litter.

• How much litter does your cat use in a month's time? Keep track, so you'll know how much to stow for an extended trip.

Clumping Litter

Clumping litter was introduced as an innovation for cat care; you remove only the used litter, which clumps together from dampness, rather than changing the whole box. While there are probably levels of clumpability, ordinary litter always did stick to itself when wet. Because it was a precarious "stick," you couldn't remove litter from the box using the traditional slotted litter scoop sold at pet stores. But a solid spoon worked fine. Buy a large plastic mixing/serving spoon from a housewares store, and dedicate it to the job.

Litter Stowage

To pack litter for an extended trip, buy the 25-pound bags for their dollar savings, then repack into three or four sacks. The size depends on your allotted space. If you save the original litter bags for a few months, you'll have as many as you need for repacking. Cut away the top half of the bags so you're not packing excess paper.

Once the litter is divided, tape the bags shut and put each one into the heaviest plastic bags you have. (Save these from hardware, housewares, or boat supply stores.) Try to stow the sacks where they are least likely to come into contact with sharp edges.

Litter Substitute

If you pick up beach sand to use for cat litter, you'll have to heat it in the oven to kill fleas. Fleas shouldn't be a problem if you scoop up *wet* sand instead of dry. Bring the wet sand on board, and let it dry out on deck.

Cat Box Motto

Keep it clean, clean, clean.

Litterless Box

Train your cat to use a box with no litter. Set up a system similar to the dog display cages in pet shops, where a metal grid raises the animal off the bottom of the cage, leaving space for the collection and cleanup of doggy mess.

First, put some litter in the box so the cat makes the proper association. Gradually reduce the amount of litter, eventually placing the grid on top of the box. Being a creature of habit and instinctive neatness, the cat will come to the box, whether or not the litter is reachable. Finally, remove all the litter.

Drill a hole near the top of one end of the box; tie a line to it, and douse the box in the water for a quick rinse.

Litter Access

If you keep the litter box in the head, consider installing a pet door in the bottom of the head door, so the cat is always assured access.

You could also use a long hook-and-eye near the top of the door, to hold the door open.

BIRDS

Bird Talk

Though it's harder to relate to birds than to fluffy kittens or playful puppies, birds will thrive on attention (and get depressed without it). Give them toys, and talk to them a lot. They'll repay you with a cheerful chatter to add to the background of boat noise.

Tweety Surprise

Recognizing the gender of birds is a challenge to experts and amateurs alike. If you thought you bought a male bird, don't be too surprised if eggs appear in the cage. (Have a good reference book for your bird's species, so you can refer to the chapter on egg-dropping.)

Bird Escape

If your bird escapes its cage inside the boat, watch it and wait for it to land. The bird is probably as surprised as you about its newfound freedom. Take advantage of this confusion, and try to cover it with a very lightweight cloth. If you're successful, pick up the bird very carefully—they're fragile—and return it to the cage.

Bird Bedroom

Birds are very sensitive to drafts. Covering the cage for protection is standard; giving the bird a separate "bedroom" off the main cage is a custom idea. The addition is just a small box tacked onto the side of a cockatiel's cage. With three sides solid wood, there are no drafts and very little light, making a true hideaway for one lucky bird.

Fume Detector

Birds are also very sensitive to fumes of all kinds. (Remember the canary-in-the-coal mine stories?) If you have any small birds on board, be careful not to leave empty nonstick pans over a stove flame; they could create fumes toxic to ultrasensitive birds.

WATER RATS

Gerbils, hamsters, guinea pigs, and ordinary mice may seem odd as boat pets, but like the others, if you owned them BB (before boat) they're yours for their duration.

• If children are on board, any pet is a good teaching tool. Small rodents are generally undemanding and often entertaining. Even adults can use the smiles that come with watching the little critters play on their in-house roller coasters, spending happy hours running around in circles.

• Any rodent needs to chew; one tiny gerbil can demolish the cardboard from a paper towel roll in an amazingly short time. Too much glue is probably not a great dietary supplement, so give them chewy sticks or vegetable treats instead.

• Get a plastic wheel "run" toy for the pet. Even if he doesn't like to play in it, it's a good place to keep him while you clean the cage. Or park him in the bathtub; he probably can't run up the slick sides.

• If the gerbil gets out of the wheel, plant some favorite food to coax the escapee into a box turned sideways, then zap on a cover as you flip the box right side up.

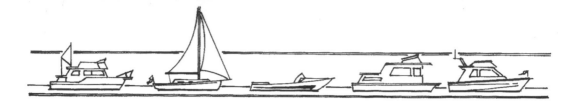

24 Worst Enemies

Nobody thinks cockroach babies are cute. There is no overwhelming effort to save the rat. Fish and dragonflies might miss mosquitoes, but people certainly would not. And even though ants may someday inherit the earth, it doesn't have to be soon.

Pests hide on board and attack on shore. Fortunately, rights activists have yet to make a stand in their favor. As long as they keep buzzing, biting, chewing, crawling, and transporting germs, we'll keep spraying, dusting, fogging, trapping, and chasing them away.

MORE THAN YOU WANT TO KNOW ABOUT COCKROACHES

Boric acid powder is the old reliable roach killer.

• Put it in small containers (like bottle caps) in all back-corner places where roaches might run or hide. You'll know where they've been by the telltale brown spots described as roach dirt by polite persons.

• To make it more inviting, mix the powder with some sugar and sprinkle it around. Or mix boric acid with water and a bit of honey or molasses and paint the goo wherever you want it. (Luckily, boric acid is also a weapon against ants, because the sweet mixes that might attract roaches would certainly draw ants.)

• A wise manufacturer provides boric acid in tablet form, just for roach-killing purposes, making it much neater to scatter about. Look for Harris Roach Tablets in the bug-spray section of the supermarket.

Petrified Roaches

A reportedly foolproof roach-getter is a mix of cornstarch and a quick-setting plaster (about equal parts). In theory, the bugs turn to stone once they ingest this irresistible treat. All that's left to do is to sweep up a bunch of roach rocks.

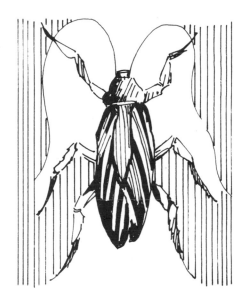

Roach Traps

• The easiest roach trap is a soda can with a tempting bit of soda left inside. You can't see them too readily, but you'll hear them. A glass jar, preferably one with a narrow taper at the top, gets the same results. Bugs jump in after the food and cannot climb out the slippery sides.

• Many boatowners have good luck keeping roaches controlled with Combat roach traps. Place the neat plastic traps wherever roaches hide, and replace the traps every few months.

• Besides poison placement, take the precautions of not bringing corrugated cardboard boxes or brown paper bags on board; both are favorite hideouts for roach egg cases. When stowing food items, repackage the dry foods; put them in plastic containers, or at least remove inner bags from cardboard boxes and repackage into doubled zip-top bags. (Roaches love the glue on those outer cardboard boxes.)

• Despite the roach risk, some people keep brown bags or corrugated boxes. Assuming you're not keeping them for food storage, spray bag or box interior with roach spray, and/or leave a few roach tablets in the bottom.

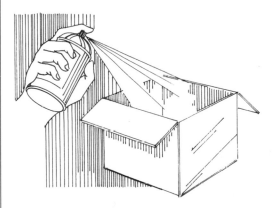

• When scattering your favorite poison, don't skip the bookshelves; the glue used in book binding, and sometimes the sizing in hardcovers, must be like candy to roach babies.

Flying Insect Fighter

• It may come as an unpleasant surprise to learn that roaches can fly, so all the bag and box precautions will not guarantee a bug-free environment. For those occasions when a flutter of brown whooshes in through an open port or hatch, antiroach spray is a boon. A quick spritz (or four or five) has a better chance of actually killing the intruder than a shaky fly swatter in the hands of a screaming attacker.

• Ditto for flying (stinging) insect spray. But try to keep track of each place you spritz, so you can clean it up after getting your bug. (Most important with children or pets on board.)

ANTS

Many kinds of ants find their way onto boats, and they don't all respond to ant traps in exactly the way advertisers would suggest.

Ant Trails

• If a succession of baited traps fails to encourage their exit, try to trace their travel routes and pour some vinegar along the trails. This will confuse them, at least temporarily, and may force them to find new territory. You can pour boric acid powder on an ant trail too. Or borax, oil of clove, or cream of tartar.

• If you're dockside for any length of time in an ant-hardy environment, spray docklines periodically with ant poison spray to discourage their parades.

• Be careful what you use on deck, dock, or lines. Many bug sprays are also toxic to fish. Also be careful of wandering pets.

Ant Nests

The large half-red variety is the carpenter ant. These do not demolish wood to the same extent that termites can, but you don't want to see them. They make nests in damp wood, and damp wood means rotting wood. Piles of sawdust may help you locate the ant nest; dust the area with boric acid powder, then try to find and replace the wet wood.

Ant Colony

Big ants sometimes take up residence in the head plumbing while the boat is in storage. This is the easiest problem to get rid of; normal use of the plumbing mechanism proves too great a deterrent for even the most determined ant colony.

In theory, ant baits work better than spraying a line of ants. It is hoped the hiking ants will take poison back to the nest, thereby dispatching all the ants, not just the walkers. This seems to work for fire ants in the yard, but indoor ants are less predictable.

WEEVILS

Certain foods often hide weevils. Even if they're not visible when you open the package, their eggs may be there, in which case, in a few weeks, you'll find little weevils happily munching holes in the pasta or swimming through drifts of flour or cornmeal.

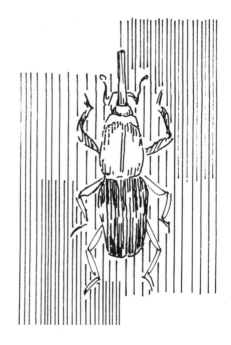

- Keep all dry food in separate canisters so bugs cannot travel from one to another.

- A house solution is to put food into the freezer for a week to kill invisible weevils. More practical on most boats: put bay leaves in the containers of flour, oatmeal, cornmeal, and other dry foods.

- If you did not store things separately in plastic containers, you may have a more far-reaching problem than one box of pasta. The bugs may have taken up permanent residence in the entire locker, moving from one open box to the next, as taste buds dictate. (Wheat flour seems more susceptible to weevils than white, but nothing is immune.)

- To get rid of weevils in the locker, take everything out and dump whatever is obviously infested. If food looks okay, do the freezer treatment, or put it in the oven for half an hour at 175°F to kill any remaining eggs. Scrub the locker, spray with an appropriate poison (or fog the whole boat), and start over with everything in airtight, bug-tight containers.

SPICE LOVERS

Check spices very carefully from time to time. Tiny specks may be burrowing through the chili powder, paprika, vegetable bouillon, and anything else that looks appetizing.

MOSQUITO CONTROL

- Ordinary screens are effective against the little buzzers, if all holes and gaps are properly plugged.

- Smoke from a mosquito coil deters them, as does citronella, which is easier on the crew.

- Mosquito coils now burn in their own round, flat metal can. The top is punctured to allow smoke to escape and do its job. Messy ashes are confined until you choose to empty them; no more grinding into cockpit or cabin sole.

- In Florida, you can buy hats with all-around mosquito-screened veils. Not much of a fashion statement, but if you ever got caught in the Everglades, particularly in "their" season, you wouldn't care diddly how you looked.

NO-SEE-UM STOP-EM

- You'll need a special fine mesh screen to keep out no-see-ums, the nasty gnats that literally hang in the still air of a Chesapeake or Carolina summer. Unfortunately, you do feel 'em when they dig into your scalp and hide in your ears and drive you bonkers. Look for the screening in army/navy surplus stores, or call Sailrite Kits: 800-348-2769.

- The best repellent (a coincidental side effect) is Avon's Skin So Soft moisturizer.

FLY CONTROL

- Fly swatters help get rid of aggression, even if you miss the fly. Fly paper is still available and still does its job, if you can stand the buzzing.

- If you have the misfortune of meeting a bunch of large greenhead flies, you'll think seriously about screening in the entire cockpit or bridge deck. Sprays help the fly problem temporarily, but they do not help the fabric or fiberglass surfaces that catch the overspray.

- To keep off the nasty blackflies of Canada and the border states, use Muskol

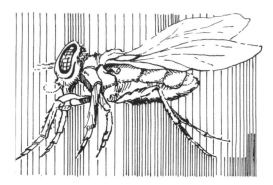

(but keep it off your varnish.) Blackflies are much smaller than the common housefly, but what they lack in size, they more than compensate for in ferocity. They are mean and pesty.

• An entomologist from New Hampshire is trying to eradicate the blackfly population of the northeastern U.S. If you're in an area where he's not yet been, wear long sleeves, long pants, and high socks, and cover yourself with repellent.

WASPS

Wasps and mud daubers sneak into the tiniest cracks to find nesting sites. Every week, shake out sails and folded canvas dodgers and biminis to stop them before their nests grow into condos. Check under locker lids, behind drawers, inside air horns.

GNAT TRAPS

Put some gnat bait (fruit peelings) into a small glass, then wrap plastic wrap around the top. (A rubber band can hold it on if you're not using superstick wrap.) Poke a small hole in the plastic. With the sweet food to direct them, the resourceful gnats will find their way in, but the exit route escapes them. (A task force will study the viability of this for no-see-ums.)

SPIDERS AND FRIENDS

• Spiders can't hang around without a web, so daily sweeping usually takes care of them. On the other hand, consider keeping a few around for bug control. Spiders not only like flies, some of them are aggressive cockroach catchers.

• If you're cruising in the southland, you can also adopt another natural predator in the form of a particularly enthusiastic miniature lizard called a gecko. This won't work if you have a cat on board. You'll start your own private food chain.

SHORE EXCURSIONS

If you're trying to have a shore lunch and some flying pests want to join you, set something sweet on a paper plate off to one side and try to convince them to go to their place setting, not yours.

BUG STORAGE

When leaving the boat for any length of time in a southern climate, leave it with a bug bomb or two. Repeat the process when you rejoin the boat, *before* you unpack. This should give you a good, clean start for the cruising season.

MOUSE CONTROL

• Rodents are discouraged naturally by the presence of a cat or dog. (This is not guaranteed.)

• If you see evidence of a mouse invasion, use peanut butter to lure them to traps. If you don't have any traps, put the peanut butter on a piece of cardboard, then put the cardboard in a plastic bag. When you hear the plastic crinkle, grab the bag, spin it closed, and relocate the mouse.

RODENT CATCHER

Fill a pail about ¾ full with water. Put some food into a small saucer, and float the dish on top of the water. The animal is attracted to the food, reaches for it, and falls into the pail and drowns.

BIRD CHASER

The scare-owl was designed to keep birds and their droppings away from boat or dock. Now you can also discourage birds and rodents with a phony falcon, a fake snake, or a counterfeit cat. The birds are fooled only for a short time; then you are left with a piece of dock sculpture of questionable merit. Better to adopt a New Englander's philosophical attitude: If a bird makes your boat his target, consider it good luck. We don't know the reasoning behind this; perhaps it has something to do with bluebirds.

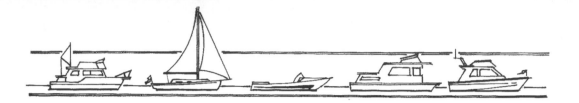

For Sailors

Besides providing the much preferred form of propulsion, all that rigging gives sailors more things to clean and polish and grease and check and replace. Sailors can read a whole other section of boating catalogs and browse in a whole different area of boating supply stores, searching for bits of hardware or pieces of line. They can ponder the virtues of one cleat over another, question the strength of a new composite, and study the results of a metal stress test. Sailors can come up with more ways to accomplish the same task than would seem possible, and most of them work.

All of which is their way of showing they like to take care of their boats.

SHORTEN MAST

As much as sailors like to sail, there are times when they'd like to have a shorter mast. Nonopening bridges block a lot of cruising areas that are put into one's memory bank as a someday thing. A tabernacle could shift that plan back to the present.

• The simplest arrangement tips the mast forward. The mast sits on its plate, held in place by the hinge pin. When you want to dip the mast, undo the backstay and the upper and aft lower shrouds. Snug the boom with a vang to keep it as centered as possible. The boom will be your lever, the mainsheet your control line. If you have running backstays, good; you'll have extra control of sideways motion.

When you're ready, slack off the mainsheet and backstays a bit; push or pull the mast to get it started; then, as it lowers, control the speed with the mainsheet and backstays. It's not necessary to lower it completely, just enough to clear the bridge. Once you're through, pull everything back and the mast pops up straight.

• To lower the mast completely and to prevent side shifting would require additional fittings on the shrouds at the height of the mast step.

RATLINES

Make ratlines so you can climb to the spreaders. Measure the width between lower shrouds at the top (just under spreader) and bottom (at deck level). Determine how many steps you want leading up, then lay out a pattern, using your two width measurements and the height of mast to spreaders.

Cut the steps to correct widths, using 1 × 2 pressure-treated pine. Put a notch or groove into both ends of each step so shroud cable can fit into the groove.

Using ⅜-inch low-stretch line, tie the steps into a portable A-frame shape that you will raise and tie under the spreaders. Knots placed over and under each step hold steps in place; the whole assembly remains independent of shrouds, even though it fits snugly between the lowers.

With the steps attached to a separate line, no hardware needs to be put onto the shrouds, so the wire stays intact.

MAST STEPS

Mast steps are a favorite of midsize children. They like to climb the mast; they like to be the lookout. And they're probably best suited for the job, because their eyesight is so much better.

SAIL STOP

When lowering the main, grasp the halyard where it attaches to the sail; bring it down and wrap it once around the winch

so the main can't ride back up the mast with a good wind puff, and you have both hands free to start furling.

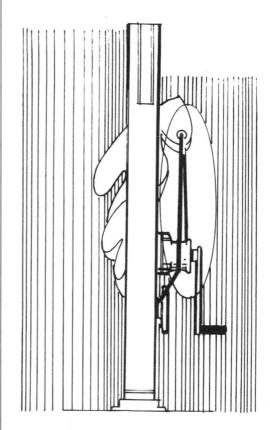

CHAFE GUARD

• Put a double thickness of sailcloth at potential chafe places (where sail touches spreaders or bow pulpit).

• If you have room to raise the tack away from the pulpit, you'll avoid the chafing problem. Add a tack line between sail tack and bow fitting.

SAIL SAVER

Luffing is really bad for your sail.

SAIL REPAIR

Keep the sail repair kit intact so you're able to fix a ripped or blown-out sail if you're not close to a sail loft. Too often, the kit has been filed for so long that the thread is coated with mold, the needles are rusted, and the leather palm is crumbling with age and water damage.

• A sailor's palm is more than a salty-looking bit of nautical trivia. Just try stitching sailcloth without it. Replace yours if need be so you're sure to have a usable palm on board.

• Watch the stitching on all sails and canvas. If you catch a break early, you may prevent a ripped-out seam.

• Hand-sew a temporary seam repair by using the sewing machine holes already in the fabric.

• To repair small rips in the fabric itself, use herringbone stitching to connect the fabric's torn edges. Sewing perpendicular to the rip, alternate long and short stitches, so the thread goes through different parts of the weave. Each stitch should interlock with the last.

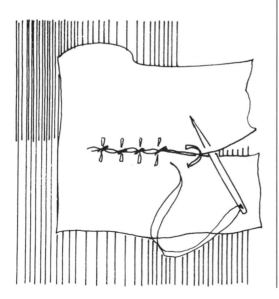

• If you're able to sew-it-yourself, check Sailrite Kits when you're ready for new sails, or cover, or dodger, or assorted bags. Call for a catalog: 800-348-2769.

FURL SAVER

Roll out your furling headsail once a week, even if the boat's sitting at a dock or at anchor, so the bearings in the furling drum don't freeze up. This is the only maintenance possible on furling units that are completely closed.

With furling drums that are not totally encapsulated, give them a good freshwater rinsing every couple of weeks.

SAILBAGS

To save more interior storage space for liveaboard use, buy or have made zipper-opening boat-acrylic sail storage bags. Sails can stow on the foredeck, protected from excess UV, but ready to hoist.

SHEET BAGS

Make two canvas bags to hold coiled jib-sheets. Tie the bags to pulpit or lifelines. When you're dockside or anchored awhile, sheets are out of the sun and out of the way, neatly bagged on deck.

SHEET SAVER

To get maximum use from the line you use for jibsheets, turn each sheet end-for-end halfway through each season.

SAIL CLEANER

Small sails can be machine-washed on a gentle cycle. Spread large sails on a clean, flat surface and scrub spots with a soft brush and mild detergent. Hose them down well to rid them of soap or salt residue. Mildew doesn't eat synthetics like it does cotton, but it will stain. Scrub with bleach or a stain-removing product made for synthetic fabrics.

PROTECTORS

• Cover the compass if it's exposed to excess sunlight. A small, inverted plastic bucket will protect it from light as well as bumps and scratches, especially when you're working on something close by. A custom-made boat-acrylic cover will look neater.

• Make matching fabric covers for sheet winches too, to keep chrome shiny and discourage saltwater corrosion.

BOOM GALLOWS

Custom fit a boom gallows. When measuring for proper height, be sure the boom will clear the gallows when you tack, even when sail is reefed.

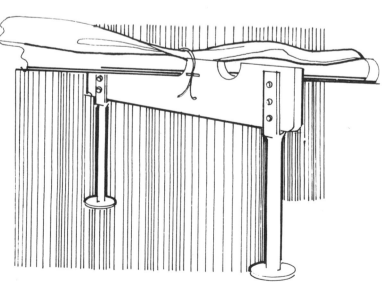

For side supports, have stainless steel stanchions made, and weld elongated U-shaped fittings at the top. Stanchion bases may need to be tilted so they'll match the curve of the cabintop when stanchions are vertical.

Use a substantial teak plank for the gallows, sized to accommodate your boom. Cut circular dips in three places so the boom can rest centered or off to either side. Set the teak into the U-shaped fittings, and through-bolt.

Besides providing a solid platform for the boom, the gallows is a sturdy hand-hold and often finds secondary use as a place to tie an awning or hang a bell. (If the boom is painted, pad each slot with leather to prevent scratching.)

NOISE PREVENTION

Prevent the clacking noise that in-mast wiring makes as the boat bobs at anchor. Cover the wiring with foam-rubber pipe insulation. Use enough to cover the complete length, or tape sections at regular intervals. Or tape on pieces of sponge rubber every 2 feet (the pieces should be wide enough to touch the sides of the mast). When you pull the wires up, all will fit snugly, precluding any shifting.

SAFETY CHECKS

• Check chainplates occasionally; look for signs of rust or corrosion on plates and hardware.

• Use a magnifying glass to check

swages on shrouds. Ask a rigger about the dye that shows hairline cracks. If you're preparing for a long trip, it's best to remove the rigging and take it to the rigger for a stretch or stress test.

• Don't forget to check shroud rollers occasionally. If they start to shred, your sails may suffer.

• If your stays have swages top and bottom, remove and end-for-end them each season. Water accumulates at the bottom fitting, so give each end a chance to stay dry.

SHROUD COVERS

When you put on wood shroud rollers, tape them twice: first use reinforced strapping tape (for strength); then cover the strapping tape with white plastic tape. It looks nice, and it protects the holding tape from the sun. Change the outer tape whenever necessary.

CABLE CUTTERS

Magazine articles abound telling sailors to buy cable cutters for the worst-case scenario of having to cut stays to release a fallen mast. The message has been misplaced by many sailors, who admit they *should* have cutters . . . but don't.

• Real rigging cutters are obviously best, but they are very expensive and you don't need the quality; you won't be trying to get a superclean cut for rigging purposes. Go to a hardware store and buy the largest size you can carry; buy an "up" size from the so-called right size for your rigging. Take a piece of your rigging wire with you and ask to have it cut with the cutters you're looking to buy, so you'll be sure they work.

• Defender sells an economy cutter that will cut stainless wire.

• It's fairly easy to cut stays when there's a lot of tension on the wire, but stand clear in case the wire snaps back.

INTERNAL HALYARDS

To replace an internal halyard, sew together the ends of the old and the new halyard. Pull the new one through, then cut away the old one. (With the ends sewn, there's no bump in the line, so it can pass through the sheave at the masthead.)

HALYARD STORAGE

• If you're storing the boat for an extended time, you might want to store halyards too, rather than expose them to months of UV. As you remove each line, leave another line in its place. Take a line roughly the same length as the halyard (¼-inch nylon should do) and *tape* it to one end of a halyard so you can pull it up and through the sheave as you remove the halyard. The thinner line stays on the mast till you want to put the halyard back up. Connect the two lines with at least 6 inches of taped surface, so the thin line doesn't slide out. Do a neat, flat taping job; otherwise, the lines won't clear the sheave.

• Put cleats into the toerail to tie off flag halyards so they don't bang against the mast. Replace flag halyards each season.

HALYARD TIE-OFF

Some sailors claim they like the sound of clacking halyards. Not many. Tie the halyards as far off the mast as is practical.

The main is easy. Remove the halyard from the sail; take the "hoisting" end aft

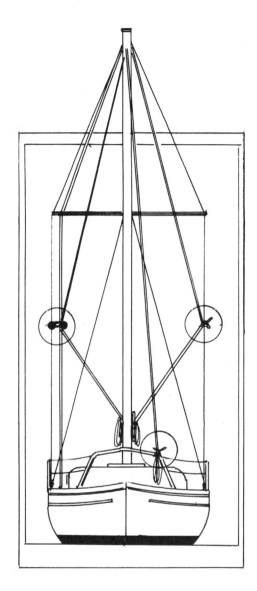

Since the spinnaker halyard leads through a block at the forward part of the mast, both ends of the halyard can be tied onto the bow pulpit.

• Some people weld O-rings to the pulpit so the shackles on halyard ends can snap on.

BOSUN'S CHAIR

• When buying a bosun's chair, choose the one with the shortest distance between the seat and the point where the halyard connects; when you're up the mast, you'll be as close to the masthead as possible. If you're sitting 2 feet beneath the masthead, you can't see or reach to fix whatever forced you to go to the masthead in the first place.

• When you go up the mast for a maintenance check or a specific repair, tie a canvas bucket onto the chair to hold all your tools. Then trail a long line from the bucket, so when you realize what you forgot, the person on deck can tie it on and you can hoist it up.

• A canvas bag works just as well as a bucket.

DRY DAYSAILOR

Replace interior seat cushions with covered closed-cell foam. On good sailing days, water always manages to find its way inside. If bunks can't absorb water, you're assured of a dry place to sleep.

BACKUP STEERER

Put an eyebolt on each side of the rudder near the top, so if the wheel steering breaks, you can tie into the eyebolts for an emergency steering system.

and cleat it on the boom gallows or a lifeline or the outhaul area on the boom. Tie the other end around the bow pulpit.

If you have a roller-furling headsail, take tension off the halyard. Pull it out and tie it to the outer shroud with a separate piece of line. Pull it snug and cleat it back on the mast, off the winch, so the sail cover can fit over the winch.

PROP CHOICE

• Compared to a two-bladed prop, a three-bladed prop allows smoother running, you might go faster at lower rpm, it provides more power in reverse, and the boat will stop faster. The downside is that it drags more when the boat is under sail.

• If you have a two-bladed prop, position it vertically sometime when the boat is out of the water. Then mark a line at the top of the shaft, visible from inside. Later, when you see that line on top of the shaft, you'll know the prop is lined up.

• To mark the shaft, tape off a 4-inch-long, ½-inch-wide strip, and paint it.

YARD DEBATE

Though sailboats are often stored with masts in place, it might be better for the boat if the mast was pulled. When a sailboat is in the water and a side wind hits—even with bare poles—the boat heels, changing the surface directly facing the wind and easing some of the pressure on the rigging and hull. When the boat is sitting on a cradle in a yard, wind can overstress the rigging, the chainplates, and the hull.

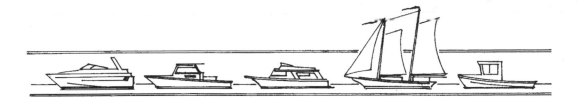

Good Kidkeeping

Boating families are together families. On a small boat, there's no place for pettiness, no room for rivalry. There *is* opportunity to work with parents and siblings as equal members of a team; there is also opportunity to chase private rainbows.

Watch the delight in a four-year-old's eyes as a fear of water turns to a love of swimming. Listen as the seven-year-old patiently points out the finer points of seashells. Admire the preteen who steers a 44-foot boat into an anchorage, bouncing to the beat of Caribbean soul, but making a perfect landing nonetheless. By the time they're teens, they'll handle the boat as well as the captain. And they'll have a good start on handling themselves, too.

FAMILY CONFERENCE

Regardless of the time you allot to boating, get input from the whole family during the planning stages. Everyone should have a voice in where you'll go and what you'll see and do as you travel.

RULES AND RESPONSIBILITIES

Establish boat rules early, and don't make them all "don'ts." To function as a good boating team, you give, and children accept, responsibility—not in general but in specific. Give them chores and jobs: a mix of the have-to-do and the want-to-do. Nobody shirks, or everybody suffers.

WORK FIRST

The cliché about work before play is a standard for good reason. If schooling is involved, the order of the day is study, chores, and play. Play always gets the most time anyway.

GOOD PLAY

Often what starts as play evolves into a learning activity, so encourage the trend. Children's minds have been described as sponges: the more they see, the more they absorb. As long as what they're seeing isn't called education, they'll learn happily and well.

Take their natural curiosity and channel it into an awareness of the world around the boat. Soon they won't miss the malls.

SCRAPBOOK LOG

Have each child keep a combination log, diary, and photo album; include postcards, pressed seaweed (but no smelly starfish), or whatever fits. The book will become a permanent, personal record of a unique time and special places.

NATURE PRESERVES

• Put some state or national parks on your itinerary. When you get there, find a ranger and ask for the full tour. Park rangers frequently have an enthusiasm for their work that is refreshing and contagious.

• If the park is not staffed, find local information and have your own expedition, perhaps organized with a few other boating families.

• Explore caves and cliffs and blowholes; go to the local library or school or natural history museum and find out how nature carved each sculpture.

ANTHROPOLOGY

Explore ruins—and go to the local library, school, historical society, or museum to find out how and why people settled (and unsettled) the area.

FOR REFERENCE

• Keep a supply of books about various aspects of where you are and where you're going, so children—and adults—can learn about things that exist beyond the beach border of a state or country.

• Most libraries have a regional shelf or section, a focused presentation about what makes each region unique. Here you'll often find books not available elsewhere, and some

are true treasures. Don't forget to check out the children's book section too.

- After a day of shelling or snorkeling, come back to the boat and get out the marine-life books; identify what was sighted or collected, and write the information on each child's personal list.

- Do an informal "pop quiz" occasionally—on fish or birds or coral formations or whatever else has recently sparked the children's interest.

FINDING THEIR WAY

Teach the children basic piloting and navigation skills as soon as they show interest.

- Chart number one has enough information to keep you all busy a long time.

- When it comes to electronics, the older children will probably outperform you.

- Whoever's interested can plot courses for the next day's trip. The more involved the children are, the more fun they'll have and the more accomplished they'll feel.

- At night, have a star seminar from your own private observatory. If you carry star charts for the latitude you're cruising, you'll have a whole new world to learn about—a fascinating mix of natural science, natural art, and supernatural myth.

- Instead of a Monopoly game, you might try a family code-learning hour. Or study the phonetic alphabet. Or semaphore.

A PLACE IN THE BOAT

- Lots of new moms bring babies on board. Babies have no problem adapting to boat life—they have nothing stored in their memory banks for comparison. (Only nonboating grandparents have problems, because it is their job to worry.) And babies seldom get seasick. Perhaps the boat is reminiscent of their former natural habitat.

V-bunks are well shaped for wedging a portable cradle or crib.

- Each child needs a place to hide or hibernate, no matter what the space's size.

- Children love boat bunks. Their bunk is probably the only place they can live in total chaos and be left alone. There is no room for anyone to come in and attempt to clean or organize.

- Before the child moves in, build in a bunch of small shelves or compartments or drawers. Hang baskets and mesh bags and net hammocks to hold toys and books and mystery stuff.

PRIVACY REMINDER

Give each child a "Do Not Disturb" indicator so that the concept of privacy can exist even if the reality is marginal. Explain emphatically to the other children the importance of respecting the intent. (This shouldn't be too difficult; children have no trouble understanding the concept of getting even.)

COMMUNICATION

Encourage children to write regularly to a friend at home, or to their former school class. When sharing an experience this way on an ongoing basis, they're more likely to pay more attention to the details of each new discovery. (Ask the recipient to save the letters for your child's return.)

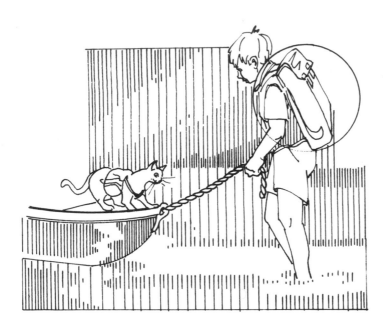

the extra effort to meet other children; then parents get together too.

• Boat children learn early to be assertive, not in a pushy way, but enough not to be shy about meeting people. They're able to talk to people of all ages, frequently on a more mature level than might be expected.

BAG PACK

For weekend boating, give each child a master list and master packing bags to fill each weekend. If they are responsible for their own things, you won't have to listen to two days of whining. And they will develop the start of independence.

VISITORS

• If you've started a long cruise and there's a best friend back home, talk to the friend's parents about arranging some visits. The anticipation of seeing friends can chase the sometime blues.

• Let the children camp out on the foredeck or in the cockpit under a tarp tent. Sleeping out is always more fun than sharing a room—an impossibility in any case.

NEIGHBORHOOD WELCOME

• Often, the children will be your introduction to new friends. They will make

WATER SAFETY AND SPORTS

• Before a cruising trip, the whole family should go to a local YMCA or sports club pool to learn swimming safety and CPR.

• An ideal place to teach children to snorkel would be a coral reef or a spring-fed lake. Clear water helps to calm any apprehensive feelings about floating face down in water. Once a normal breathing pace is established, confidence is sure to follow. (A swimming pool may seem a logical place to practice snorkeling, but there's not much reward in watching the bottom of a cement box.)

• In your cruising budget, try to build in an allotment so children can learn scuba diving in Tobago, boardsailing in Antigua, or deep-sea fishing in Cozumel. It may actually be less expensive than taking courses at home before you leave, and it will be more fun.

• Don't buy equipment until you're sure your child wants to pursue whichever interest.

WATER CAUTIONS

• Record the following subliminal messages to play while the children are asleep:

Swim with a buddy.
Watch the tidal current.
Don't step on jellyfish.
Anchor the dinghy well.

• Warn the children not to run along the shallow-water line when exploring beaches in barracuda land. Barracuda probably don't know the mass of bubbles they see is a running child; they probably think they're striking at a dinner fish. Regardless of what they may be thinking, the end result could be a nasty barracuda bite.

• Children should wear some kind of beach shoes that will grip slick rocks and save foot bottoms from beach glass, beach litter, and sea urchin spikes. If their feet are growing too fast to make nylon water shoes a practical choice, a succession of throwaway sneakers should see them through.

IN-HARBOR COMPETITION

When you are with a group of cruisers for awhile, organize a day of sailing-dinghy races or rowing regattas.

• If you're very ambitious, you could make a junior yacht club event out of it, with trophies (or at least prizes) for the winners.

• One boat might provide the platform for spinnaker flying.

COMMON SENSE

When children use the dinghy, or if they're allowed on a jet bike, let them know you expect them to operate the craft safely and in a considerate way. If it's necessary to spell out what you consider considerate, they probably shouldn't be in the dinghy or on the bike. You can't teach too much boating courtesy.

SHORE SPORTS

• When you're staying in a town for awhile, look for a group of local children to organize sports or games—against or with—the visiting boat children.

• Bring a volleyball. If you don't have a real net, a line between two trees will suffice. Great for getting rid of excess energy.

ONBOARD BUSYWORK

• Without the structure of crosswords or Scrabble, you can organize word games for the children, with rhyming lists or with synonyms and antonyms.

• On a cold or rainy day when everyone is confined to quarters, try card games or board games, or plan a pizza or a cookie party. (Either will take a long time to fix and will be a big treat when done. Plus, the doing will keep the boat warm.)

• A teenager may volunteer to take over the job of videomaker. The perspective will probably be different from yours, but the tapes are usually fun and always interesting. Videotapes and audiotape cassettes provide special opportunities to communicate with friends and family.

• Counting contests are more difficult on water than on land (you can't count cows along a roadway when you're on a boat), but animals often can be found in the clouds. Studying the formations is good imagination training (as if a child needed such a thing).

• If young children want to use paints, put the brush-washing water in a squatty container (like a cottage cheese carton) so it can't spill readily. Or set the water container into a cake pan. Or cut a hole in an empty tissue box or a large sponge.

• Young children enjoy making home movies. Use a roll of white shelf-lining paper. Have the children paint a continuous picture, with scene changes pulled from the boat's recent travels.

If you planned ahead, you'll have a couple of pieces of ½-inch to 1-inch PVC tubing, about 2 feet long. Or substitute wood dowel rods, or relatively straight sticks from shore. Tape one end of the movie art to one of the dowels, and wind the paper around. As child "shows" the movie, the "film" rolls up on the second dowel. (It will be necessary to tape the leading edge to the second dowel, and the rolling will require a certain amount of coordination on the part of the film technician.)

SHORE FUN

• Shore lunches or beach fish-fries are family affairs that start with fish-catching, go through fish-cleaning to the favorite

part of cooking and eating, and end with a general cleanup.

• Encourage the children to stake out their bonfire location for the later marshmallow roast. Assign a designated firebuilder. Remind them to bring out any trash that doesn't burn.

• A group sing or a storytelling session is fun for all ages.

• If the children are old enough to take the dinghy to shore by themselves, remind them to tie the painter to a tree or else dig the anchor in, even though they've dragged the dinghy up on the beach. If the tide is rising, it could take the dinghy back to sea, a common and frustrating occurrence.

SHOWTIME

Old-fashioned family get-togethers often included sending the children out for an entire afternoon at a local movie theater, a treat for both generations. New-fashioned get-togethers can bring parents to one boat for a grown-up conversation while children have a VCR party on another boat. With a bunch of friends and a bucket of popcorn, an extended afternoon moviefest is always a hit.

SOUL SOOTHERS

• While you may prefer to promote real music, played with real instruments, children will want their own listening music, too, whether or not you define it as music.

A parent must have invented the Walkman. Everyone on board should have one—a small concession to the tech world, it will keep your inner world on an even keel.

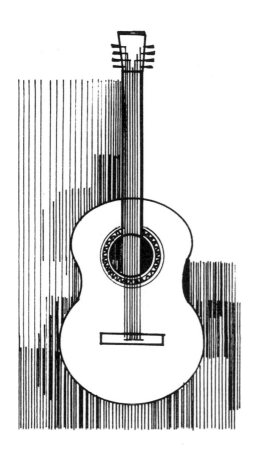

PERSONAL SIGNALS

Develop some easily recognized ship-to-shore signals (for dinghy pickups or general attention-getters), because not all boaters necessarily have a personal handheld radio, and because even if they do, radio batteries sometimes run out of power.

One family has fine-tuned a distinctive "whoop" that works equally well in shopping malls, video stores, or flea markets. They don't even mind the questioning looks the "whoop" always brings, or the purposeful ignoring that says "Leave the strange people alone."

PERSONAL I.D.

If you have small children on board, sew boat-name tags into their clothes. Give visiting friends' children a boat-name bracelet and hats or visors imprinted with the boat name. Nobody ever plans to misplace a child, but they can wander off at a shoreside picnic as casily as at a shopping mall.

SHORE WARNINGS

• If teens go to shore in a foreign country to shop or sightsee, explain why they shouldn't drink the water, and remind them how popsicles are made. Stress that eating forbidden food is not a test of individual toughness; it is a risk not worth taking. Show them pictures of awful-looking parasites, or explain symptoms in frightening detail, if that's what it takes.

• By example, instill in children some awareness of and respect for local customs: when they're in someone's home, they should abide by house rules; behavior that's normal in one place may be unacceptable in another; what they see as

• A boat trip provides time and incentive for learning to play music. Siblings in one family formed a duo of classical guitar and flute. A basic harmonica can produce a surprising variety of sounds. And the background sounds of banjo or guitar are the core of countless songfests, still a source of fun for every generation.

VERY PERSONAL PFD

If children like something, they'll wear it until it wears out or they outgrow it. Take advantage of that devotion by letting them choose their own PFD. Choices go beyond basic orange to include likenesses of mermaids, turtles, or a particular batperson.

mischievous might be a jail offense; etc., etc., etc.

Enough horror stories have been publicized that teens should realize you're not trying a phony scare tactic to ensure obedience. Hope the messages get through.

• Even in home port, if teenagers are out, especially with the dinghy at night, check-in time is not an approximate, for all the reasons they should be old enough to recognize. Give each child a handheld radio for his or her 13th birthday, and explain that parents don't choose to be worriers—it just goes with the job.

FORMAL LEARNING

Children's education should not be a reason to postpone an extended cruise. Between the teaching aids of correspondence schools and children's natural ability to adapt, they will learn (more and better, by their own judgment in hindsight).

• Growing numbers of parents are choosing home-teaching for reasons that have nothing to do with a boat trip. In some places, school is not the best environment for children, academically, socially, or from the standpoint of basic safety.

• With onboard schooling, concentrated effort for four hours a day can accomplish the same academic results as eight hours spent at a school.

• Most parents schedule schoolwork early, leaving the rest of the day for living and learning.

• Of necessity, boat students learn how to do research, whether from onboard reference material, shore libraries, or a tour of the marina or anchorage, looking for teacher's aids. (With luck, they may find help from a chemist, an electronics buff, or a math professor on sabbatical.)

Short-Term Schooling

• If the children will be away from their regular school for only a few months, or even for one full school year, talk to the teachers to get lesson plans, or at least a comprehensive description of the material to be covered. This will assure the easiest return.

• One couple used their own curriculum for a year of school; they did not want the pressure of trying to complete a given number of papers. Their advice: "Put good reference books on board. Study what's available—science, weather, sea creatures, coral formations, and history—wherever you go." For the more formal schooling, they took a math book for their daughter's grade level, and a history book.

Part of English class was a monthly letter to the school relating the happenings of the month past. The parents used the letter to teach grammar, spelling, and sentence structure; by encouraging the inclusion of maps, charts, and sketches in the correspondence, they were able to add art lessons, too.

• If you'll be spending a month in a new place, ask the local school if they accept visiting students. Classes may not follow your prescribed educational schedule, but it will satisfy a social need while introducing your child to a new region or culture.

Long-Term Schooling

For long-term onboard education, a recognized correspondence school is the way to ensure a complete course of study.

For grades through 8, contact:

Calvert School
105 Tuscany Road
Baltimore, MD 21210

For high school, write:

American School
850 East 58th Street
Chicago, IL 60637

Results

A year of cruising sparked the natural interest of one teen who went on to earn a doctorate in geochemical oceanography; he now lectures around the world on his chosen subject. Two girls educated on board through high school received scholarships from a college whose administrators were interested in studying the results of correspondence education. Two other boat-educated children are now published authors. And on and on and on.

• One downside: there was no access to labs for high school science courses such as biology, chemistry, and physics. In general, though, there were very few complaints about the correspondence schooling; most found it to be a positive experience.

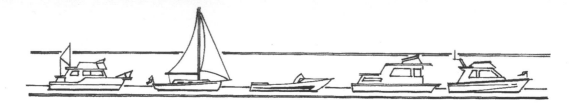

Catch All

PERSONAL LOGS

Real ship's logs take many forms (engine, radio, navigation), but for most pleasure boats the popular form is a personal record of cruise highlights.

• Use a good scrapbook; you can write on its pages, add postcards or newspaper articles, and include photographs, or whatever else pertains.

• A "chummy" log highlights daily events: an especially delicious meal, an unusual happening, the day's travel details, wildlife or marine-life sightings.

PHOTO LOGS

Photo scrapbooks of cruising time are a family history, even without words. One family has a 16-year accumulation of photo books. Entertaining to outsiders, they are a priceless collection for the family.

GUEST LOG

• A guestbook is a nice way to remember new friends, but it's not much good sitting blank in a drawer. Keep it on an obvious shelf near the entry, and try to catch people as they arrive.

• Keep a separate record of people you meet. *You* enter their names, along with the boat name and any other notes you want to help your memory.

• Take Polaroid pictures of new friends. Put their names and the boat name on the back, and keep the photos in a file box or their own separate scrapbook. (Include information about where you met, and you'll be more likely to place the people later.)

PAPER PROTECTORS

• Important papers (personal and boat) should be kept in a lockable fireproof box or, at the very least, in a zip-top bag to prevent mildew attacks.

• Photocopy the information page of your passport. If you lose the passport, you'll have the information you need to replace it quickly.

• Make a list of all credit card numbers and issuer's phone numbers, and keep a copy on the boat. If your wallet or purse is lost or stolen, one shore trip can take care of all calls promptly.

MONEY CARRIERS

• A waist-pack bike purse is a good way to carry necessities; a bumpy dinghy ride won't ruin it or the contents, and it foils a would-be pickpocket.

• A floating wallet is an obvious wise idea. You might avoid the need for the floating aspect by wearing a flat wallet on a line around your neck.

• Money belts are sometimes useful on shore treks, but make it a *thin* belt, worn *under* trousers, holding most of your money and all cards.

• If you carry a wallet, keep it in a front pocket, though even this is risky; thieves do a "squeeze" play, with two people working together in a crowded bus or train.

• The personal watercraft people brought a choice of waterproof floating holders for cards, keys, and cash for those days when you're dressed in a swimsuit all day. There's a watertight fanny-pack, too.

KEY CARRIER

Floating key rings have prevented a lot of broken locks. This is a small item that can make a big difference.

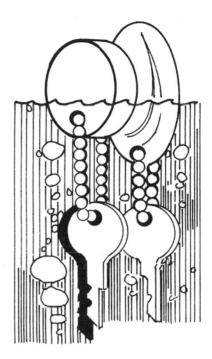

MAIL HANDLERS

• If you'll be traveling places where mail is not reliable, make out checks (dated, signed, and in dated envelopes) to leave with the trustworthy person who is handling your mail. Insurance premiums, credit card payments, and phone bills are too important to worry about having them chase you around.

• You could leave a bunch of signed but otherwise blank checks, too, but nobody feels comfortable about that. The simplest solution—almost necessary for extended cruising—is to add the name of the trusted mail forwarder/bill payer to the list of authorized signatures on your checking account.

- Unless you're cruising in really remote places, take along U.S. stamps. You can usually find vacationing tourists who will take correspondence back to the states and mail it for you, and there's less chance of delay if it's ready for the mailbox.

- When cruising in the states, keep the outgoing mail in an assigned spot near the entryway, already filed in a plastic bag. Anytime anyone goes to shore and/or to town, they might remember to check the mail shelf.

COMMUNICATION

- Keep a record of letters sent to friends. You'll stop repeating yourself, and you'll avoid forgetting anyone. A write-in calendar is one way to keep track of letters sent, but a running list (for each person) gives information at a glance. (A laundromat is a good place to write letters, automatically putting you on a fairly regular schedule.)

- Snapshots sent home on a regular basis give families real pictures of your travels. Cassette recordings are also a personal form of communication; videos are best of all.

- Before a lengthy cruise, give your family-back-home a map of the area you'll be cruising. Mount it on a cork board and get a bunch of pushpins. When you later write or send photos, they can pop in a pin to make a connection to the places your letter describes, relating them to the locale of your last correspondence.

- You'll probably write most often to one or two friends or family members. Ask them to save your letters. Later, you'll be surprised to read how many things have been left out of your own personal log; the letters give you an opportunity to enjoy the trip all over again.

NONSTICK SOLUTIONS

Ordinary envelopes do not store well in a humid environment; glue is too eager to oblige.

- Keep them in zippered plastic bags (but don't pack tight).

- Open all the flaps first (but don't pack tight).

- If you have room, put them in sturdy boxes (where they won't pack tight).

- For really important envelopes, put strips of waxed paper next to all glue flaps.

- Or bring a lot of cellophane tape.

- Best solution: bring self-stick envelopes with their own wax paper flaps.

- When you buy a supermarket box of envelopes, unfold all the flaps, then slip the whole box (with the top now opened because flaps are sticking out) into a plastic bag containing a desiccant packet.

STAMP COLLECTING

To keep stamps usable, follow the example of the postal experts: keep them in folders of waxed paper. If you buy stamps by the roll, lay them flat and fold rows of 8 or 10 in an accordion-pleated folder. Also carry glue, to use after you practice teapot steaming.

- The U.S. Postal Service now offers pregummed peel-and-stick stamps.

IDENTIFIERS

Have some personal cards printed with your boat's name and your own name (to give to all the people who forgot to ask you to sign their guest books).

• Have an artist design a personal logo that reflects the meaning of the boat name. Use the logo on your cards, and also for a rubber stamp—a handy "signer" for traveling documents.

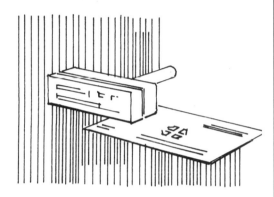

• On the subject of identifying marks: The traveling boating community is still a surprisingly small world. If you care about your good name, behave accordingly. Your reputation will follow (and eventually precede) you.

FOUL-WEATHER GEAR

• Always buy a size larger than you normally wear. When it's 40° and sleeting, you will want to wear four layers of clothes underneath. When the weather's mild, you can always roll up cuffs and sleeves.

• Always buy bright colors; no seawater blue, green, or white.

• To extend the life of the inexpensive foul-weather gear you bought for temporary use: rinse often with fresh water. Coat metal rivets with nail polish or varnish to delay rust. Coat zippers with WD-40 or soap or wax, also often. Coat snaps with an anticorrosive each time you put the outfit away for any length of time.

• The elastic straps that hold up foul-weather pants eventually lose their elasticity. Keep pants on with suspenders. (The metal clips will rust, so don't buy the best pair; you'll be replacing them soon enough.)

• Patch foul-weather gear with pieces of the same fabric (save an old jacket for this purpose) and a *good* contact cement formulated for use on rubberized fabrics. Try the one you use to patch your inflatable dinghy.

WATCH TIME

• Use a timer for man-on-watch naps. Set it for a five- to eight-minute doze when everything looks quiet. (The time span depends on location and common sense.)

• Night watch is one more reason why everyone on board should have their own radio/cassette player with headset. When on watch, you can enjoy the job (and stay awake) while others sleep.

WATCH BAG

Make a rectangular canvas bag, open on one long side. (Or buy a bag meant for stowing sheets; these measure about 1½ feet by 10 inches.) Mount the bag alongside and within easy reaching distance of the helm seat. Inside, keep binoculars, note pad (for course changes, loran plots), pencils, snacks, red-lensed flashlight, and other necessities. For day watches, add some reading material.

WATCH LIGHT

• For night vision, color a flashlight lens red with paint, fingernail polish, or a marker pen. Use the light to read charts or search for lost items without bothering your night vision.

• If the chart table light below blinds the man at the wheel, do the same thing with an ordinary lightbulb over the table.

CHART CHOICE

• For intracoastal travel, the government's small-craft charts are most everyone's favorites: They're clear and printed on good-quality paper to last a long time. But they are expensive.

• Compare the charts sold in book form for size, color, clarity of information, and legibility. It's important that you feel comfortable with the charts you're using.

• Have some overall charts as well as the separate strip or page sections; sometimes you want the overall picture.

• If you're using a book chart and find the book awkward, pull out the pages; cut off the spiral edging and keep the charts folded between outer covers made of posterboard or other lightweight cardboard.

• When comparing charts, look at the number of detail inserts.

• If charts get rain-soaked, dry them and iron them. This works for badly wrinkled or creased charts too; iron through a cloth if you're worried about ink on the iron, but it won't hurt the paper if you do it directly.

• If a chart falls into salt water and you're able to retrieve it, rinse it with fresh water, and iron it when dry. (It will not return to its crisp, new-paper state, but it will be usable with care.)

• Or, buy waterproof charts, one of the better product ideas. If your marine store doesn't carry them, call for a catalog: Waterproof Charts, International Sailing Supply; 800-423-9026.

CHART FILE

• Full-size charts can be rolled, four or five together, and kept in long tubes (available at blueprint or art supply stores, or through a packaging service). Store the tubes in brackets against the overhead above a bunk, or wherever there's room. Velcro straps can also hold tubes in position against bulkhead or hull side.

When unrolled, the charts need to be weighted in many places so they'll stay flat enough to use. Diving weights find secondary use here.

• Those who hate to fight curling charts favor flat storage. Fold charts to a convenient size. Write the chart number and area covered on as many corners as you want, and store by geographic groups in large, flat plastic bags under a bunk mattress.

OUTSIDE CHART FILE

Get a clear plastic folder to keep charts in when you're using them outside. One heavyweight bag is sold at boat stores for keeping Chart Kit's books. An art gallery might order a larger size for you, though they don't usually sell their print display folders.

CHART READING

Get a magnifying glass for help with reading chart details. For night reading, use a lighted magnifier to focus light on the specific area you're studying.

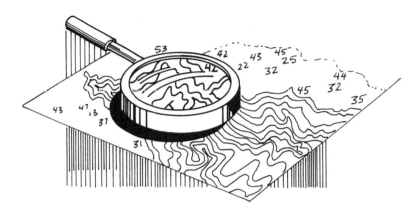

CHART WRITING

• Write down entry headings and information about an anchorage on an unused portion of the chart. You won't remember details from one time to the next, and you'll be sorry to have to guess the second time around. (Entering information in a log is fine, but then you have to look it up; if it's on the chart, it's immediately available.)

• Wrap a piece of tape around a pencil, leaving a short tab sticking out so the pencil won't roll away to oblivion.

ELECTRONIC HELP

• Once you start using loran, you *do* wonder how you found your way without it. For coastal travel, if there's a way to fit a loran into the budget, fit it. Justify the expense for the safety factor so you won't feel guilty about enjoying the new toy. But don't abandon dead reckoning, the original and still workable method of navigation.

• GPS has taken too much of the worry out of offshore navigation. The system is so fast and so accurate that people no longer consider alternative methods, such as the original position finder, celestial navigation.

Electronics are mini-miracles, and they are mostly reliable, but they are not infallible. Everyone knows that, but they still assume that fallible will happen to somebody else. If you're going offshore, don't rely on only one navigation system. (A spare GPS doesn't count; you could lose power.) Learn the basics of celestial navigation, and have the necessary publications on board. With the plastic sextants made by Davis Instruments, purchase of a sextant need not be a major investment.

• "Everyone" also knows that GPS positions will probably *not* match chart indications exactly; don't be tempted to assume a greater accuracy than exists.

WEATHER INFORMATION

• If you have a single-sideband receiver, you may listen to the offshore forecasts broadcast every six hours from Portsmouth, Virginia. The broadcasts cover a lot of area; make notes (in your own private shorthand) from the radio report, or copy it on a cassette so you'll have all the information to study afterward. Do this daily to note developing weather patterns.

- When listening to offshore weather broadcasts, keep an 8½ × 11 tracking chart in a plastic sleeve close to the radio. Use a grease pencil to mark the path of a low-pressure system.

- Most boaters don't need to listen to offshore reports; the regional NOAA reports are broadcast continuously over local VHF channels. Local television weather reports are another good source of information on the movement of weather systems coming your way.

- Keep a road atlas on board. NOAA reports are often located by counties; with a land map, you can track weather more accurately.

CUSTOMS HINTS

If you're going out of the United States, you'll need to obtain a decal that will allow you to come back in. Get an application from the U.S. Customs Service, then return it with a check for $25 (processing fee). For an application, write to:

U.S. Customs Service
P.O. Box 198151
Atlanta, GA 30384

The U.S. Customs Service publishes a pamphlet called "Know Before You Go." Get a copy so you'll have no surprises regarding what items can, or more specifically cannot, be brought into the United States from other countries. Listed along with narcotics, obscene material, and toxic substances is liquor-filled candy (though that restriction is applicable only where prohibited by *state* law). Call a local customs office or write:

U.S. Customs
P.O. Box 7407
Washington, DC 20044

TRAVEL HINTS

- The U.S. Department of State publishes "Tips for Travelers" pamphlets covering a number of areas of the world. The pamphlets cost $1 each. For a list, write to:

Superintendent of Documents
U.S. Government Printing Office
Washington, DC 20402

- Carry a road map and buy land guidebooks covering the areas you cruise. You'll be able to see where you are relative to more commonly recognized landmarks, and you can make note of those places you might want to sightsee while you're in the neighborhood.

- To see as much as you can on a limited budget, eat out (but do it at breakfast or lunch) or buy a local book and local food to experiment with regional tastes (make it a school project).

- Wherever you cruise, look for church picnics or fund-raisers, whether you are a member of the denomination or not. It gives you a chance to try a variety of local or ethnic food; you can talk to people and learn what *they* like about their country, where *they* go for fun on a weekend. A church "sing" is another good meeting place, and you *might* be allowed to join in.

- Go to the library and study the local shelf. You may not come that way again; you don't want to miss a thing.

EXPANDING TERRITORY

Weekend boaters can expand their cruising grounds by taking the boat to a new port one weekend, then leaving it there and taking a bus home. Next week, bring it back or go farther.

WELCOME SOUVENIRS

As you travel, look for small, decorative things that could be used to trim a tiny Christmas tree. Many handmade or found-object items make a unique tree. Some examples: a tiny Seminole doll, meant to pin onto a dress; tiny birch bark canoes or beaded moccasins, made to be necklaces; fish-scale earrings.

WAVING BANNERS

• Don't let your U.S. ensign become one of those things you stop seeing because of familiarity. Replace it *before* it becomes faded and tattered.

• The same applies most emphatically to the courtesy flag of the country you are visiting. If you put up a shabby flag, don't expect a warm welcome.

• Don't fly a state flag (or any flag other than the national flag) from the stern unless you think it's clever to be wrong. The state flag belongs on the bow staff or at masthead.

WASTE MANAGEMENT

• Specific laws regarding marine pollution have been in effect since 1990. Commonly called MARPOL, the regulations are part of an international agreement. The condensed version is: Dump nothing in inland waters or within 3 miles of shore. Beyond that (3 to 12 miles), dump only garbage that is broken up into pieces of less than 1 inch. Exception: Don't dump any kind of plastic anywhere on earth, ever.

Dunnage (the packing material used to protect cargo) has some special restrictions too, but since dunnage is seldom found on pleasure boats, it is not a major concern.

• For the coastal boater, MARPOL means you must keep all garbage until you can dump it in an assigned place, which is not too far removed from what neat people have always done.

TRASH FILING

• Since you may be keeping trash for a while, rinse the stinky cans, at least with salt water (or river, lake, or creek water). You don't want to encourage crawlers or nose pollution.

• Keep smelly garbage separate from cans, bottles, and paper, so you'll have fewer objectionable garbage bags to store. (Double, triple, or quadruple these bags, as necessary.)

• Practice crushing, compacting, and shredding trash. Crush aluminum cans and keep them all together for later recycling. (Some marinas—though not enough—provide separate trash cans for aluminum.) Take off the top and the bottom of regular cans, then flatten the can. (They will take less space in the trash storage. Plus, when they get to the shore dumpster, visiting animals won't get their noses caught or cut on sharp lids.) Tear cardboard and paper into easily compacted sizes. The energy expended on such destructive practices is a welcome way to vent some of the frustration that occasionally surfaces when two people spend time in a small space alone together.

TRASH CONTAINERS

• Buy a frame on which to hang small plastic garbage bags inside the galley's undersink locker.

• A sprinkle of baking soda in the bottom of the garbage pail helps deodorize spills.

• Put a lid on any wastebasket. Cut a piece of wood (doorskin or thin-ply) slightly larger than the top opening. Varnish or paint it to match the decor. Drill two holes in one of the long sides of the wood, and cut matching holes in the back of the wastebasket, about ¼ inch down from the lip. "Hinge" the lid by tying line or coated wire through each pair of holes.

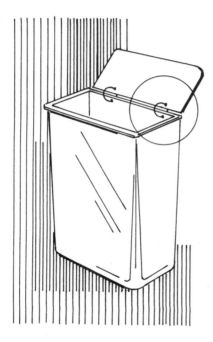

TRASH HIDING

In the master storage plan, you saved space for trash. Keep the smelly bags where they will be least noticeable (perhaps riding in the dinghy trailing downwind).

TRASH CLEANUPS

If you think the concern about trash is exaggerated, think again. In less than a decade, hundreds of beach miles have gone from pristine to plastics-dump as the ocean tries to rid itself of garbage. If you can give some time to beach cleanups, write for information:

Center for Marine Conservation
1725 DeSales Street N.W., Suite 500
Washington, DC 20036
202-429-5609

STICKERMANIA

Stickers have become an obvious if not important part of boat life. Annually updated decals in bright, noticeable colors are required to prove that the boat has some registered status. *State* status usually adds double sets of sticky numbers and letters; even dinghies declare their statehood and alphanumeric code in duplicate. Federal documentation papers leave carefully captioned blank spaces where boatowners affix yearly confirmations in the form of colorful ministickers.

In the early years of Pollution Awareness, the larger "no-oil-discharge" sticker/placard became a legislated necessity, stuck close to potential oil dumping areas to guarantee sticky-free waters. MARPOL regulations added the official garbage-deposit-rules sticker/sign, thereby assuring even cleaner wakes.

Foreign-bound cruising boats must include one more decal in their sticky lineup, so U.S. Customs can collect their foreign fee.

A temporary addition to the collection—the government's user fee—is now history, thanks in great part to continued complaints from organized stickees.

Other sticky options have long been available and privately encouraged. Stickers of support for Cousteau or Greenpeace. Membership decals for boating clubs. An "I Passed" the Coast Guard

Auxiliary's courtesy exam, or the "I Gave" to South Florida's mosquitoes. A firm "No Smoking" is many an owner's favorite, and a "Zero Tolerance" sticker may serve as a positive influence in a potentially sticky situation.

The key word about these, of course, is optional, which the user fee was not. Its repeal is a notable first, suggesting that if boaters stick together, they may have a voice in preventing future regulatory sticky wickets.

Your Ideas

Everyone who spends time on a boat knows something that belongs in *Good Boatkeeping*. With a little help from our readers, future editions will fill out data and fill in voids to provide an ongoing information exchange.

Send us your ideas. If we use one or more of your suggestions, International Marine will send you a complimentary copy of the next edition.

Good Boating!

Zora and David Aiken

Mail ideas to:
The Aikens
c/o International Marine
P.O. Box 220
Camden, Maine 04843

Index

A

abandon-boat plan, 182
ABYC. *See* American Boat and
    Yacht Council
acupressure, 217
Adventure Foods, 17, 47
aerobics, 211–12
air catchers, 122–23
air conditioning, 118–23
airing out, 84, 104
alarm systems, 178, 181
allergies, 218
aloe vera, 216–17
American Association of
    Naturopathic Physicians,
    217
American Boat and Yacht
    Council, 115
*The American Medical Associa-
    tion Family Medical Guide,*
    217
American Red Cross, 182
American School, 261
anchoring, 135–39, 155–56,
    177–78
antiboarding devices, 182
ants, 242
Aqua Lather, 101, 150
Aquaseal #3, 89, 125
ASPCA Education Depart-
    ment, 231
Avon's Skin So Soft moistur-
    izer, 243

B

back stretches, 219–20
Bahamian mooring, 136, 137
bailers, 156
baking, 39, 46
baking soda, 86, 93, 96, 178,
    216
barbecue grills, 5–6
Bar Keepers Friend, 87, 88
barnacles, 157
batteries, 114–15, 206–07
bedding, 66–67, 93, 225–26

bell brackets, 131
biking, 211
bilges, 87, 110
binoculars, 177
Biobor fuel additive, 107
bird counts, 167, 257
birds, 209, 238–39, 245
blistering, 189, 204–05
blocking, 199
boarding steps, 133
Boater Safety Hotline, 116,
    182
boat hooks, 134
boating courses, 182
BoatLIFE's Life Calk, 79, 196
boat storage, 206–09, 252
Boat/U.S. Boating Safety
    Foundation, 182, 215
boatyards, 198–209, 252
Boeshield T-9, 106, 115
Bon Ami, 87, 88
"Books Aboard" burgee, 167
boom gallows, 249
boric acid, 240, 242
bosun's chair, 251
breads, 40, 42
bronze wool, 184
Brown, "Fatsco," 119
brushes, 192, 194
bug controls, 69, 89, 209, 244
bunks, 66, 74–75, 76, 77
Bushnell binoculars, 177
busywork, for children,
    257–58
butane stove. *See* stoves,
    propane

C

cable cutters, 250
Calvert School, 261
camera gear, 160–62, 223
Camping World, 95
Campmor, 17
Carradine, David, 211
carryalls, 19, 147–48, 155,
    201, 230–31, 265–66

castor oil, 216
cats, 235–37
caulking, 196
C Cushions, 130
Center for Marine Conserva-
    tion, 270
chafing, 141, 154, 247
chainplates, 249
charts, 266–67
children on board, 222, 239,
    253–61
chroming, 197
ciguatera, 24, 25, 219
Citizen's Emergency Center,
    183
clams, 26
cleaners, 86–87, 88, 89, 96,
    98, 157, 194
cleaning, 81–90, 111, 138,
    140, 148, 248–49
cleaning kit, 82, 111–12
cleats, 140
clothespins, 95
clothes wringers, 95
clothing, 203, 222, 226
cockroaches, 240–42, 244
Combat roach traps, 241
communications, 172,
    181–82, 255, 259, 264
compasses, 176–77, 249
compressed natural gas stove.
    See CNG stove
conch, 30
condensation, 75, 84–85
cone of protection, 116
cooking, 35–47, 257; less-
    water, 148–49; one-pot, 37
cooling foods, 48–57
Corning's Corelle dinner-
    ware, 9
Corrosion X, 105–06, 115
Cousteau, Jacques, 87
covers, 124–26, 141, 249
crabs, 27–29
CRC Instant Galvanize, 138
crewkeeping, 210–20

crew-overboard pole, 175
curtains, 75
cushions, 75–76, 129–30, 251
customizing, 79–80, 132–33
customs, 268
Cutless bearing, 112
cutting boards, 11

D

dairy products, 54–55, 56
Dairy Queen's insulated bags, 101
dancing, 212
davits, 152, 158
Dawn dish detergent, 87
decals, 154, 268, 270–71
decks, 87–88, 131–32, 188–89, 205
decommissioning, 206
decorative art, 163
desalinators, 91, 143
desks, 77
desserts, 38
detergents, 92, 96, 101, 125, 203
deviation table, 176
Dickinson Stoves, 3
dinghies, 151–59; folding, 152; glass-bottomed, 157; hard, 152, 153; inflatable, 151–52, 153, 157–58; locking, 159
dinnerware, 9
dishwashing, 85–86
dividers, 59–60, 66, 77–78, 104
docking, 142
documents, 223, 231, 263, 270–71. *See also* registration papers
dogs, 233–35
doors, 61, 76, 79–80, 238
drains, 131–32, 208
drinking alcohol, 172–73
drinks, 41–42
dry box, 10
drydocks, 199–200
dryers, 95
dry rot, 204
dusting, 83

E

eggs, 55
electric cords, 201–02
electrolysis, 204
electronics, 115, 206, 267
Elizabethan collar, 232
engines, 106, 109–10, 112, 206
Epifanes varnish, 195
exercising, 210–12, 234
expense sharing, 222
exterior modifications, 124–34
eyeglasses, 202. *See also* sunglasses

F

fabric art, 163
fabrics, 89, 93–94
Fantastik, 87
fenders, 141–42, 153
Ferris Power Survey, 114
fiberglass, 90, 185–88, 204
fids, 60–61
filters, water, 145–46
fingerholds, 71
firearms, 183
fire extinguishers, 179–80
first-aid kit, 217, 218
fishing, 23–25, 170–71
fish pot, 25
flags, 134, 269
flares, 181
fleas, 232–33
Flexipaint, 157
flies, 243–44
Flitz metal polish, 88
float plan, 172
flooring, 78–79, 102–03
Florida Center for the Book, 167
flying, model plane, 167
fondue pot, 5
Food and Drug Administration Seafood Hotline, 45
foods: canned, 35, 38; canning, 16, 20, 25, 44–45; cooling, 48–57; dehydrating, 33; dried, 36, 47; freezing, 53–54; fresh, 23–34; packaging, 17, 18, 19, 20; prepared, 14–22; pre-prepared, 40; storing, 207; substituting, 46–47
foot pedals, 103
foul-weather gear, 174, 265
fruits, 34, 56
fuel, 107–08
fume detectors, and pets, 239
furling drums, 248

G

galley gear, 1–13, 173
galvanizing, 138
games: board, 166, 257; card, 166–67, 257; stowing, 19
gardening, 31–32, 236
gauges, 112
generators, 113–14
gifts, 222
ginger, 214, 216
glass, 79–80, 86, 89
glass art, 163
glassware, 9
glazing, 186
gloves, 202–03
glues, 196–97
gnats, 244
goggles, 202
Goop, 93
GPS navigation, 267
grounding systems, 115–16, 117, 180, 205
guests, 67, 221–28, 256, 262–63

H

Halon (FE-241) gas systems, 179
halyards, 250–51
Hamilton Ferris Company, 114
hammocks, 58, 65, 107
handholds, 70, 110
handwork opportunities, 160–71
harnesses, 174–75
Harris Roach Tablets, 240
hatches, 68, 69–70, 132, 133
haulouts, 199
heads, 86–87, 97–104
heat escape lessening position

(H.E.L.P.), 215
heat gun, 185
heating, 119–22; AC-powered, 119; alcohol-powered, 120; coal-powered, 119; diesel-powered, 120; kerosene-powered, 120; propane-powered, 120, 132; trans-ferring, 120
heat shield, 121–22
H.E.L.P. *See* heat escape less-ening position
herbs, 31–32, 36, 47
hiking, 210
Hold-A-Bag box, 18
holding plates, 50, 51–52
homeopathy, 217
horseshoes, 212
hoses, 145, 201, 204
hulls, 90, 192, 193
hypothermia, 215

I
ice, 48–49
"ICW mustache," 88, 90
ideas, 273
identifying marks, 183, 233, 259, 265
Inland Marine's Inflatable Boat Sealant Kit, 157
insurance, 183
interior modifications, 58–80, 192
Interlux Jet Speed Varnish, 195
Interlux #223 Eggshell enamel, 84
inventory, 21–22
inverters, 6, 113
in-water storage, 209
itineraries, 222, 253, 254

J
Jack Rabbit Marine energy systems, 114
jellyfish, 215–16
jetboating, 171
jogging, 210–11
joker valves, 98–99
Joy dish detergent, 101, 149–50

Joy of Cooking, 45
jumping rope, 212

K
keys, 112, 263
kick plates, 71
knee pads, 203
knife racks, 72–73
knotwork, 140, 165
"Know Before You Go," 268
Kodak's one-time-use camera, 161

L
ladders, 71, 130–31, 152, 173, 199
lanterns, 71–72, 121
latches, 62
latex housepaint, 192
laundromats, 91–92
laundry, 91–96
laundry basket, 92–93
leaks, 127
Lemon Pledge, 89
Le Pet Bag, 231
lifelines, 173–74
Lifesling rescue system, 175
lightning, 115–16, 180
lights, 110, 129, 139, 156, 165, 177, 266
lines, 139–41; care, 140–41; coiling, 140; handling, 135–42, 177–78; lead, 155, 176; towing, 152–54
lint, 82
Liquid Nails, 196–97
Liquid Steel, 109
Liquid Wrench, 109
lists: child's, 255; communica-tion, 172, 264; document, 263; identification, 183; master, 15, 19, 21; paint, 195; provisions, 14, 15, 19; self-survey, 203; storage, 209; to-do, 81–82, 198, 200
litter boxes, 237–38
lobsters, 29
lockers, 10, 14–22, 59, 65, 133
locks, 159, 182

logkeeping, 225, 254, 262–63
look bucket, 30, 168–69, 178
loran, 267
Lyme disease, 220, 235

M
M-1 Additive, 84, 192
Mace gun, 183
magnets, 111
magnifying glass, 267
mail handling, 263–64
maintenance chores, 184–97
Man Overboard Module res-cue system, 175
Marine-Tex putty, 185
The Marlinspike Sailor (Smith), 165
MARPOL regulations, 269, 270
Marvel Mystery Oil, 108
Marykate cleaner, 157
masking tape, 191
masts, 246–47, 249, 252
matches, 13
mats, 83, 200
MDR antifouling coating, for inflatables, 157
meats, 55–56
mechanical maintenance, 105–17
medications, 217–18, 223, 231–32
metalcraft, 163
metals, 203–04
mildew, 84, 93–94, 192, 208; M-1 additive, 85, 192
Minolta waterproof camera, 161
MOM. *See* Man Overboard Module rescue system
money, 223, 263
mops, 134
mosquitoes, 243
mud daubers, 244
mugs, 9–10
muriatic acid, 87
music, 166, 257, 258–59
Muskol insect repellent, 243–44
mussels, 26

N

National Center for Home-
opathy, 217
nature preserves, 254
naturopathy, 217
Naval Jelly, 87, 109
navigation, 255, 267
needlework, 164–65
Nevr-Dull metal polish, 88
Nikon's Nikonos waterproof
camera, 160–61
NOAA weather reports, 268
no-see-ums, 243, 244

O

oar holders, 155
oil, 106–07
Origo stove, 5
outboard-hoisting systems,
131, 158
overboard procedures, 173,
175, 233
oysters, 30

P

packing bags, 222
paddling, 155, 211
painters. *See* lines
painting, 162–63, 258
paints, 192, 193, 195, 202
pans, 7
patching repairs, on inflatables, 157–58
pattern transfers, 189–90
Peel-Away stripper, 185
Penn #5500 spinning reel, 24
pepper spray, 183
pets, 223, 229–39
Pet Taxi, 231
PFDs, 156, 174, 181, 233, 259
photography, 160–62
picture frames, 63
pillows, 226
piloting, 255
plants, 80. *See also* gardening
Plasti-Kote spray paint, 129
plate holders, 85
plugs, 180, 188, 190
plumbing, 117, 150
poisoning, 218–19, 232
polishing, 86, 88–89

Pooper Scooper, 235
Portuguese man-of-war,
215–16
pot holders, 8, 73–74
pots, 7
preventive maintenance,
105–06
preventive safety. *See* seamanship
priests, 25
prisms, 70, 84
privacy, 174, 225, 228, 255
progressive meal, 43
props, 112–13, 204, 252
provisioning, 14–22
pumps: bilge, 110, 180–81;
oil, 107; seawater, 150;
sump, 101; water, 146
putties, 185–89, 218

R

racks, 72–73, 78
radios, 156, 173, 182
rafting up, 142
rags, 83, 84, 92, 111, 202
rain-catching systems, 144–45
Rain-X, 89
ratlines, 247
rattle stops, 126–27, 249,
250–51
reference books, 254–55
refrigerators, 49–52; AC-powered, 51; DC/AC-powered,
51; DC-powered, 50–51;
holding plate, 50, 51–52;
three-way-powered, 51
registration papers, 154
repairs. *See* maintenance
chores
resin thickeners, 185–89
Resolve carpet cleaner, 83
respirators, 202
responsibilities, 81–82, 253
rigging cutters, 250
rodents, 239, 244–45
Ross Electronics, 115
rowing, 211
Rubba Weld tape, 109
rubrails, 157
rudders, 205, 251–52
ruins exploration, 254

S

safety checks, 110, 156,
203–04, 224–25, 249–50
sail bags, 248
sailboarding, 171
sailboats, 246–52
sailing dinghies, 152
sailor's palm, 248
Sailrite Kits, 125, 243, 248
sails, 205–06, 247–49
sanding, 190–91
scale models, 167–68
scare-owls, 245
scheduling, 200, 221, 226
scherenschnitte, 163
schooling, 260–61. *See also*
boating courses
screens, 69, 127–28, 197
screw holes, 197
scrubbers, 89
scuba diving, 169–70
scuffing, 191
scuppers, 208
Sea & Sea waterproof camera,
161
Seacook stove, 5
Seacurity inflatable PFDs, 174
seafood, 23–30; pickling,
25–26; smoking, 26
seamanship, 172–83
seasickness, 214–15, 223
Sea Swing stove, 5
seats, 78, 128–29
sea urchins, 216
Seventh Generation, 96
sewing, 165–66
shakers, salt and pepper,
12–13
Shaklee Company, 87
ShapeMate exerciser, 212
sheet bags, 248
shell collecting, 168–69
shellfish, 26, 218–19
shelves, 60–61, 64–65, 77,
104, 108–09
shoes, 223, 227
shopping, 16–17
shore sports, 212, 257
showers, 86, 87, 100–04,
224
shrimp, 27

shroud rollers, 250
sightseeing, 227
signals: distress, 181–82; personal, 259
Simple Green, 87
Simpson-Lawrence windlass, 138
sinks, 73, 103
sketching, 162
skin cancer, 213
Sludge & Slime Control, 107
Smith, Hervey Garrett: *The Marlinspike Sailor,* 165
smoke detectors, 180
smoking, 223
smudge guards, 192
snorkeling, 169, 256
Soda Syphon bottle, 6
Soft Scrub, 86, 87, 89
solar-powered systems, 113–14, 131, 139
Solartex sun-screening fabric, 126
SOS. *See* signals
soups, 38
souvenirs, 269
spatter guards, 191
spices, 63, 243
spiders, 244
Spill Saver pour spout, 106
sprouts, 31
Sta-Bil fuel additive, 108
stains, 87, 93–94
stamp collecting, 264
Standard Homeopathic Co., 217
Starbrite's Inflatable Boat and Fender Cleaner/Protector, 157
Starbrite's Premium Marine Polish, 90
star study, 167, 255
steering aids, 158, 251
Sterno, 5
stingrays, 215
storage spaces, 58–67; box, 133; bunk, 76; desk, 77; hanging, 58–59, 63–64; helm seat, 128; seat, 134; shifting, 62; stacking, 60, 104

stoves, 1–6; alcohol, 1–2, 179; alternative, 4–5, 7; charcoal, 5–6; CNG, 4; electric, 2, 6; kerosene, 2; propane, 3–4; two-for, 2–3
STP gasoline treatment, 107, 112
strippers, 184–85
suggestion box, 228
Sunbrella acrylic, 125
sunglasses, 213–14
sun protection, 212–13, 223
Sun Shower, 100–01, 147
Sun Shower Soap, 101, 150
surveys, 183, 203
swabbing decks, 87–88
swages, 249–50
swimmer's ear, 216
swimming, 234, 256
swim platforms, 131, 152
Swing-A-Way can opener, 11

T
tables, 73, 129
tack cloth, 191
Tai Chi, 211
Tank-ette Head-O-Matic, 99
tanks: dive, 169–70; fuel, 108, 207; holding, 99–100; water, 99–100, 145, 146–47, 148
tanning, 212–13
tarps, 207–08
teak wood, 190, 195
3M's 5200 caulking, 196
3M's Long Mask tape, 191
3M's synthetic steel wool, 184
through-hulls, 90, 150, 180, 188, 203–04
ticks, 235
tiles, 73
"Tips for Travelers," 268
toasting, 40
toilets, 97–99
toilet tissue, 100, 104
tools, 108–10, 190
towels, 74, 96, 103–04, 225
towing, 153–54
toys, 222, 236, 239
travel advisories, 183, 259–60, 268

"Traveling with Your Pet," 231
treats, 18, 42, 43, 44, 56–57
trip lines, 137

U
Uncle John's Foods, 17
U.S. Coast Guard Auxiliary, 182
U.S. Customs, 268, 270
U.S. Department of Agriculture Meat and Poultry Hotline, 45
U.S. Department of State, 268
U.S. Mattress Company, 75
U.S. Power Squadrons, 182
utensils, 9, 11, 12, 74

V
varnish, 184–85, 189, 195, 200
vegetables, 32–33, 42, 52–53
ventilation, 119, 120, 122–23, 202, 208–09
vents: cowl, 209; mushroom, 123, 209; solar, 123, 208–09
vertical clearance, 130
VHF. *See* radios
videotapes, 166, 257, 258, 264
vinegar, 86, 98, 242
vinyl, 89, 197
VinylKote spray paint, 129
vitamin supplements, 218, 236
V.L.P., 197

W
warranties, 206
washing: clothes, 94–95; dishes, 149; laundry and baths, 94, 101–02; pets, 234
Washington State University Creamery, 55
wasps, 244
waste management, 67, 269–70
water conservation, 148–50
waterlines, 205
watermaking, 143–50

water-powered generator systems, 114
waterproof charts, 266
water safety, 256–57
water skiing, 171
water-workouts, 212
WD-40, 93, 105, 109
wearable art, 164
weather information, 267–68

weevils, 242–43
weight lifting, 212
WEST System, 185–86
wet suits, 169
winches, 249
windlasses, 137–38
wind-powered systems, 114
Windscoop, 122
wind tunnels, 123

wiring, 116–17, 204, 249
wood, 189–90, 204
woodworking, 164
workshops, 109

Z
Zero Tolerance, 224, 271
Z-Spar, 105, 192
Zud, 87